by the same author
Politics in West Africa
Economic Survey 1919–1939
The Principles of Economic Planning
The Theory of Economic Growth
Overhead Costs (*out of print*)

DEVELOPMENT PLAN

THE ESSENTIALS OF ECONO

W. Arthur Lewis

Development Planning

The Essentials of Economic Policy

HARPER & ROW, PUBLISHERS, NEW YORK

278 pp

CONTENTS

TABLES

PREFACE

Many books have been published on the theory of economic development, but very little has appeared on how a Development Plan is made, what the chief snags are, and what distinguishes good planning from bad. Academic journals have carried a few esoteric articles on some parts of the subject, but the man in the street, whose life is affected by those Plans, needs a short and simple introduction which can help him.

I have written for the intelligent layman, presupposing the equivalent of one year's courses in Economics. About a third of the book is given over to an arithmetical exercise, which explains the statistical framework of a Plan. This is set out in some detail, so that students can work it out for themselves with pencil and paper, if they so desire. In order to show how errors of judgment reveal themselves, I sometimes do the same thing more than once, with different policy assumptions.

In making a Plan, technique is subsidiary to policy. Hence, although the basic techniques are displayed, the emphasis is throughout on policy. The Economics of development is not very complicated; the secret of successful planning lies more in sensible politics and good public administration.

This book does not overlap with my earlier book, *The Theory of Economic Growth*, published in 1955, partly because the first book is philosophical while the second is operational, but mainly because I had not yet had experience of most of the problems discussed in the second book while I was writing the first. In order to be comprehensive the second book would need the extensive discussion of economic institutions and their improvement which appears in the first, but I have resisted the temptation to repeat myself, since most readers of this book will also have access to the earlier one.

Professors W. J. Baumol, Hollis B. Chenery and F. C. Shorter read an earlier version of this book, and gave me wise advice; they have not seen the present version, and are not responsible for it. I am grateful to successive Secretaries, Mrs Pamela Phipps and Mrs Dorothy Rieger, for arduous but elegant preparation of the manuscript.

W.A.L.
Princeton June 1965

DEVELOPMENT PLANNING
THE ESSENTIALS OF ECONOMIC POLICY

CHAPTER I

Patterns of Planning

Since the end of Second World War most countries of Asia, Africa and Latin America have published one or more 'Development Plans'. These Plans differ so much in structure and content that the title 'Development Plan' no longer conveys a meaning. The first task is therefore to sort out the characteristics of development planning.

A Development Plan may contain any or all of the following parts:

  (i) a survey of current economic conditions;
  (ii) a list of proposed public expenditures;
 (iii) a discussion of likely developments in the private sector;
 (iv) a macroeconomic projection of the economy.
  (v) a review of government policies.

Economic Survey
The Plan normally begins by reviewing progress in recent years, especially since the last Plan was issued. Changes are noted in population, national output, investment, saving, consumption, Government expenditure, taxation, the balance of payments, and the performance of each of the major industries. Giving this information is not one of the purposes of the Plan; many governments produce some kind of Annual Economic Survey with this material, and many also produce Plan Evaluations from time to time, which examine the progress of the economy in various spheres, in the light of proposals in the Plan. In the Development Plan document such information is merely a curtain raiser, suggesting the problems which must be selected for further attention.

Government Expenditure

When the first Development Plans were issued at the end of the war, the emphasis was on determining priorities in the public sector. A review of public expenditure is still an essential part of any Plan. The first move in preparing a Plan is normally to ask each Government department or agency to submit its proposals for expenditure over the period of the Plan. Most of the routine work on the Plan consists of costing each proposal as carefully as possible, and estimating potential benefits, financial and otherwise. The total of the sums requested always greatly exceeds the money the Government is likely to have; hence the prime object of this part of the Plan is to assign priorities, deciding what is to be included, and what shall be postponed or rejected.

Hardly anybody doubts the value of this kind of periodic re-assessment of what Government departments are planning to do, even though it is realized that modifications have to be made in between Plans. It is very easy for Government agencies, like any other institutions, to drift from day to day. The periodic call to look ahead, and to make and defend proposals before the planning authorities, in competition with the proposals of other agencies, helps departments to keep their sense of direction.

Private Sector Targets

The passage from planning the public sector to reviewing the private sector was made at an early stage. It was inevitable, partly because these sectors are inter-related, but still more because the rate of economic development depends more on what happens in the private sector than it does on expenditures in the public sector.

Most Development Plans contain chapters reviewing each of the major industries, analysing their prospects and their difficulties, and formulating programmes for increased output or sales. Special attention is given to promoting new industries which are thought to have good prospects, having regard to current estimates of markets and resources. Some of these reviews include specific targets in quantitative terms (e.g. investment, employment or output).

Sometimes these quantitative targets are used for making policy decisions; more often they are not. A statement that the output of a particular industry is expected to increase by 45 per cent during the next five years may have no significance whatsoever; or may serve merely as propaganda, intended to encourage producers in that industry to redouble their efforts. If the figure becomes the basis of policies, such as import controls, or building licences, or subsidies, it then becomes important to know how the target of 45 per cent was chosen. Most such figures are taken out of the air, but some more solid method becomes essential if the figures are to determine policy.

To prepare a reasonable set of private sector targets for a Development Plan involves a great deal of work. Markets and costs must be analysed with the same accounting and statistical techniques that private firms use for this purpose; and, in addition, adjustments must be made wherever the gain or loss to the economy as a whole is thought to be greater or less than that which accrues to private firms. This must be done for each industry separately; and then a check has to be made to ensure that the predictions for each industry are consistent with each other and with what is predicted for the economy as a whole.

Each industry buys from some other industries at home, and also buys some imports; it sells to other industries, to consumers and perhaps to exporters. It generates savings, pays taxes, and absorbs investment. The sum of the output predicted for each industry must equal what is predicted for total output; so also with investment in each industry, consumption of its product, exports, and so on. The only way to test the consistency of targets is to make a set of interlocking tables for each industry and for the economy as a whole. This is done by projecting national income, using standard national income and input-output procedures.[1]

Exercises of this kind have gained rapidly in popularity among professional planners, mainly because macroeconomic planning provides a consistent framework for all the quantitative aspects of the Plan. In extreme cases the shape of the Plan is completely transformed. We are told in detail how much each industry will produce, import, export and invest; but there is no list of Government projects, and no indication of the policies which might bring the predicted results.

This evolution of planning concepts, from listing public expenditures, through reviewing industrial and agricultural policies, to

[1]See Chapter III, section 5 below.

15

making macroeconomic models, has not been unaccompanied by controversy. For one thing these different kinds of planning are done by different kinds of persons, each proud of his own methods, and somewhat contemptuous of the others'. A plan for public expenditure is best made by a man with Treasury experience, who is used to dealing with Government departments, and knows their tricks. A Plan centred on public policy is best made by a 'practical' economist, who knows the kinds of problems that emerge in developing economies, the various solutions which have been tried in various places, and the extent of their failures and successes. A Plan consisting of interdependent tables needs an econometrician, who can invent figures when they do not exist, make interdependent models, and solve any number of simultaneous equations. As these three types of men have jostled one another, they have snarled at each other, and made hostile remarks about each others' work. Here is an example from an august source: the *Report to the President of the United States from the Committee to Strengthen the Security of the Free World* (known as the Clay Report) on *The Scope and Distribution of United States Military and Economic Assistance Programmes*:

> There is a difference between sound national budgeting in economic and social terms on the one hand and theoretical long-term national development planning as it is often encountered. Extrapolations of mathematical models based on questionable statistics for debatable base periods seem to have a way of going wrong, even when it is possible to find economists who agree with each other. Furthermore these long-term projections have been of little or doubtful value and frequently have proved harmful by directing attention to the theory of economic development at the expense of its practical implementation. Sound governmental planning consists of establishing intelligent priorities for the public investment programme and formulating a sensible and consistent set of public policies to encourage growth in the private sector (p. 16).

Macroeconomic Planning

The principal danger of a macroeconomic exercise lies in its propensity to dazzle. The more figures there are in a Plan, produced by an army of professionals who have laboured mightily to make them consistent, the more persuasive the Plan becomes. Attention shifts from policy to arithmetic. Consistency can be mistaken for truth. Revision is resisted. Yet the Plan is not necessarily right merely because its figures are mutually consistent. However, this is a psychological rather than an intellectual danger. Once the point is grasped that mathematical exercises do not of themselves produce truth, a Plan with figures is no more dangerous than a Plan without figures.

The question remains: what useful purpose is served by producing doubtful target figures for the private sector? The answer turns on a number of factors, especially on the degree of interrelationship between private and public sectors, on the amount of control exercised over the private sector, on the persuasiveness of the planning process, and on the availability of reliable statistics.

That the public and private sectors are interrelated cannot be doubted, but it does not follow that one must make a mathematical model of the whole economy. Each public agency must take account of private plans when making its own. The Electricity Department must consult all potential major uses of power, in order to forecast demand. The Water Department must try to find out where new industries are to be located. Transport and other communications must also be integrated with the private sector, and so on, all along the line. This calls for much consultation with the private sector, but to include the results of this consultation in the plans of the public sector is relatively simple. Large-scale investors in the private sector have to meet the same problem every day; they have to know, or guess, how others will behave, in both the private and the public sectors. In small countries where all the chief decision makers know each other, and consultation is easily arranged, co-ordination can be achieved without elaborate models. In larger countries, like Britain or France or the United States, this argument for models is much stronger.

Public and private sectors are also interrelated in that the total size of the public sector programme must depend on what the private economy can bear. Most public sector programmes are too large. Typically a new Government comes into office having promised everybody schools, hospitals, water supplies, electricity, roads, houses, jobs and all the other good things of life. Undaunted by finding that the Treasury is empty, and that taxes bring in only 9 per cent of the national income, it proceeds to make a Plan. Postulate that the national income, now rising by 3 per cent, will rise by 7 per cent per annum through the Plan period, and you can programme on the basis that public revenue may be as much as 50 per cent larger within five years. The postulate is absurd, but that may not be obvious. Ask the planners to produce a programme for the economy as a whole, showing how all the various sectors are to expand, and this type of absurdity then becomes less plausible. But this is like using a steam hammer to crack a nut. One does not have to make elaborate models of the whole economy to come out with a reasonable basis for estimating what the public revenue will be.

The second argument for comprehensive planning turns on the degree of control which the Government exercises over the private sector. If the Government controls the private sector, through licenses, quotas and price-fixing, or attempts to influence the private sector through subsidies, it needs a well-articulated model to ensure that its decisions are both efficient and mutually consistent. A controlled private sector is like the public sector in that, if sensible decisions are to be made, they should be made in accordance with some programme. Now there is no doubt that the market economy, left to itself, gives the wrong answers in underdeveloped countries. Prices do not correctly reflect relative costs. Opportunities for reducing risks through co-ordinated action are neglected. Insufficient allowance is made for the value of knowledge acquired through unprofitable activities, and so on. The temptation to control the private sector, or at least to induce businessmen to do what they would not otherwise do, is therefore almost irresistible. Of course, an equally impressive case can be made against Government control of business; the Government is inefficient, corrupt, wasteful, not impartial, and so on. However, Government controls or influences business behaviour to some extent in every country in the world. We note merely that if the Government exercises extensive control over the private sector, it will need a programme for the private sector to ensure that its decisions are efficient and mutually consistent.

The Government may not require to forecast the prospective behaviour of the whole economy for its own decision-making; yet such a forecast may be useful in other ways. For there is a third argument in favour of such predictions, namely that the result may persuade private individuals to act more adventurously than they otherwise would. This argument turns on the interdependence of investment decisions. Suppose Firm A contemplates building a refrigerated storeroom. Its success may depend on whether Firm B goes ahead with its fishing trawlers, whether Firm C will bring down cattle from the North for slaughter, whether Firms D and E carry out their plans for employing 1,000 men, who will eat meat and fish stored in refrigerated space, and so on. For any one of these firms to go ahead it is necessary first to estimate what demand and supply will be if the others also go ahead, and secondly to be given some assurance that there will be a general forward movement. Forecasts for the whole economy help all concerned to see the possibilities created by a general expansion. The forecast cannot always provide full assurance of a general movement, but if it is constructed co-operatively, with private and public decision makers consulted at all crucial stages, the very planning process may help to give investors confidence. When a macroeconomic forecast is made for this purpose, it is known as 'indicative planning'.

Indicative planning presupposes that the economy responds mainly to domestic demand, as is the case in mature economies. In very poor economies exports are most usually the engine of growth, and development depends mainly on opening up new export possibilities, or making better use of existing possibilities. The planners can therefore take the market for granted, and concentrate on opening up new natural resources for development, or improving the utilization of existing resources. An interrelated model begins to be useful as the economy begins to exploit the opportunities for import substitution, and to develop a complex pattern of inter-industrial relationships. The greater the interrelationships the more necessary it becomes to have an input-output model to reveal results which are no longer obvious. But in the average small, underdeveloped economy, input-output manipulations are not likely to tell the planners much that they do not already know.

The distinction between an 'indicative' and a 'controlling' Plan is important. The Plans made by Communist countries are documents of authorization; they tell each industrial unit what it must produce and how much it may invest. A Development Plan, on the other hand, authorizes nothing. Even public expenditure is authorized not by the Plan but only by the Annual Budget passed by Parliament. The figures in a Development Plan indicate expectations, aspirations and intentions, but are not binding commitments. This (as we shall see later) is one reason for the irresponsible tendency to use grossly inflated figures, intended to impress the reader, without committing the writer. On the other hand, the fact that the indicative Plan does not commit helps it to ride changing circumstances better than a document which seeks to effect control.

Finally, the value of a macroeconomic exercise depends on how much confidence one has in the figures. Even in countries which are rich in statistics, forecasts of the economy have usually turned out poorly. In poor countries the econometrician has to invent many of the crucial figures. He says: 'The income elasticity of demand for food has not been measured; let us assume it to be 0.8.' Or: 'We do not know what the ore content will turn out to be; let us assume it to be 48 per cent.' Or: 'It seems reasonable to assume a marginal savings ratio of 0.2.' Unfortunately, even if each of the basic assumptions were right to within 1 per cent, the final results could be highly erroneous, because so many crucial magnitudes are found by difference. For example, if we subtract 10,000 from 10,300, the answer is 300. But if we are told that each of the basic figures may be 1 per cent out, we can only be sure that the answer lies between 97 and 593, which is a range of 600 per cent! Many important magnitudes in economics are found by subtractions involving two nearly equal quantities; the balance of trade is the difference between imports and exports; personal saving is the difference between disposable income and consumption; the budget surplus is the difference between revenues and expenditures. Relatively small errors are therefore easily magnified.

The conclusion must be that it is useful to undertake statistical exercises where we have plenty of fairly reliable statistics; but the same exercises would be pointless where we would have to invent most of the statistics. It is useful to go through these exercises where we have plenty of statistics, even though we know that statistics are never completely reliable. For one thing, statistics can serve as cross-checks for each other, so reliability increases in something like geometrical proportion to the number of available figures. Furthermore, the larger and more complex the economy, the less easy it is to keep the whole thing in one's head, and make interrelated decisions without calculation. In poor economies the statistics may easily mislead. One frequently rejects the statistics one is offered because one believes them to be wrong, having regard to what one knows about other economies at a similar level of development. (For example, we have had plenty of wild estimates of population growth, national income per head, numbers engaged in agriculture, growth of productivity, etc.) A sensible person, familiar with the economy, can often give a more correct quantitative answer than one would get from the available statistics. Also, since the economy is fairly simple, its interrelations are fairly obvious, and one can reach good conclusions without elaborate models.

In a country with poor statistics, the first Development Plan, and even the second, should concentrate on bringing order into the public sector's programmes, and into economic policy. This is largely a matter of improving administrative machinery. The Cabinet has to learn not to take an important economic decision until civil servants and technical advisers have examined the matter from every angle. Ministries must be staffed with people competent to analyze the policies which they administer, and to prepare or have prepared, good feasibility studies of proposed projects. Experience must be acquired in planning a project, getting it started, keeping it on schedule, amending it to take account of unforeseen snags, and evaluating its results from time to time. Without a reasonably competent administrative machine, there is no basis for development planning.

Meanwhile, collection of useful statistics should also be accelerated. Then by the time one makes the Third Development Plan, there may be enough reliable statistics to justify attempting to construct an interdependent model for the whole economy. Much depends on the country's size, and on the degree of interrelationship between its industries, since one can carry in one's head the interrelationships of a small simple economy, but not of a large or complex country. Whether the economy responds mainly to export demands, or grows mainly in response to home demand, is also important. India is certainly ready for an elaborate mathematical model; whereas in most of the simpler African economies such a model would do no good, and, as the Clay Committee suggests, might well do harm, by deflecting attention from the major task of evolving useful policies and institutions.

Policy

In the private sector statistics may help, but what really counts is policy. The Government is seeking to induce people to do what they would otherwise not do—invest more in physical resources or in their own skills; change their jobs; switch from one crop to another; adopt new technologies; and so on. The set of policies which it will adopt to bring about these results is the core of private sector planning.

Can a Government really contribute to raising the rate of growth in the private sector of the economy? The first task of a Development Plan is to bring order, priority and foresight into Government expenditure; any Plan which achieves this is already making a substantial contribution. Can a Government usefully do more? The answer is in the affirmative. The main elements of development policy may be listed as follows:

1. Investigation of development potential: surveys of natural resources; scientific research; market research.
2. Provision of adequate infrastructure (water, power, transport and communications) whether by public or private agencies.
3. Provision of specialized training facilities, as well as adequate general education, thereby ensuring necessary skills.
4. Improving the legal framework of economic activity, especially laws relating to land tenure, corporations, and commercial transactions.
5. Helping to create more and better markets, including commodity markets, security exchanges, banking, insurance and credit facilities.
6. Seeking out and assisting potential entrepreneurs, domestic and foreign.
7. Promoting better utilization of resources, both by offering inducements and by operating controls against misuse.
8. Promoting an increase in saving, both private and public.

The quality of a Development Plan should be tested mainly by examining what is proposed under each of these heads. The recent trend towards putting more figures into Development Plans has unfortunately tended to obscure the fact that what matters in planning is not mainly figures but mainly policy. It is possible to write a good Development Plan without using any figures, by concentrating on policies which will stimulate an upward movement of the economy. It is also possible to write a Development Plan which is mathematically completely consistent, but which will nevertheless achieve nothing, because policies are lacking.

Success is hard to measure. If private enterprise moves ahead vigorously, the critics of planning are likely to say that the Plan made no difference; that private entrepreneurs would have acted even if there had been no Plan. Even if growth is slow, it might have been slower but for the Government's effort, but this is not easily proved.

Neither can success be guaranteed, even by the best policies. We do not really know why some countries are more dynamic than others. Some countries experience phases of great activity in literature, painting, music, war or religion; and dynamism in economic affairs may spring from the same deep and uncharted sources. It is probably no easier or more difficult to plan an artistic renaissance than to plan economic development. Good policies help, but do not ensure success. Development planning is in this respect like medicine; the good practitioner knows some useful tricks; but it is still the case that many patients die who are expected to live, and many live who are expected to die.

Summary

1. A Development Plan may contain any or all of the following features: (i) a survey of the current economic situation; (ii) proposals for improving the institutional framework of economic activity; (iii) a list of proposed Government expenditures; (iv) a review of major industries; (v) a set of targets for the private sector; (vi) a macroeconomic projection for the whole economy.

2. The macroeconomic projection is useful for testing the mutual consistency of the quantitative assumptions and proposals in the Plan; and may also stimulate investment by revealing unsuspected relationships. Its usefulness depends on the quality of the statistics which go into it. Given adequate statistics, it is useful in large, complex economies; not useful in small, simple economies. The danger of the exercise lies in the possibility of being dazzled by an array of doubtful figures.

3. The core of planning for higher productivity in the private sector lies in a set of policies which induce private persons to employ their time and resources more productively. The quality

of a Plan depends on the quality of its policies, rather than on the quality or quantity of its arithmetic.

FOR FURTHER READING: GENERAL WORKS

Hagen, E. E. (Editor). *Planning Economic Development.* Homewood, Ill., 1960.
Hirschman, A. O. *The Strategy of Economic Development.* New Haven, 1958.
Lewis, J. P. *Quiet Crisis in India.* Washington, D.C., 1962.
Tinbergen, J. *The Design of Development.* Baltimore, 1958.
United Nations. *Planning for Economic Development.* New York, 1963.

CHAPTER II

Plan Strategy

In the course of preparing a Plan, the Planning Agency is flooded with proposals: projects for Government expenditure, cost and market analyses for possible new industries, schemes for revising the laws affecting economic institutions, reports on newly discovered natural resources, analyses of social need, and so on. All this material has to be sorted, assessed, and assigned priorities in some consistent fashion.

There is no simple formula for making a Development Plan. In the first place a Plan is essentially a set of guesses about the future, since the assignment of priorities requires uncertain estimates of likely results, benefits and costs. There is no formula for predicting the future; the best we can do is to seek parallels in the past. Development economics compares past and present in search of guidelines for the future. Thus a Development Plan is made in the light of a general philosophy of how development takes place; this philosophy underlies the guesses which must be made in assessing individual projects.

Even if the future could be predicted, planning is complicated by the absence of a single, precise objective. In elementary economics the student learns that resources should be allocated in such a way as to maximize the national income. The planner cannot work with such a simple rule. He has to distinguish between maximizing income now, and maximizing income later by accelerating growth at the expense of current income; hence he is as much interested in productive capacity as in income. Productive capacity can be increased at the expense of consumption, now or in the future; this, as well as effects on employment, or on the distribution of income between persons, classes or regions cannot be ignored. The objectives of planning often clash with one another—productive capacity with current consumption, output with employment, growth with income distribution, present with future benefits. They cannot then be reconciled but must instead be arbitrated in an essentially political process. Development planning is only in part an economic art; to an important extent it is also an exercise in political compromise.

A discussion of development strategy can therefore have no single unifying theme. One lists the things which seem important. Avoiding those which are generally agreed, one concentrates on those which may be controversial, judging by the frequency of errors of omission or commission. Each list is therefore personal, deriving from its author's experience in making Development Plans, or in assessing Plans made by others.

I. INTERDEPENDENCE

Leading Sectors

In planning growth one looks first for the two or three industries whose rapid expansion is going to supply drive to the rest of the system. An economy does not grow at the same rate in all its sectors. The average may be 5 per cent, but the challenge and stimulus is coming from a few places where the rate is 10 per cent or more.

For this there are two main reasons. First, the opportunities for development are unequal. If a country has just discovered new rich reserves of iron but not of coal, the iron ore industry can grow much faster than the coal industry. The discovery of new resources, the introduction of new technologies, the opening of new trade routes or facilities, changes in institutional barriers to growth, and other such opportunities, affect some industries more than others, and therefore promote different rates of growth.

The second set of reasons for differential growth rates can be grouped under the heading of economies of scale. An industry which is growing rapidly creates self-reinforcing tendencies which make it grow even faster—up to a point. It attracts entrepreneurs, inventors and resources. Specialized facilities (railway lines, harbours, banking, research institutes, training schools, marketing institutions, etc.) are set up to deal with its problems and reduce its costs. Brains and money are poured into it. The human mind is a machine which responds to stimuli; it gives thought to the problems which are most pressing, and these tend to be the problems of the industries which are growing fastest; so these are the industries where the greatest progress occurs, creating still greater opportunities for new investment. This works up to a point, but opportunities are exhaustible; the growth of almost any industry resembles a logistic curve; at first it is slow; then it accelerates; and finally with age it falls again.

How much stimulus a new industry imparts to the rest of the economy depends partly on how far it uses local resources, on whether its product can be processed locally, on how far the incomes it generates are spent on local goods and services, on how far the facilities which are created for it (railways, ports, water supplies, etc.) improve the climate for other industries, and on how far the novelty of its technology or institutions is imitated in other sectors. In these respects there are wide differences among industries, and among countries. One of the most fruitful consequences of planning can be the exploitation of potentials which might otherwise escape, so that the impact of major or expanding industries may spread as widely as possible.

This is why development planning begins not by projecting consumer demands, but by seeking the most fruitful production possibilities. Which are the two or three major industries whose high rate of growth is expected to carry the whole economy forward at 5 or 6 per cent? What are the obstacles in their path, and how can the opportunities they present be exploited most widely? Planning starts here, and then spreads out to the rest of the economy. It does not stop here; in due course all opportunities and needs, big and small, must pass under review, and be dealt with according to priority. But it is safe to say that if the planners do not have two or three industries on which to rely for vigorous growth, the prospect of raising the overall growth rate of the economy from 3 per cent to 5 per cent is very small.

In the course of economic growth the economy becomes more complex, in the sense that production for intermediate use (one firm selling commodities and services to another) grows faster than production for sale to the final buyer. Investments designed to exploit industrial interrelations are an important source of growth. Normally the market will seek out and handle these possibilities but it can be greatly aided by good planning. The natural resources of an underdeveloped economy remain to be explored; surveys and pre-investment studies turn up possibilities which would otherwise not be known. Market research, and the efforts of Development Corporations to induce new entrepreneural interest also pay off in investments which would not otherwise occur. Ignorance is one of the chief obstacles to development.

Given the information, the market will take care of most situations involving interdependence unless the sums involved are very large, or some of the parts of doubtful profitability. The exploitation of new natural resources in previously underdeveloped areas tends to involve large investments because infrastructure has to be created (roads, water supplies, power, hospitals, schools, residential housing). Entrepreneurs are willing to invest in some parts of the complex, but not in others. The Government has to be involved in these big deals, partly as the broker bringing different interests together, but also because some of the needed investments are in what is normally the Government's sphere.

That planners must play an active role in investigating new possibilities is now generally accepted. The theoretical problem posed by interdependence is economic: in what circumstances is it justifiable to subsidize activity A, which is unprofitable, on the ground that activity A increases the profitability of B? The obvious answer—whenever the increase in the profitability of B exceeds the required subsidy—happens to be wrong; but the right answer —whenever this is the most productive use of the resources required for A and B together—requires further analysis if it is to be helpful.

The Price System

If the price system is functioning perfectly, the price of any resource will be its value in the most productive marginal use to which it can be put. Any enterprise which can make a profit (over and above the cost of interest on capital and normal remuneration to managerial skills) will therefore represent a superior use of resources; and any which operates at a loss is making an inferior use of resources. If all resources are scarce and fully utilized, the set of projects which maximizes output will also be the set that maximizes the average product of each resource taken separately; it will also be the set that yields the highest return to each resource taken separately; so it matters not whether we take the most profitable set of projects (from the standpoint of returns to capital), or the projects which can pay the highest wages; the result is the same. However, this presupposes that all prices correctly reflect relative scarcities, benefits and costs.

In practice, prices provide a useful first approximation to costs and returns, but since the price mechanism does not function perfectly, the test of profitability is not decisive. An enterprise may make a profit because it is paying less for its resources than they are worth in alternative uses; or it may make a loss because it is paying more than their worth in alternative uses; this must be checked before profit or loss can be identified with superior or inferior use of resources. It would be impossible to check every use of every resource, because prices and uses are innumerable. We make do with an imperfect system of prices, checking only major projects and a few crucial prices.

Some examples will illustrate the analysis, and the typical sources of error in the price system:

(a) Costing of a new project to extract mineral ores shows a loss. Investigation indicates that this is because the owners of the land are demanding a royalty of five dollars on each ton extracted. It further appears that the land is idle, and has no other use. The project is therefore justified. If the lands were planted in crops yielding as much as could be derived from the five-dollar royalty, converting them to mineral extraction would not be justified.

(b) A certain factory, burning its own wastes, is driving out of business another factory burning fuel oil, which is taxed. The tax must be deducted from costs in order to compare efficiencies in the use of resources.

(c) It is proposed to import machinery to take over an operation now done by hand. Unemployment will not result, since the labour displaced will be absorbed in other uses. If there is a shortage of foreign exchange, the real cost of the imported machinery is understated.

(d) The costs of generating electricity from a hydroelectric scheme (to last eighty years) and from diesel plants (to last thirty years) are being compared. If the rate of interest understates the real scarcity of capital, the cost of the hydroelectric scheme will be understated.

(e) Two investments, using the same amount of capital, yield different rates of return to capital. The investment with the lower yield provides employment for twice as many persons. If full employment prevails, the number employed is irrelevant. But if unemployment prevails, wage rates overstate the value of the labour, since there is no alternative use. The amounts paid out in wages should therefore be included when comparing the productivity of the two investments.

The argument most often cited to justify projects which show a financial loss is the contribution they make to employment either directly, or through making other investments possible. The point is made either by arguing the difference between money and real costs, or by arguing that additional employment will circulate additional purchasing power to the advantage of other enterprises. This is the core of the famous Rosenstein-Rodan argument for the balanced planning of industrial growth.[1] If X starts a shoe factory and pays out $1,000 a year in wages, his employees will spend only a part of their earnings on the purchase of shoes. The rest they spend on other commodities, and X gets back his $1,000 only if total employment increases sufficiently in the rest of the economy to raise total expenditure on shoes to $1,000. Thus, if the marginal propensity to spend on shoes were 0.01, it follows that total expenditure must increase to $100,000, or the shoe factory will fail.

Fundamentally, the Rosenstein-Rodan case is an aspect of the general proposition that if labour and capital are unemployed, an increase in the monetary circulation will increase real output; the same result could be achieved, as Keynes showed, by digging holes in the ground and filling them up again; making shoes is all the more advantageous. The argument would not hold if resources were fully employed, since the failure of the shoe factory would then indicate only that the resources were more highly valued in other employments. Even with unemployed labour, the argument will not hold if the workers spend money on imports, or on buying additional food from farmers who do not increase their output, since this merely leads to structural inflation[2] (if the shoes can be exported there is no problem); Rosenstein-Rodan is assuming a closed economy which is capable of meeting all its needs if only adequate demand is generated. Given these assumptions, it is

[1] P. N. Rosenstein-Rodan, 'Problems of Industrialization of Southern and South Eastern Europe', *Economic Journal*, June-September 1943.
[2] See below, page 43.

desirable for X to offer employment in producing shoes, but he will make a loss by doing so unless other employers also increase their production in the right proportions. The situation is ripe for 'indicative planning'.[1]

The validity of arguments based on the existence of unemployment depends on the situation in the labour market, which varies greatly among underdeveloped countries. Several countries in Asia and the Middle East have extreme population pressure in the countryside. The conventional wage rate for unskilled labour exceeds the marginal product of labour on the land, from which innumerable workers could be drawn. By contrast, in the southern parts of West Africa, where rainfall is adequate, cultivable land is abundant, and such unemployment as exists in the towns is due to errors of social policy rather than to absence of uses for labour. The argument that a project provides employment should not be entertained if the wages which would be paid to unskilled labour are not significantly different from the marginal product of labour on the land.

External Economies

We pass now from arguments that the money costs of a firm are greater than its real costs, to arguments that the benefits it produces are worth more than its monetary receipts. For the purpose of what follows we shall assume that resources are fully employed, and that the prices an entrepreneur pays for factors of production are equal to their marginal values in other uses. To justify an unprofitable investment one must then demonstrate that the value of what it produces exceeds the cost, and the loss is due to

(1) not being able to charge the consumer for the benefits he receives; or
(2) preferring for political reasons not to charge enough to cover costs although this can be done; or
(3) economies of scale (average cost exceeding marginal cost).

Services yielding indivisible benefits are an example of the first condition. A lighthouse yields indivisible benefits; any ship which passes benefits, and one cannot charge in proportion to benefit. Unscrambled radio is another example. Services for which one cannot charge in proportion to use are normally in the public sector. Perhaps the most important benefit which private indus-

[1] See above, page 19.

trial firms still produce without payment is education. Any new large-scale enterprise serves as a school. Insofar as it keeps the staff it trains, the cost of training them is a part of its investment which may or may not pay. But it also trains people who leave and carry their skills elsewhere, whether to other enterprises or to businesses of their own. Even people who do not work in the enterprise learn from it; they observe its way of doing business, the superior quality of the seeds it uses, its technological practices, its handling of staff, its codes of commercial behaviour. Some loss may therefore be justified as an educational investment.

If one assumes that factor prices correctly reflect real costs, that costs are constant or upward sloping throughout the economy, and that all products are priced at marginal cost, then there are no external economies. It is true that if one firm expands another may in consequence make losses; but these losses signify that the second firm cannot produce a commodity which the public values as highly as it values other commodities which can be made with the same resources. Hence these losses are not to be deducted when evaluating the change from the community's point of view. Similarly, expansion of one firm may bring profits to others producing complementary goods; these profits are 'rents' in the economist's sense; they must not enter into the marginal calculations which alone (in the absence of economies of scale) decide the correct allocation of resources.

Interdependence of profits is an argument for interdependence in planning—for indicative planning or some other information device which will enable entrepreneurs to know more about each others' intentions. In the absence of economies of scale, or the possibility of employing additional resources, it is not an argument for subsidizing one activity at the expense of others.

These remarks hold equally for public projects, the value of which is always exaggerated in argument by bringing in the rents which accrue to some members of the public as a result of any project. If water can be produced at constant cost (e.g. by desalinization) the fact that deserts will bloom is no reason to sell it for irrigation below cost. If the water increases output by more than it costs, the farmers will be able to pay for it; if they cannot pay for the water, it is not justifying its cost. The Government may find it convenient (politically or administratively) to sell water below cost to the farmers, and recoup itself by taxing the landlords; but administrative convenience must not be confused with economic analysis of the most productive use of resources. In assessing proposed public investments one should always start by trying to estimate what the situation would be if all divisible services and commodities were charged for at cost. If the Government wishes to sell below cost, it must justify this to itself not in terms of rents accruing to third parties, but in terms of political or administrative considerations.

This analysis assumes constant or rising costs; economies of scale change the result. In deciding whether to start an enterprise with economies of scale, it is necessary to take into account the rents which will accrue to others if it is established. For full utilization requires that, if it be established, any demand be supplied which can pay its marginal cost; but it should on the other hand be established only if the rents it creates exceed the cost of establishing it. And since some people will benefit more than others, it is customary and appropriate to levy discriminatory charges which fall heaviest on those who benefit most. Indeed it is easily shown that, where rents are adequate, it may be in the social interest to establish the enterprise even though there is no practicable price which would cover average cost if everybody paid the same price. Thus investors in large undertakings which will raise surrounding land values have an incentive to buy up property and include expected increases in land values when calculating whether the investment will be profitable. The social argument does not hold in the absence of economies of scale. If one intends to make an investment which will raise surrounding land values it always pays to buy up the surrounding land before the information leaks out; but if the enterprise will be producing at constant cost, the socially desirable output is determined solely by the public's willingness to pay a price equal to marginal cost (which is also average cost), and rents have no place in this calculation.

Most of the larger investments which are made in underdeveloped countries involve economies of scale, and cannot therefore be assessed in isolation from investments in other industries from which they will buy, or to which they will sell, unless the opportunities for foreign trade make it possible to operate economically without regard to local demands or supplies. An input-output matrix can help, but only if one keeps changing the coefficients with each different level of output considered. Such investments also often involve considerable doubtful guesswork about the future. Whether it pays to develop a railway-iron ore-port-complex, or a road-hydroelectric-aluminium-chemicals-port complex, is subject to some fairly precise figuring, compared with what is involved when one guesses whether it will pay to build a road from A to B to open up new agricultural land; or what will be the total benefit accruing from a large irrigation project.

Uncertainty apart, such calculations tend to be bedevilled by double counting. For example:

(a) The increase in output is calculated, and summed over the expected life of the investment; then something is added for increased capital values. Since an increase in capital values merely reflects future rents due to increased outputs, these rents are thereby counted twice. Or,

(b) In calculating the increase in output, intermediate products are counted twice; for example the investment is credited with the value of the raw material which it produces and also with the full price of the commodity which is manufactured from that raw material. Or,

(c) The investment is credited with the full value of the additional output, without deductions for other factors of production which are used in the process. This is justifiable for factors otherwise unemployable, such as surplus labour; but is not justifiable for factors deflected from other uses.

To calculate the true net social benefit of an investment calls for skepticism as well as skill. The figures submitted to governments almost always involve exaggerated optimism and double counting.[1]

Infant Industries

The 'infant industry' argument has elements both of unrecovered benefits and also of economies of scale. Let us begin by assuming the presence of constant costs per unit of output, the absence of unemployment, and correct factor pricing. Suppose that a new firm would make a loss when established, but could convert this loss into a profit, say, over ten years. This may deter private operation in several ways. Even if there are no unrecovered benefits, the firm may feel that ten years is too long to wait. It may argue

[1] For further discussion see Chapter IV, section 4 below.

that society as a whole has a greater interest in the future than it has. Effectively this means that society should use a lower rate of interest than the current market rate. This is an important element in the infant industry argument.

Next, the prospective fall in the firm's future costs may be due to the training of the workers. If they remain with the firm, the cost of training them is merely a part of the investment, which must pay for itself in higher output later. If the firm pays the workers in accordance with their productivity, its only case for a subsidy will be that society should use a lower rate of interest. If it has to pay trained and untrained workers the same, the latter earning more than they produce, there is an unrecovered benefit to the workers. Also if the workers leave when trained, and put their training to work in other enterprises, the firm is serving partly as a school, and if it has to pay trainees more than the value of their product, it deserves a grant for this purpose.

The fall in the company's costs may be due to the increased efficiency of outside suppliers as they become more familiar with the needs of this industry and better specialized to serve it. Banks, raw material suppliers, engineers, wholesale and retail distributors, university research workers and others give their minds to the problems of the new firm, and serve it better with the passage of time. This may be simply a function of time and not of size. It is part of the learning process, and from the standpoint of the firm is an uncompensated benefit, if it is expected to make a loss over ten years in order to give the rest of the economy the experience of learning to be more efficient.

The fall in costs may also be a function of size, either because the firm's costs fall with the magnitude of its operations, or because suppliers' costs fall as the firm's demands increase. Then one has to consider the rents of all those who would benefit if facilities were now built on a large scale, and output sold at marginal cost. We are back with interdependent planning of investment.

The fact that suppliers become more efficient as they become more familiar with new industrial needs, and the fact that industrial services fall in cost as they operate on a larger scale, combine to convert the 'infant industry' into an 'infant industrialization' argument; i.e. to emphasize that a country which has hitherto specialized in agriculture needs to approach industrialization not by calculating the cost of each project separately, but by calculating what could happen to costs if a whole complex were established, and time and effort allowed for the specialization, research and learning which pay dividends. It has even been argued that a country which took the industry-by-industry approach could never break out of the agricultural circle, in competition with established industrial producers, and if the terms of trade were moving against agriculture, might find itself becoming poorer and poorer merely because of its failure to make a concerted effort. This is rather an extreme statement of a range of possibilities. We need not examine all the assumptions it involves, but may rest content with the proposition that, in the early days of industrialization the costs of any industry are likely to look quite different when considered as an isolated possibility from how they might look if considered as part of a new industrial complex.

Public Policy
This analysis of costs and interrelated benefits brings out the extent to which assessments depend on individual guesses. Yet the Government cannot avoid making decisions in the private sector, on issues of this kind. For if money costs and real social costs diverge significantly, or there are differences between private and public benefits, there is a positive duty to encourage socially justifiable enterprises which would not otherwise be undertaken or continued; otherwise the desirable rate of investment and of economic growth cannot be attained. There is a parallel duty to discourage cases where private benefit exceeds public benefit. One of the major tasks of development agencies is to seek out and investigate suitable investment projects, and to seek out, investigate and assist suitable investors for these projects. Where the public benefit exceeds the private, it is necessary to establish a set of development policies of various kinds, such as tariff protection, tax exemptions, and subsidies, to encourage investments which would not otherwise occur. And where success depends on the simultaneous planning of a complex of interlocking projects, the development agency may have an important role as intermediary and co-ordinator. Besides, every Government is asked to support new enterprises in one way or another, by tax exemption, or priority licensing, or subsidy or the building of ancillary public services; and it cannot make these decisions without making its

own assessment of how much the enterprise will contribute to the economy, both directly and indirectly. Given the aggressiveness of capitalists seeking favours, the planners are unlikely to have to think up arguments in favour of projects which would not otherwise be profitable. The greater danger is that of being taken in by fallacies, especially by double counting, and by dragging in rents in situations where changes in rents are not relevant to resource allocation.

One of the sadder aspects of this type of problem is that it is not possible to make simple administrative rules which make the decision of each case clear and obvious to all. Each project has to be assessed in its particular context, and subjective assessments cannot be excluded. This opens the door wide to both honest error and dishonesty; this is, indeed, the sphere where Governments are most prone to corruption, since there is opportunity for large sums of money to change hands surreptitiously as a reward for favourable decisions. If project evaluation cannot be accomplished honestly, the community would sometimes be better off if the Government kept out of it as much as possible, leaving the regulation of investment to the admittedly imperfect price mechanism.

Summary
1. Investments designed to exploit the interrelationship of industries and services are an important source of economic growth. To exploit some of these opportunities requires simultaneous operations by different interests; planners should seek out such opportunities and promote collaboration.

2. Losses in one undertaking may give rise to profits in others; arguments for subsidies in these cases need to pass stringent tests.

3. Whether or not interrelationship is claimed, a subsidy can be justified if money costs exceed real costs because prices do not reflect the real scarcity of resources, especially foreign exchange, capital, or labour. The argument with regard to the price of labour is often stated in the form of justifying a project because it creates employment; the argument is valid in those underdeveloped countries where the conventional wage of unskilled labour exceeds the marginal product of labour on the land but not otherwise.

4. Even if prices reflect real costs correctly, interdependence will justify a subsidy if services or commodities whose benefit exceeds their cost are distributed below cost (*a*) because charges

cannot be collected for use; or (b) there are economies of scale or (c) charges can be collected but there are good political or administrative reasons for charging less than marginal cost. Except in these three cases, the fact that investment in one project increases profits of losses in other projects is irrelevant when allocating resources, if prices reflect real costs.

5. Education is one of the more important benefits for which a firm may not be able to recoup its costs; education and economies of scale are the twin pillars of the infant industries argument.

6. Assessment of differences between real and money costs and differences between benefits and money receipts cannot be made precisely, and opens the door to arbitrary decisions; but cannot be avoided if resources are to be allocated to their most productive uses.

2. FOREIGN TRADE

Economic growth and foreign trade are intimately connected. Trade can stimulate growth, if exports are tending to increase faster than imports, or be a brake on growth, if imports are tending to increase faster than exports. One of the important objectives of development planning is therefore to ensure that the rate of growth of output, the propensity to import and the rate of growth of exports are mutually consistent.

Stages of Foreign Trade

Exports play different roles in different stages of development. One can distinguish five such stages: a first stage where exports are the engine of growth; a second stage where import substitution sets the pace; stage three, where unbalanced growth may set off structural inflation; stage four, where the propensity to import is reduced by breaking bottlenecks; and stage five, where, despite a low import propensity, a ceiling is set to the growth rate of a mature economy by the potential rate of growth of exports. These are not historical stages; an economy may skip a stage, or may move backwards; division into stages is merely a way of distinguishing the situations in which an economy may find itself.

Exports are the engine of the first stage of economic growth. A country cannot begin development from a subsistence level by producing for the home market only. An increase in *per capita* income increases the demand for nearly everything, but no country can produce nearly everything, since no country has every kind of mineral, climate and soil. Hence an increase in *per capita* income causes imports to increase. Income which has been generated in producing goods for the home market only is spent instead on buying imports. Some of the goods are unsold; producers are bankrupted, and development stops. Self-sustaining progress can continue only if the increase in imports is matched by an increase in exports.

In the neo-classical model the possibility that the rate of growth of exports can be a brake on the rate of growth of output is usually ignored, because it is customary to assume first that total demand is maintained, and secondly that small changes in prices will effect big changes in quantities. Thus, if an increase in output increases imports, there is a deficit of home spending. This releases goods which are automatically exported. A high elasticity of supply is assumed, such that resources can switch easily from supplying the home market to supplying exports. Also the demand for exports is assumed to increase to the necessary level, partly because of the additional income which the increase in imports has put into foreigners' hands, and partly because a small fall in the price of exports will in any case do the trick. It is recognized that an increase in the propensity to import may move the terms of trade against a country, whether by lowering its money income (if it is on the gold standard) or by effecting a devaluation, but the relevant demand and supply elasticities are assumed to be such that full employment is maintained with only slight changes in prices.

These assumptions do not always hold in the real world. Export income may grow too slowly, whether because the elasticity of supply is too low, or because the foreigner's elasticity of demand is too low (this matters to countries which are supplying a large proportion of the trade in one commodity) or because the demand for one's exports depends on factors other than price which are difficult to change (industrial countries may have difficulties in selling which are unrelated to price). If exports do not grow fast enough, the deflation in the home market remains. This deflation discourages investment; so equilibrium may be restored in the balance of payments not as a result of exports growing, but as a result of output (and so imports) declining. One cannot predict whether the balance of payments problem will be solved easily or only with great difficulty unless one knows all the relevant elasticities. At one extreme exports are no problem and cannot brake growth; at the other extreme difficulties with exports are the major obstacle to growth.

An economy cannot start its economic development by producing for the home market alone because some exporting would also be required. It is much easier to start by exporting, and this is why historically the beginnings of economic development in every country have been generated by an increase in exports. Of course not every increase in exports spurs development. Suppose that the landlords have been taking 50 per cent of the peasants' output, and using it to maintain handicraftsmen, musicians, artists, priests, soldiers and other retainers. If now the landlords acquire instead a taste for foreign goods, they will export some of what they take from the peasants, and the result is not development, but unemployment for the retainers whom they previously maintained. What helps growth is not a mere diversion of output to exports, but rather an increase of output to meet an increased demand for exports.

Production for exports can bring considerable prosperity to a subsistence economy. Exports raise the incomes of all those who are directly involved—small farmers, wage-earners, middlemen and investors, since nobody need be involved (outside a slave society) unless involvement raises his income. These incomes also provide a base from which to move forward to other stages of development, both by increasing productive capacity, and also by creating a challenging home market.

Productive capacity is increased because these incomes support considerable improvement of infrastructure and of skills, whose benefits are not confined to the products which pay for them. Capital is invested in transportation (harbours, roads, railways, telecommunications), in electric power, in banking and commercial institutions, and in public services (schools, hospitals, water supplies and general administration). The community acquires a new set of resources and skills which would serve it to produce new commodities even if the original exports disappeared. (This is why it pays to mine and export ores, even though this disposes of a wasting asset.)

The proceeds of exports are used to buy imports. Thus import substitution becomes a challenge to domestic producers. The export industry buys many commodities to use up in production (fuels, chemicals, timber, machines, ores, fibres, etc.). It is thus linked, on the production side, to many other industries, whose output is thereby stimulated. The industry also pays out incomes to farmers, wage-earners and others, whose expenditure is also a challenge to consumer goods industries. At first, much of this income goes in importing consumer goods, but as productive capacity increases, import substitution takes place.

Import Substitution

Thus the second stage of economic development is import substitution, producing for the home market. A country cannot start its development by producing for the home market, but given export production, can generate further progress by substituting home production for imports. The range of possibilities is wide. Import substitution is not confined to manufactured goods and industrial equipment. Production of raw materials can also be stimulated. Also, increasing income changes the pattern of food consumption (from roots to cereals, meat, milk, vegetables and fruits) and the failure of farmers to keep up with these changes is reflected in increased imports of food.

Now developing countries differ immensely in the extent to which they seize the opportunities created by expanded exports, and move into the import substitution stage. For this there are both technical and political reasons.

It is technically easier to produce some commodities rather than others. Generally speaking, it is easier at low levels of development to start growing agricultural crops for export than to start manufacturing industrial commodities for export. Agriculture requires special soils and climates, but industry requires only skills and equipment, which can be duplicated anywhere; hence it is easier to be superior in agriculture than to be superior in manufacturing, at low levels of development. So in the beginning, the engine of growth is always not only exports, but exports of agricultural or mineral raw materials in which the country has some geographical advantage. In drawing up a Development Plan for a subsistence economy, the first task is to discover, by surveying its natural resources, what geographical advantages it may have.

Once having started with some favourable commodity, it is very easy to overspecialize; this is why so many countries pass through a stage of monoculture. Specialization pays; it is the secret of economic success. So all the resources associated with the new export tend to specialize in its requirements. Transport is designed to serve it, geographically. Banks, commodity exchanges, legal contracts, research institutes, training facilities, universities and practically everything else, specialize in the problems of this one export commodity, to the neglect of most other opportunities. The community maximizes its gain from this commodity, at the expense not merely of other potential gain, but also of becoming dependent on a market which may easily disappear for reasons beyond its control.

A sensible community should fight against over-specialization. This requires a deliberate and expensive effort. Money must be spent on research, training and investment in commodities which are not now as profitable, or do not now seem as promising, as the dominant export. Such money would have to be raised by taxing the dominant export. But those associated with this export —not only the capitalists but also the farmers and wage-earners —tend to be powerful politically, and therefore prevent efforts to develop other forms of production. They demand that these others 'stand on their own feet', while forgetting how much effort, Governmental and otherwise, had to be put into the now dominant export before it learnt how to stand on its own feet. Failures in this respect can be especially damaging to incipient industrial production for all the reasons enshrined in the infant industries argument for protection (economies of scale, investment in skills, external economies) as well as in those cases where manufacturing costs are high because firms are required to pay wages in excess of what their workers could produce in alternative occupations.

The institutional structure of foreign trade can also be important. Where exports come to be handled by a few big foreign wholesalers, who also bring in most of the imports, perhaps even using their own ships, there is small chance that the challenge of import substitution will be met. For the interest of these traders in imports and shipping will make them hostile to measures aimed at reducing imports.

Failure to pursue import substitution is associated with imperialism, but is not confined to that political system. Imperialism virtually ensures that measures will not be taken to pursue import substitution, but political independence does not ensure that the challenge will be taken up, since those associated with the dominant export are not necessarily foreigners, and can be just as powerful in a sovereign state as in a colony.

The Great Depression of the 1930's, followed by the Second World War, did more to promote import substitution than any political change, since both these events emphasized the dangers of over-specialization and destroyed the ideological scheme (misuse of a static Law of Comparative Costs) on which the defence of over-specialization was based. Since the Second World War most countries have progressed rapidly along the path of import substitution, confining themselves, unfortunately, mainly to manufactures, while tending to ignore raw materials and food. Annual rates of increase of industrial production of 8 to 10 per cent have become quite common, in countries where agricultural output increases only by 3 per cent or less. Thus, in several, the possibilities of import substitution of manufactures are already exhausted, or about to be exhausted, and development must move into a new stage, or decelerate.

Structural Inflation

In an underdeveloped economy the possibilities for manufacturing are limited on the one hand by technical factors, and on the other hand by the size of the market. Technical factors include absence of the heavy raw materials needed by some industries, absence of specialized skills needed by others, and the large scale of output of still others. Thus, it will always pay to specialize: the biggest importers of manufactures are the countries which themselves export manufactures.

Apart from these technical factors, which determine which manufactures to make at home and which to import, the market for manufactures as a whole (domestic and imported) is limited by the standard of living. In a country where half the people are subsistence farmers, with no surplus to spend on manufactures, the scope for industrial production is inevitably limited.

Agriculture and industry depend on each other. This is clearest in the closed economy. An increase in industrial production raises the demand for food and raw materials from the farmers. If farm output is stagnant, this raises agricultural prices. This in turn raises wages, reducing the profitability of industrial production, even perhaps to the point of bringing industrial growth to a standstill. In an open economy the required food and raw materials can be imported, without prices rising; but they must then be paid for by exporting industrial products. Industrialization thus demands either a balanced growth of industry and agriculture, or increased exports, or some combination of both.

Industrialization for import substitution is viable until the economy is substituting for all the manufactures it can produce economically. In this stage the increased imports generated by increased income are paid for with the foreign exchange released by import substitution. But this is only a temporary stage. When import substitution is exhausted the economy reverts to stage one, where exports are again the engine of growth.

Countries which have exhausted import substitution without achieving a breakthrough in agriculture are ripe for what is now called structural inflation. Further investment in manufacturing raises real income and therefore the imports of food (and other commodities). This causes both a balance of payments deficit and also deflation in the home market (income generated in producing manufactures being used instead to purchase imports). The action taken to eliminate the balance of payments deficit (devaluation or tariffs) raises the cost of living, and thus starts an inflationary spiral, in which wages and prices chase each other. Alternative action directed in the first instance at eliminating the home deflation (increased monetary circulation, budgetary deficit) has the same effect. Persistence along these paths, to maintain continued growth of industrial production, must produce persistent spiralling inflation. Growth without inflation requires either balanced development of industry and agriculture, or a breakthrough in export trade.

The essence of structural inflation is that a more rapid growth of the economy is prevented by the low growth rate of exports and a too high propensity to import. The way out is either to reduce the propensity to import, by breaking the bottlenecks which prevent domestic supplies from increasing in response to domestic demands, or else to increase the rate of growth of exports to whatever level would be consistent with the growth of output and the propensity to import taken together. An economy which is solving its problem by eliminating bottlenecks is in stage four. When this stage is completed, elasticities of supply will be fairly high, but the country will still not be able to produce everything it consumes. In this final stage the limiting factor on the rate of growth, given the propensity to import and a high propensity to invest, will again be the rate at which exports can be expanded. Exports, from being the engine of growth in the subsistence economy (stage one), can become the brake on growth in the mature economy (stage five).

Latin America furnishes examples of economies in the first four stages. Venezuela is in stage one; an economy growing at over 6 per cent per annum, with exports (oil) as the engine of growth. Brazil was in stage two through the 1950's; a high growth rate based on import substitution of manufactures. Chile has been in stage three, structural inflation; the limits of import substitution of manufactures have been reached; further growth requires either an agricultural breakthrough or a renewed drive to export manufactures and minerals. Mexico has achieved the agricultural breakthrough, and is in stage four.

Farm Policy

A breakthrough in agriculture is especially crucial and especially difficult. It is especially crucial because the slow growth of agricultural output is usually the chief brake on the rest of the economy, and especially difficult because it is necessary to influence the decisions of hundreds of thousands or millions of uneducated peasants.

Small farmers are very responsive to price changes; the problem lies not here but in their slow response to new technology. There is little difficulty in getting them to abandon less profitable for more profitable crops; the large output of cocoa, peanuts, rubber and other such exported crops in Asia and Africa supplies ample proof. Discovering such crops, and introducing them to small farmers is a well trodden road towards higher levels of living.

But the ground is more difficult when the problem is not more of one crop and less of another, but more of all, i.e. an increase in productivity per acre (or per man) measured at constant prices. For this requires new technology, and small farmers are slow to absorb new technology.

Sometimes the answer may be to raise the average level of prices received by farmers. This is not always effective. While farmers will grow more of A and less of B if A's price rises relatively to B's, it does not follow that they will grow more of A and B if the price of both rises. Moreover, even if this policy is effective, its cost may be too high. If farmers get more of the national income, other classes get less. To increase farm incomes at the expense of industrial profits, or savings, or public expenditure on services, may indeed reduce the rate of growth, rather than raise it. Paying more to farmers is a good strategy if it will increase their productivity, and especially if a small price increase brings a large increase in output. But if a large increase in prices brings only a small increase in output, the result may only be to slow down the overall rate of economic growth. Even in this case, however, the conclusion is not that it is wrong to raise farm prices, but only that it is wrong to rely exclusively on this weapon, instead of using also other means of raising productivity. While it is true that an increase in farm prices by itself will not necessarily raise farm productivity significantly, it is equally true that keeping farm prices low can be disastrous.

Setting the scene for higher productivity requires a wide variety of measures: adequate prices; public investment in physical facilities such as roads, water conservation, reclamation, drainage and irrigation; public or private investment in warehouses and processing plants; agricultural credit facilities; research into crops, pests, diseases, fertilizers, rotations, etc.; an agricultural education programme, including agricultural extension staff, and, perhaps even more important, farm institutes which adult farmers may attend for short residential courses; measures forcing landowners to disgorge cultivable lands which they are holding idle, including land taxation, and the dismemberment of large estates for land settlement schemes. And, of course, in countries where landlords or moneylenders are parasitical on farm initiative, land reform is needed to ensure that the farmer keeps the produce of his labour and investment. The catalogue is as familiar as it is extensive.[1]

That it is difficult to raise the productivity of small farmers is often said, but the truth is rather that the appropriate effort has seldom been made. Few underdeveloped countries have come near to setting the scene as it needs to be set. Particularly notable is the failure in regard to farmer education. It is taken for granted

[1] For an excellent survey see David Hapgood and Max Millikan, *Policies for Promoting Agricultural Growth*, 1965.

that industrial workers need training, and much money is spent on building trade schools, and organizing industrial apprenticeship. But it is assumed that anybody can farm without prior institutional training, subject only to an occasional visit from an extension agent. The modern trend towards farm institutes, where leading villagers spend months receiving practical training is showing good results. The productivity of small farmers can be increased sharply if men and money are allocated to the task in adequate proportions.

However, creating an agricultural service takes time; men must be trained, and institutions developed. Such is the period of gestation that results must be sought in years, not months. This causes impatience among politicians seeking short cuts to a 7 per cent growth rate. Coercing the farmers seems to some a possible shortcut. Why not force all the farmers into collective farms, and appoint trained scientists to decide what to plant and how? Will not this bring quicker results? The answer is emphatically not. All the countries which have tried this method have found it a failure. Compulsory collectivization makes it easier to control farmers politically, and to tax them, whether directly or through adverse terms of trade; but its effect on agricultural output is to reduce it.

Another alternative, practicable in countries which have unexploited lands, but not in overpopulated countries, is to ignore the small farmers, concentrating resources instead on opening up virgin lands in large-scale farms, using the latest machinery and the latest scientific knowledge. Here also failure is common, though it is not inevitable. Failure has two main sources. First, to keep machinery running in virgin lands far from established engineering service centres, it is necessary to create a system for bringing damaged machinery in and sending it out with minimum delay. This is a major administrative problem, obviously not insoluble, but obviously difficult to solve in countries where skilled engineers and mechanics are in short supply, and administrative ability not noticeably in surplus. The other failure is that of science. Virgin lands are usually virgin because over the centuries farmers have found them marginal; maybe rainfall is erratic, or the soils are difficult, or trace elements are lacking. The scientists have concentrated on studying the agricultural problems of the areas which are under cultivation. When suddenly sent into the virgin lands, with orders to cultivate immediately hundreds of thousands of acres, they may not even know what problems to expect, let alone what solutions to apply.

Opening up new lands for cultivation is indeed an essential part of agricultural policy, but only in areas whose fertility has been tested. In some of these countries population grows by 30 per cent over ten years; most of this increase can be absorbed only by agriculture. Thus planning must commence with soil maps, rainfall and other fertility data, in search of new lands of known potential whose development is hindered only by lack of roads, drainage or other facilities. Also, in most of these countries increases in agricultural output come more easily from larger acreage than from higher productivity. These two can and should be linked. Where large sums are to be invested in opening new land, steps must be taken to ensure high productivity. If small farmers are settled on such lands, tenure can be made conditional on good husbandry—even to the extent of prescribing fertilizers, crop rotations, seeds, or plant protection measures. The choice between establishing large farms or settling small farmers under controlled tenures then depends mainly on political sentiment.

Export Promotion

By the time a country has passed through the import substitution stage exports will normally have ceased to be the main engine of growth. Production for the home market will have grown in relative importance, and investment for the home market will have become an autonomous source of economic growth. It is still necessary for the propensity to import, the rate of growth of exports and the rate of growth of output to be consistent with each other, but a mature economy adjusts foreign trade to growth rather than depending on foreign trade for growth.

Most developed countries are therefore in stages four or five, maintaining high growth rates either by keeping the propensity to import low (e.g. the USSR) or, since the range of climates and minerals required for a low propensity to import is rare, more often by keeping the rate of growth of exports high (Germany, Japan). Failure to do either of these (e.g. Britain) causes exports (or the propensity to import) to become a brake on the rate of growth of output.

Taking the underdeveloped world as a whole, exports of primary products have not since the Second World War played quite the dominating role as engine of growth that they did before the First World War. This is due partly to concentration during the last fifteen years on exploiting the opportunities for import substitution in manufacturing. But it is also due partly to having higher growth targets than exports of primary products can sustain (taking the group as a whole). During the 1950's the exports of underdeveloped countries increased at an average annual rate of 3.6 per cent. This is probably as high as at any time in the past, but it is not high enough to sustain the growth rates which underdeveloped countries would now like to achieve.

The underdeveloped countries have so far exported mainly to the developed, and mainly primary products—minerals, fuels and tropical agricultural commodities. The demand for these is limited in the developed world; and there is in any case no reason why the growth rate of the underdeveloped countries should be tied to the growth of demand for their products in developed countries. If the underdeveloped can achieve among themselves balanced growth of their manufactures, minerals and agriculture, their rate of growth will not be tied to exports to the developed world.

Most underdeveloped countries are small enough to be able to sell all they want to in the world market without affecting prices adversely. The current tendency of planners to neglect exports is based more on psychology than on objective reality. Exports behaved unfavourably during the 1930's and '40's, and therefore fell into bad odour. Instinctively a planner therefore tends to seek a development strategy which minimizes imports and exports, if this can at all be achieved. Such a strategy is appropriate for those stages of development where economic growth can be based on substitution for imports or on breaking the agricultural bottleneck; in other stages neglect of exports ultimately brakes the rate of growth itself.

Countries which command a large proportion of world trade in some particular commodity—say, copper, cocoa, tea or coffee—are in a special position; as are also countries which sell in protected markets with limited absorptive capacity. If a country's share of the market is 40 per cent, and the elasticity of demand for the commodity is less than 0.4, any increase in sales will reduce its total receipts. A country in this position should not seek to export more of this particular commodity; its policy should be to diversify its exports.

Recently, several underdeveloped countries have begun to export manufactures. Those which suffer from population pressure have no option; they are bound to develop as net importers of agricultural commodities and net exporters of manufactures, but any country is liable to want to export some manufactures since, as its skills and resources increase, there will be some manufactures in which it has a relative advantage. Rapid industrialization since the Second World War has brought this situation to a head, and caused some shift of emphasis in the discussion between developed and underdeveloped countries of the barriers to international trade. When it was assumed that the underdeveloped world must concentrate on primary products, remaining forever in stage one, this discussion centred on methods by which the developed protect their agriculture, and on measures to stabilize the prices of primary commodities. But the United Nations World Trade Conference of 1964 found underdeveloped countries concentrating as well, for the first time, on the developed countries' tariffs against manufactured goods. This problem will grow in importance.

Most underdeveloped countries are not good at exporting manufactures. Primary commodities can be sold in unlimited amounts on the world's produce exchanges, but manufactures have to be sold through a network of distributive channels, which take time and skill to construct. Considering how large world trade in manufactures already is, failure to capture an adequate share despite competitive prices must be explained in terms of poor salesmanship rather than in terms of the height of tariffs.

Customs unions and other regional arrangements are a means by which countries help each other to industrialize, by offering protection in each others' markets, and are of special value to industries in which the market of any one country, by itself, is not large enough for production on an economic scale. Such arrangements, however, are very difficult to organize, since the benefits are seldom divided equally between the countries which would participate. Progress is being made on these lines, but its rate is determined more by political than by economic considerations.

The Price Level

For countries which are open to international trade a rising price level can be the chief obstacle to economic development. Rising costs hold down exports and also make it difficult for the import substituting industries to compete with imports. Shortage of foreign exchange then leads to licensing of imports, which may in turn restrict investment.

Keeping domestic costs low does not raise for most under-developed countries the terms of trade complication which it raises for some industrial countries. If a country has some mono-poly power in markets where it buys or sells, an increase in its prices relatively to those of its customers will not necessarily diminish its net profit from trading, since what it loses in volume it may more than make up in improved terms of trade. Most underdeveloped countries are not in this position. The prices they receive for exports or pay for imports are determined in world markets where their participation is relatively small. Whether they devalue or appreciate their currencies, world prices remain the same, and so their terms of trade remain the same. The level of their domestic costs determines not what they receive for exports, but how profitable it is to produce their exports. Hence if they wish to stay in production they must keep their costs in line with costs in similar countries.

Keeping in line does not mean price stability because prices fluctuate widely in the world commodity markets where under-developed countries buy their imports and sell their exports. These price fluctuations enter directly into the domestic cost structure, pressing prices upwards and downwards in irregular succession. Various measures are designed to reduce the impact of such fluctuations (such as Government purchase of exportable commodities at constant prices, or export taxes which vary in-directly with export prices, or import duties and subsidies which vary indirectly with prices), but these have only limited coverage and partial effect. At times when world commodity markets are active, the price levels of underdeveloped countries rise, and at other times the price levels fall. These fluctuations produce many difficulties—including uncontrollable variations in the yield of taxes, changes in the terms of trade, changes in the level of employment, and so on. But fortunately they are not relevant to the competitiveness of different countries producing or capable of producing the same commodities, since their general effect is to keep prices everywhere in line. From the competitive point of of view what matters is not the fluctuations but the trend.

Even the trend is not necessarily constant. World prices are subject to deep secular swings, in which a long period of rising prices, lasting one or two decades or more, may be succeeded by an equally long downward movement; and to these swings are added other deep movements generated by wars, gold discoveries and other such influences. At present, thanks to high investment levels and active trade unionism all over the world, prices are tending to move upward in most countries, so the policy of keeping in line actually involves a slight upward trend.

If a country's domestic costs rise faster than those of competing countries, it can stay in line only by devaluing its currency to the extent of the divergence. Getting back into line is not easy, because devaluation itself raises domestic prices further. Devaluation raises the cost of imports, and therefore the cost of living. This provokes demands for higher wages and other incomes. If these are granted, part or all of the devaluation will have been cancelled out by the increase of domestic costs. Granting these demands therefore raises the cost of living further, and so sets in motion the spiral in which prices and incomes chase each other. Most countries which resort to devaluation find that it is not a once-for-all, but at best a converging process, in which it takes a series of devaluations, some severe, to reach the desired equilibrium between domestic costs and foreign prices, even though the original divergence may not have been very large. Hence devaluation, essential as it is once prices have got out of line, is something to be avoided if one can manage without it.

In deciding whether to devalue, costs in export industries and in import substituting industries must be considered separately. It is not necessary to devalue merely to stimulate import substitution, for this can be achieved equally well by controlling imports (whether by import duties or by licensing), which is less likely to start a price-wages spiral than is devaluation. One devalues if costs are out of line in export industries, for the alternative, a wages subsidy, is too costly for the budget. But costs can be out of line in import-substituting industries without being out of line in export industries: indeed, if the exports are produced by small farmers who hire no labour, their 'costs' are a dubious concept. There is no point in devaluing unless this will increase the volume of exports; so the elasticity of supply of exports, and the elasticity of world demand are the two factors which determine whether a country should devalue or apply import controls instead. In most cases both these factors will indicate devaluation. Unless the farmers are very depressed indeed, higher prices will call forth larger supplies for export. And unless the country is the major supplier of some particular commodity, the elasticity of world demand for its exports will exceed unity, and the larger supplies will earn more foreign exchange. One can avoid devaluation for some time by devices which raise prices to the exporters (such as Government purchases for export at prices in excess of the world price, or differential exchange rates favourable to exporters and unfavourable to importers). But if the gap between domestic and foreign prices gets wider and wider, such devices become increasingly more cumbersome, and devaluation is inevitable.

The importance of keeping domestic costs in line with world prices can hardly be exaggerated. An incorrect foreign exchange rate can be the chief cause of economic stagnation.

Balanced Growth

Extreme and persistent shortages of foreign exchange during the 1950's have forced Governments to give higher priority to foreign trade. Special measures are being taken to promote exports (subsidies, foreign exchange premia, credits, advertising). The fact that the foreign trade of developed countries has been expanding twice as fast as the trade of the underdeveloped has helped to remove from foreign trade such stigma as it acquired during the great depression of the 1930's.

The appropriate strategy for foreign trade in a Development Plan depends on the stage at which the country finds itself. At low levels of development, where both imports and exports are small, the planners should look for industries which will contribute a large increase in exports. At the next stage, one may concentrate on import substitution. The attack on agricultural stagnation should begin as soon as possible, not only to enrich the farmers, but also because the economy must soon bog down in general stagnation unless the agricultural problem is solved. Import substitution and increased agricultural output, taken together, will give the planners a long breathing space during which they can concentrate on the home market, neglecting exports; but as the economy matures, the danger of exports becoming a brake on output will again be faced.

The Plan must provide such a balance between different industries as will keep the rates of growth of output, imports and exports in equilibrium (but not necessarily equality) with each other. Many Plans fail this test. The planners write down output targets for various industries without considering their mutual consistency. They propose large increases in industrial output, forgetting that this would raise the demand for food and raw materials; or rates of growth of the output of services which are out of line with the rates proposed for commodities. One of the merits of macroeconomic forecasting is that it focuses attention on this issue. The impact of every industry on every other is taken into account automatically, and the exercise is not complete until demand equals supply in the economy as a whole.

Summary

1. The propensity to import, the rate of growth of exports, and the rate of growth of output must be mutually consistent. Imbalance causes either stagnation or structural inflation.

2. At low levels of development exports are the engine of growth. The planners' chief task is to find new natural resources, or new methods of utilization which will cause a rapid growth of exports.

3. At the next level high growth rates are possible without relying on exports, by reducing the propensity to import (import substitution). However, the limits to industrialization for the home market are reached quickly if there is no simultaneous breakthrough in agriculture, to absorb the increased output of manufactures and meet the demand for food and raw materials.

4. The main obstacle to agricultural improvement is inadequate effort by Governments; the means to success are well known.

5. Given the propensity to import, the rate of growth of exports may become the brake on the rate of growth of output. Every Development Plan should pay special attention to measures for increasing exports.

6. Both exports and import substitution are impeded by rapidly

rising prices and costs. Overvaluation of the foreign exchange rate can be the chief reason for economic stagnation.

7. As underdeveloped countries industrialize, they will export some manufactures. This calls for increased international co-operation, both regionally and by universal agreement.

3. CAPITAL INTENSITY

Comparative Advantage
Poor countries have less physical capital per head than rich countries, and must therefore choose less capital-intensive techniques of production. It does not follow that they will have only the less capital-intensive industries. Capital works with natural resources as well as labour, and a poor country's natural resource advantage may be such that it pays to develop some rich but capital-intensive natural resources (e.g. mines) rather than poorer but less capital-intensive resources. Comparative advantage is also based on relative differences in skills; a poor country may be nearly as efficient as a rich one in some highly capitalized processes, but much less efficient in processes relying more on skill than on capital, and may then profitably specialize in the capitalized processes where it is least relatively inefficient, despite the higher relative cost of capital. Thus, in jobs where precision work is important, machine methods are even more attractive in poor countries, with low skills, than they are in richer countries with more reliable craftsmanship. If we compare processes which differ only in capital-intensity (but use the same natural resources and skills) we should expect the poor country to be further from the capital-intensive end of the spectrum than the rich country; but if we are comparing different industries, with different skill and natural resource requirements, there is no reason to expect all the capital-intensive industries to be in the country which has relatively more capital.

Underdeveloped countries are constantly criticized for putting some of their capital into capital-intensive industries. These countries make many mistakes and waste a lot of capital, but one cannot legitimately determine which industries are suitable for underdeveloped countries merely by measuring capital-intensity. In the standard case of steel, for example, the presence or absence of coking coal and iron ore, the costs of transportation, the availability of appropriate skills, and the size of the market are usually far more significant than the relative cost of capital. However, whatever industries a poor country may have, we should expect it in each industry to favour less rather than more capital-intensive techniques.

Interest Rates

The function of discriminating between more and less capital-intensive techniques falls in the first place upon the rate of interest, which determines the choice between techniques yielding returns more heavily in the near future and techniques yielding more heavily in the more distant future. Thus if one wishes to increase the electricity generating capacity by say 50,000 kW, one may have the choice between building a dam which would cost say $65,000,000 to complete, last for eighty years, and have an operating expense of say $900,000 a year, or building an oil burning station of the same capacity, costing $15,000,000 to complete, lasting for twenty years and having an operating expense of $3,000,000 a year. The two alternatives are reduced to the same base by calculating what annual rent would have to be paid for each capital structure, so as to return to the investor his original capital and the ruling rate of interest. The standard formula for calculating this annual rent is

$$a = K \frac{(1-r) \, r^n}{(1-r^n)}$$

where a is the annual rental, K is the capital invested per unit of output, r is the appropriate rate of compounding (i.e. unity plus the rate of interest) and n the expected life of the capital, in years. A little calculation will show that in this example the two methods cost the same at a rate of interest of about 5 per cent. A lower rate favours the higher initial cost (the hydro plant), and a higher rate the lower initial cost (the oil burner).

The test of whether the ruling rate of interest is the right rate is whether good borrowers (i.e. those offering excellent collateral) can borrow all they want to borrow at the ruling rate; or whether some form of rationing is applied to them. Most borrowers in less developed countries constitute a substantial risk, whether because they are not well known, or the property they offer as collateral is specially risky (the wide fluctuations in commodity prices have something to do with this), or the market in which it would have to be sold (if need be) is imperfect, or the legal systems (law or courts) are uncertain. The premium for risk is therefore much wider than in developed economies. The basic rate for excellent borrowers is not very different from the similar rate in developed countries, if only because something of an international capital market does exist. Well established Governments of good reputation can borrow at this rate, but they cannot borrow all they would like to borrow at the ruling rates, whether in London, New York, Washington, Paris or in their own money markets. The interest rate at which they borrow does not reflect the true scarcity of capital in their countries. But for many other borrowers the rate of interest is too high; these are fundamentally sound borrowers who are charged excessive rates only because market imperfections (e.g. tenure systems which prevent them from pledging their lands) exaggerate the real risk of lending to them. Some farmers try to get around market imperfections by organizing special credit institutions for sound borrowers (e.g. co-operative credit based on crop liens), leaving the less sound borrowers to money-lenders. Because of market imperfections, too much capital goes at low rates to borrowers who can offer marketable security (especially into Government projects and into luxury building in towns), while too little goes at excessive rates to other borrowers, especially in the countryside.

Wage Rates

Capital-intensity is also affected by the share of wages in output. Given the physical resources of the community, an increase in the real wage tends to lower the number of men whom it pays to employ, and a fall in the real wage increases employment per unit of physical capital. If the real wage exceeds the marginal product of labour, the ratio of capital to labour will be unduly high.

If the real wage is inflexible, it is theoretically possible that the introduction of new inventions will reduce employment. Investment which brings no new techniques cannot reduce employment; on the contrary, an increase in the amount of capital must increase employment, if wages are constant. But the substitution of new labour-saving techniques can reduce employment, and it cannot be assumed that the good effects on employment of more investment of the kind which uses existing (or even more labour-intensive) techniques will necessarily more than offset the bad effects on employment of investment of the labour-saving kind. In the neo-classical economic model full employment is always possible since the wage rate will move to whatsoever level full employment may require; but in the real world the wage rate cannot fall below the subsistence (or some higher conventional) level, and cannot be relied on to produce that degree of capital-intensity which would maximize output.

Exchange Rates

A third factor which can cause excessive capital-intensity, apart from inappropriate interest rates or wages, is an overvalued currency. If the foreign exchange rate is too high imported machinery is too cheap, relatively to labour. So the proceeds of exports, instead of providing employment for workers at home, provide employment instead for workers in the capital-goods factories of foreign countries.

Maximizing Output

The theorist's solution to these problems is simple. If the price mechanism is causing misallocation of resources because prices (the rate of interest, wages, foreign exchange) do not reflect the true scarcities, find the true set of prices, calculate the optimum capital-intensities, and use subsidies, tax incentives or licensing to bring about the right result. How does one find the true prices? In theory they could be found nearly enough by computing from some hundreds of functions. However, such calculations lie some time in the future. The number of functions is not a problem in these days of high-speed computers, but techniques for estimating the shapes of the functions, and solving the non-linear systems (linear functions do not allow adequately for declining marginal yields) are still in the experimental stage. In the absence of true 'shadow' prices, such calculations must in the meantime be based on somewhat arbitrary 'accounting' prices, relying on subjective assessment of how much actual prices diverge from what the true prices would be.

The output to be maximized by shadow pricing is not the 'domestic' but the 'national' product, after excluding income accruing to foreigners. For example, the income generated by doing a project with little capital may be less than the income generated by doing it in a different way with foreign capital. But if the difference is less than the profits which would be exported, the economy gains more from the less productive method. The proposals of foreign capitalists have to be judged not by their general profitability, but by how much they will add to domestic income. Normally the addition to domestic income is considerable, since new industries are created which increase employment. What needs watching are cases where foreign capital brings new techniques which compete with existing domestic production, and result in a net reduction of employment.

If shadow prices could be used as a basis for determining the use of capital, new investment in underdeveloped countries could hardly result in reducing employment. In order to maximize output, capital must be used only where it adds most to output. At the top of the list are new industries which could not exist but for the investment. At the bottom of the list are industries adequately served by handicraft producers, where capital would reduce cost but would not (because the handicraft producers are not now fully employed) produce any additional output that they could not also have produced. At current prices investment in these industries at the bottom of the list might well be the most profitable for investors, but from the social point of view the marginal product of capital in these industries is zero. To say that if one begins at the top of the list, and works downward, one cannot reach the bottom is therefore only to say that the real marginal product of capital cannot be zero in an underdeveloped country. There must be plenty of uses for capital in which it would add to output; to use it where it merely substitutes for already abundant labour must therefore be uneconomic. If uneconomic uses are profitable at current prices, administrative action should be taken to prevent the wasteful use of capital which will otherwise occur.

One reason for waste of capital is the tendency to build plants embodying all the latest technology used in the developed countries, instead of adapting plants to use more labour-intensive technologies. This is sometimes defended by saying that labour costs just as much in poor countries as in rich, despite lower wages, because of lower skills. This is true of some skills, but is not generally true of unskilled occupations, or of occupations whose skills are easily taught. A more sophisticated defence is that it would require new research to produce suitable labour-intensive technologies, and that the expertise which such research would need does not exist or cannot be spared from other tasks. This may be doubted. A large range of technologies already exists in any developed country, since the plants built in each decade differ from one another. It is not really very difficult to distinguish between inventions which have improved the quality or uniformity of the product, or economized the use of raw materials, or improved the precision with which the job is done, on the one hand; and improvements which have merely substituted for labour, such as mechanical transport of materials in the factory, or mechanical packaging, or mechanical bookkeeping, on the other hand. Redesigning the plant to include the former and exclude the latter could be done without great difficulty but for the fact that it is not profitable to make the necessary changes at current prices. Capital cannot be used most productively without administrative action based on some notion of what prices should be.

The big waste of capital in underdeveloped countries has tended to be not in the mechanical processes for transforming raw materials into manufactured products, since these new processes have usually also improved the product and reduced the wastage of raw materials. The waste has come mainly in substituting capital for labour in moving things about; in the handling of materials inside the factory; in packaging; in moving earth; in mining; and in building and construction. The bulldozer, the conveyor belt and the crane usually achieve nothing that labour could not do equally well. They spend scarce foreign exchange solely in order to produce unemployment. Of course, underdeveloped societies differ in the extent of their labour surplus. This is more of a problem in Asia than in Africa. One can therefore justify in some countries degrees of mechanization which cannot be justified in others. However in all the underdeveloped countries cost comparisons in money are not reliable guides to what is economically sound.

Waste of capital also results from failure to recognize the importance of small scale enterprise in economic growth, and to develop a technology appropriate to the small workshop or farm. In the industrial revolutions of the nineteenth century the rapid multiplication of small workshops was as spectacular a feature as the emergence of a few industrial giants. The absence of this feature is notable in some recent Development Plans. Nevertheless, there have also been notable successes. Perhaps the most notable is not in manufacturing industry but in fishing; all over the tropical world a marriage between the outboard motor and the fishing canoe is proving to be most fruitful. Another notable example is the famous Japanese small tractor, suitable for the small farm. Indeed Japan has done so much work on equipping the small workshop that here again progress does not have to wait on new basic research. For most countries the problem is first psychological, then economic. Psychological, in that they must stop looking towards Europe or North America for all their industrial techniques and look instead towards countries which have specialized in producing equipment for the workshop. Economic, because the problem of financing the small workshop, and enabling it to hold its own in competition with large scale mechanized output still remains. As we have seen, if prices do not accurately reflect factor scarcities, desirable labour-intensive methods will not be able to compete with less desirable capital intensive methods unless there is administrative protection.

Maximizing Growth

The purpose of shadow pricing is to maximize the national output. Suppose that the real wage exceeds the marginal product of labour, with resulting unemployment. Employment could be increased by levying a proportionate tax on profits, and subsidizing wages with the proceeds. This would increase output, but by less than the increase in wages (since the marginal product was less than the wage), and would therefore reduce profits both relatively and absolutely.

In a famous article[1] Professors Galenson and Leibenstein have argued that output maximization should not be the goal; or, more precisely, they have argued that the goal should be not to maximize current output, but to maximize output at some future date. If this is so, and if the rate of growth depends mainly on the rate of saving, and if the rate of saving depends mainly on the volume of profits, then it follows that the immediate goal should be to maximize profits; higher capital-intensity is superior to higher employment.

[1] Galenson, W., and Leibenstein, H., 'Investment Criteria, Productivity and Economic Development', *Quarterly Journal of Economics*, August 1955. The argument dates back to David Ricardo's *Principles*, Chapter XXXI.

This chain of argument can be broken at any point. Marginal profits are not necessarily saved; for example, if a mining industry makes higher profits by introducing labour-saving machinery, it is just as likely to export the extra amount to shareholders overseas as to use it to extend its operations. If capitalists use marginal profits to buy more foreign goods, while workers buy more from farmers, who therefore save and invest more, employment will do more for saving than will extra profits. Taxation can be a source of saving, or can be spent to improve human resources in ways which increase productivity; if the Government can raise more taxes from a larger income than from a smaller irrespective of the share of profits, then a larger income may do more for the rate of growth than a smaller income. There are countries where the rate of growth depends mainly on the share of profits, but there are no doubt other cases where it does not.

Neither can it be taken as a universal rule that it is more important to maximize future output then present output. How far ahead one looks is of course relevant; there is less to argue about if the future year is next year than if it is ten years ahead. How far ahead one can afford to calculate depends on how urgent is the need for current output. If the level of living is already pitiably low, the present must have greater priority than in countries with a greater sustenance. If there is massive unemployment, it requires first priority. One can always provide employment, without interfering with capital-intensity, by taxing some people and using the proceeds to employ others on useful works; but for this one needs as large an output of consumer goods as possible, so a policy which simultaneously reduces output and increases investment is doubly inappropriate in these circumstances. Maximization of saving is worth considering in countries where very few people are out of work (because the mass trek from farms to towns has not yet begun) and the standard of nutrition is fairly high. It makes sense, for example, in Guinea, but not, for example, in India.

Shadow Pricing

In any case, even apart from the impossibility of calculating true shadow prices, already mentioned, the practical difficulties in the way of basing policy on such prices cannot be neglected. Suppose that at the prices actually ruling it would pay to substitute capital for labour, but that this would add nothing to output since labour is abundant. It is then clearly wasteful to use capital here to produce what labour could equally well produce, when capital could be used to increase output in sectors where its use would not create unemployment. However, in practice one must consider the relative amounts of labour used, for labour has to be paid; what it is paid helps to determine the price of the commodity; and the price determines demand and output. It may be that there are enough labourers to carry all the freight that lorries could carry, and that the use of lorries creates unemployment. But if at current prices lorries are able to charge one-tenth what porterage would cost, the fact that the same result would be achieved if porters were paid zero is not in practice relevant. Similarly even if labour were the only cost, factories must be allowed to drive out of business all small-scale production where the difference in labour utilization is considerable, and it is only in cases where the difference is not very great that it is practicable to consider protecting handicrafts. (But it must not be forgotten that some handicraft workers, especially in metals, have great potential for development into small workshop producers viably linked into the modern industrial complex. Spotting which handicraft industries have this potential, and strengthening their techniques, capital and market organization are an important part of development strategy.)

Now when one says that in practice, even though unemployment exists, an industry which uses less labour per unit of output is more efficient than one which uses more, one is, in effect, saying that the shadow price should not be zero, but should reflect the burden which using one technique rather than another imposes upon the rest of the community. One therefore ceases to analyse the economy as if it consisted only of one people, with the object of maximizing output per head of population, and divides the people instead into two classes, the employed and the unemployed.

The theorist's assumption that the employed and the unemployed are to be treated as 'one people' is political, not economic. If one asks what it 'costs' to employ a man the answer might be:

1. What he would otherwise produce; or
2. What he would have to be paid; or
3. What he would have to be paid minus such subsidy as he is already receiving.

Economists have chosen the first answer, and have used the marginal productivity theory of distribution to argue that it yields the same results as the other two. If the three answers coincide, one can work equally well with any of them. However, they do not coincide if the man is now unemployed.

Suppose that currently the man lives on the family farm where his marginal product is 10, but his consumption is 50. And further suppose that if he were given wage employment both his marginal product and his consumption would rise to 70. What is the cost of employing him?

1. The employer's answer is 70.
2. The economist's answer is 10.
3. The 'rest of society's' answer is 30, since the man is already being subsidized to the extent of 40.

Suppose that the potential employer is the Minister of Finance, calculating whether to build a dam with bulldozers or with labour. The taxpayers exert pressure on him to do it in the cheapest possible way. With bulldozers the cost comes, let us say, to $20,000,000; by hand it comes to $30,000,000. The economists wish him to use their answer, which might make the costs say $10,000,000 with bulldozers but only $5,000,000 without. If the difference between the unemployed's marginal product of 10 and consumption of 50 was financed by the Treasury paying unemployment relief, the Minister could settle for the third answer; but if the difference was met by the unemployed's family, the taxpayer would still prefer the first answer. Each of these different 'shadow' costs has an important meaning. One cannot in practice completely ignore actual prices, and the burden on the consumer or taxpayer, when making actual decisions.

Administrative Control
Given the desire to maximize output, in the face of prices which do not reflect the true scarcities, it becomes necessary to resort to administrative controls. There are several possibilities: a subsidy to wages, a tax on machinery, tax allowances varying with the share of wages in value added, and licensing the use of machinery. To apply such measures to all employment or investment is simply impracticable, because of the burden on the budget, and the administrative burden. One can at best confine one's attention to certain sectors.

First, the Government should police itself; scrutinize all its construction activity to ensure that machines are not unnecessarily substituted for labour, even though this means that its projects will cost more; do the same for all other Government employment. Merely to prohibit machinery would cause waste; the proper course is to instruct its cost accountants, when deciding how much to invest in machines, to make the calculations as if wages were x per cent lower than they are, x being whatever factor is deemed to yield the appropriate shadow price. One must not expect this to be completely effective. Government decisions are made not by one man but by many different officials in different departments and agencies, each of whom would like to get maximum results for the money allocated to his administration. The Government can expect to have as much trouble controlling its own departments as controlling private enterprise—perhaps even more, since the assumption of moral superiority with which it sometimes approaches private business is not applicable in dealing with public servants.

Next, special controls can be applied to factories which would compete with handicraft production, if there is already much surplus capacity among the handicraft workers. This is relevant only to commodities which are strictly comparable in quality; machines which improve the product, or make it more uniform perform a service for the consumer of which he should not be deprived. Also, if machine production economizes raw materials, or is much cheaper than hand production, the latter should not be protected. Factories should be licensed restrictively (or prohibited altogether) only in cases where handicraft workers (duly helped with credit, new designs, marketing institutions and other extension programmes) can produce what is required in the appropriate quantities and qualities at a price not too much higher (say not more than a third higher) than the cost of factory production. This problem is confined almost entirely to Asia, where handicraft production is extensive and subject to much surplus capacity; action of this kind is not worth considering in Africa or Latin America.

Thirdly, instead of trying to control the techniques of every new factory or other operation, one can confine attention to a few large projects or industries, scrutinize their proposed techniques, and refuse licenses for those which are excessively capital-intensive. This is such a burdensome task that it must obviously be confined to a small number of important new cases. One would have to exclude from such controls industries subject to world competition, such as export industries or industries producing substitutes for imports, where such industries can show that they cannot pay the current level of wages unless permitted to mechanize—or unless the Government will pay a subsidy to wages, or prohibit imports, or meet the cost in some other way.

Finally, the Government can operate on the consumer, persuading him to choose the more labour-intensive commodities (e.g. wooden furniture instead of steel furniture, handwoven cloth instead of machine-made cloth); or failing persuasion, it can tax capital-intensive commodities to discourage their use.

All this is easier said than done effectively and efficiently. If wage costs are too high, employers will mechanize, and labour-intensive techniques and commodities will be discouraged. It is very difficult to prevent this from happening. The planners and the unemployed will be on one side, but employers, consumers and the Minister of Finance will be on the other.

Some Fallacies

The inappropriateness of market prices explains some part of the excessive capital-intensity of development programmes, but errors of approach explain as much or more.

A major source of waste is the ambition of some Governments to acquire prestige through spectacular spending, being sometimes even genuinely persuaded that 'nothing is too good for our people'. This means choosing expensive structures, when cheaper structures would do the job equally well; building to last 100 years structures which are certain to be torn down in thirty years because by then they will be considered obsolete; or building with elaborate grandeur where a simple structure would do. This has some point. Every nation takes a pride in its monuments, and willingness to bear the costs of progress is increased when people see structures which give them pleasure or stimulate their pride. But the cost is real; obviously the more one spends on one project, the less there is to spend on others. Investment which might have provided continuing employment for 100 men, supports instead only seventy or eighty.

Another source of error is the belief that it is the most highly productive technology that maximizes output. For example, it is stated that an increase in wages will stimulate investment in improved cost-reducing technology, and so increase productivity per head. The argument confuses output per person at work with total output; maximizing the first does not maximize the second unless employment remains the same. Investing a given amount in industry A may employ 100 men with average productivity of fifty (total output 5,000). In industry B the same investment may yield average productivity of only forty, but if it provides employment for 150 men, both employment and output will be larger. This is often the case, especially as the proportion of profits going overseas tends to be larger in the more capital-intensive cases. If the degree of capital-intensity will determine the amount of employment, high productivity per person employed is not a sufficient goal.

Related to this error is the further belief that the path of economic development lies mainly through the multiplication of large-scale projects, on which attention is therefore concentrated. Plants are built on too large a scale, in anticipation of demand, so capital lies idle. Such projects employ very few people; so many countries which have had high investment levels during the 1950's are now surprised to see how few new jobs have been created. These highly capital-intensive projects are very vulnerable to wage demands, since wages are a small proportion of their costs; so the ease with which they keep raising wage rates plays havoc with wages and employment in the rest of the economy.

Given the prevalence of all these fallacies favouring high capital-intensity, plus the preference of architects, engineers and politicians for spectacular, most-up-to-date, and highly expensive structures, plus the bias given to high capital-intensity by interest rates and foreign exchange rates which are too low, and wage rates which do not reflect the abundance of labour, it is impossible for development planners to prevent waste of capital. All they can do is to throw their influence in favour of spreading capital around, a little here and a little there, rather than concentrating it on a few spectacular schemes. Their most powerful instrument is to produce the relevant figures, showing how much employment and income will be created by sensible use of capital, and how much less if the more capital-intensive proposals are adopted. With most politicians, unemployment is a sensitive spot.

DEVELOPMENT PLANNING

Summary

1. Poor countries need not avoid highly capital-intensive industries if they have natural resources or other comparative advantages whose exploitation requires high capital-intensity; but their techniques should normally be less capital-intensive than those of richer countries.

2. Current prices tend to understate the scarcity of capital and foreign exchange, and the relative abundance of labour. The correct degree of capital-intensity cannot be attained without administrative action based on shadow prices.

3. An excessive proportion of investment goes into capital-intensive urban projects rather than into labour-intensive rural projects, because the rate of interest is too low in towns and too high in the countryside. Improvement of rural credit facilities is essential to a better utilization of capital.

4. Excessive capital-intensity may reduce output and employment, but the fact that it increases the incomes of some workers or consumers is an obstacle to securing administrative action.

5. Excessive capital-intensity may raise the rate of growth of income at the expense of reducing current income. Whether this is justifiable depends on the relative urgency of present income compared with future income, and on whether it is practicable to use the other means by which the rate of growth of income can be raised without sacrificing current income.

6. Irrational prejudices favouring large and spectacular projects cause considerable waste of capital, and reduce the amount of employment created by investment. The planner's best way to resist proposals involving waste is to produce figures comparing their effects on employment and incomes with the effects of more sensible schemes.

4. REGIONAL BALANCE

Differing Potentials

In every country some regions are richer than others, and some (not necessarily the richest) are developing more rapidly than others. To make a plan which gave equal emphasis to every square mile, or spent an equal sum on every inhabitant, would be quite uneconomic. In the first place, different areas have different growth potential; some have minerals, or water, or good natural

68

harbours, while others are poorly favoured. And secondly, even if all areas started with equal resources, it would pay to concentrate development in relatively few places, because of the economies of geographical concentration. Hence, as soon as one area got ahead for any reason, however accidental (e.g. the birth there of some entrepreneurial genius, which explains the growth of motor manufacture near Oxford), it would grow faster than the rest. It could offer many services and commodities more cheaply, because produced on a large scale; it would possess an interlocking network of markets, banks, transport facilities, engineering repair services and the like; its schools, hospitals and research institutes would offer more specialized services, and so on. That some parts of the country will develop faster than the rest is a natural economic phenomenon; and so is its corollary, that some areas will contract, relatively, or even absolutely.

If the country is fully integrated, it is in the general interest that resources be invested where they are likely to prove most productive. Full integration means a right to participate equally in economic activities in any part of one's country. If the savings of citizens of county B are to be used to develop county C, on the ground that they will be most productive there, the citizens of B must be allowed to enjoy the new opportunities which their savings will be creating in C: to seek work there, to trade without customs barriers, and to enjoy any facilities (schools, hospitals, etc.) which are going to be financed out of taxes collected as a result of such development. Resistance to the proposition that resources be invested where they are most productive derives from the expectation that those who live where the resources are invested are going to benefit most. Such resistance cannot be eliminated altogether, since it is true that residents have an advantage, but it can be minimized by furthering the country's integration: by building transport facilities, and by using some of the wealth produced in the richer areas to finance improved public facilities in the poorer areas, thus buying their consent to concentration of development policies in the area with the best prospects.

The richest areas are not necessarily those with the best prospects. Some of the poorer areas may be poorer only because they have been neglected, and it is possible that if now helped they will develop so rapidly that they more than justify economically the diversion of resources to their needs. It is not always easy to recognize those backward areas which are really capable of rapid growth, given help, and distinguish them from other backward areas where expenditure would be more of the nature of subsidies; especially if the missing factor is education, which can be rather a long-term investment. The planner can try to separate out economic from other issues, but one can no more be certain which areas of a country are likely to break through economically, than one can predict which of two countries is going to grow faster over the next thirty years. Hence, while concentrating on regions which seem clearly to have the most potential, the planner must not neglect the basic infrastructure needs of the others, for economic no less than political reasons.

The approaches of the planners and of the politicians are not likely to coincide. The planners have to concentrate, in the first instance, on getting the economic facts clear; this is their most useful contribution. The politicians, on the other hand, are in the line of fire from their constituents, who are more interested in local matters than in the economy as a whole. Decisions are more likely to be made as a result of the balance of political forces than as a result of analysis of the national economy. If the Government is controlled by the richer areas, the poorer areas are likely to be neglected; if it is controlled by the rural areas, they will milk the towns with little regard for where resources can most profitably be invested. Good planning machinery helps. If all parts of the country are represented on the various committees, there is less likelihood that the Plan will reflect mainly the interests of people living in the capital city (as has happened in some Plans). And if the Planning Agency is supported by a National Planning Council which does not consist wholly of politicians, and is permitted to produce a first draft of the Plan before the politicians get to work, then proposals based on economic analysis will at least see the light of day, and cannot simply be suppressed without argument or explanation.

Equilibrating Forces
Economies of scale are a powerful force making for concentration of population; but they do not lead to the whole population coming to live in a single town. For there are also diseconomies of concentration which grow as population increases, and which

sooner or later catch up with the economies to produce a state of balance: it pays to grow, but only up to a certain point. Moreover, some economies are exhausted faster than others, so the general picture is a string of towns of different sizes. Statisticians claim to see regular patterns. The most popular is the 'law' that the distribution of towns is linear in the logarithms:[1]

$$\log y = a - k \log x$$

where x is the number of inhabitants of a town, y is the number of towns having more inhabitants than x, and a and k are constants. If one believes in using such laws for policy making (which one should not), plotting the number of towns in the country in order of size will soon show whether the existing distribution of population is 'normal'.

In a free competitive economy, where prices truly reflected social costs, a town or region could not outgrow its 'proper' size, in economic terms. As population increases, the marginal yield of resources decreases. Rents rise. The cost of supplying the city with food, water and other necessities from further and further distances increases. The cost of travelling to work increases. The streets and other facilities become congested. The cost of living rises, and this is reflected in wages. Despite the economies of concentration, the region becomes, for some purposes, a high cost area. Some industries move out; others stay out. If the price mechanism worked perfectly a balance would be achieved where only those industries remained for whom the special advantages of the area exceeded the high cost of labour, land and congested facilities. Population would grow up to a point, and then stabilize. New low cost areas would then begin their development.

Policy Errors
However, the price mechanism is not allowed to work perfectly. Rents are not allowed to rise as much as they should; the city council imposes rent control. High transport costs do not rest where they belong; flat rate charges are adopted, such that the user pays the same price irrespective of distance; or the burden of building expensive highways to reduce congestion is shifted to the central Government, instead of falling upon the city. New

[1] H. W. Singer, 'The *Courbe des Populations*: a Parallel to Pareto's Law', *Economic Journal*, June 1936.

firms coming into the area are shielded from some of the additional costs they impose (congestion, new schools, smoke, etc.), by the burden being placed upon the municipality, which levies taxes upon residential property. Above all, the cost of living differential in wages is either abolished, or greatly reduced, to meet the insistence of the large urban unions that they not be undercut by the 'sweated labour' of the less developed regions. Thus the incentive to new industry to locate outside the already congested area is diminished. The forces making for growth continue, while those making for balance are held in check. Thus the population of the town or region grows far beyond its proper economic size, at the expense of other regions where, from the economic point of view, investment of resources would be more productive. In most countries of the world nowadays, people complain about the excessive explosion of cities, and excessive development of some regions to the neglect of others; yet most of the measures which are taken to deal with this explosion, since they mainly diminish the differential disadvantages of living in the congested areas, merely make the problem worse.

To the breakdown of the price mechanism one must add acts of the central Government which favour the existing centres of population; especially the allocation of money for the development of new facilities, such as roads, water supplies, hospitals and colleges. It takes a courageous Government to say 'We will tax the inhabitants of area A, whose roads and other facilities are dreadfully overcrowded, and use the money to build an entirely new town at B,' though this is frequently the most sensible thing to do. Given the distribution of votes, it is easier to spend the money in A, justifying this not only by present overcrowding, but by showing that according to recent trends, population will be even larger in ten years' time.

Planning Balance

The planners have to walk a middle course; resisting on the one side those who want to have factories distributed evenly throughout the country, neglecting altogether the advantages of concentration; and on the other side those who are so concerned with the obvious degradation of the cities—their high unemployment, slums and shortage of all basic facilities—that they would make matters worse by concentrating all development expenditure on existing towns. A workable approach is to treat suspiciously all proposals for development in towns whose population already exceeds 500,000, or has not yet reached 5,000. The reason for the upper limit is clear. In poor countries demand is small, and does not justify any enterprises so large that they could not fit easily into a town of 500,000 people; at that level most of the economies of concentration have been exhausted, and the diseconomies of congestion are clearly felt. (Even in industrial countries most studies conclude that the most economic size of town is under 300,000.) At the other end, one has to resist proposals to build a hospital or secondary school in every village; but the countryside needs population centres in the 5,000 to 50,000 range, and emphasis on developing such centres pays off in helping to keep people in the countryside, as well as in affording facilities for small workshops and light industries. These remarks are not intended to rule out serious consideration of proposals for expenditure in towns of less than 5,000 or more than 500,000. On the contrary, they are intended to suggest that all such proposals need to be examined very seriously.

A good Development Plan should contain measures to restrict the further growth of cities with populations in excess of 500,000, and to develop other centres. For every one city so restricted, some four or five others, currently under 100,000, should be selected for special development. These should be cities which by reason of their location and natural resources (including easy transport and access to plenty of fresh water) clearly have development potential; a tendency to grow rapidly in the recent past is a good symptom, but in some cases one may even build a completely new town, starting from scratch, if location and resources are specially favourable. The special treatment consists, in the first place, of ensuring the full range of infrastructure—electricity, water, transport, secondary schools, a hospital, and other amenities. Secondly, industrialists are offered special inducements to locate there; money is set aside to lay out industrial sites, and, if necessary, build factories for rent; loans are available at low interest rates, and so on. The Ministry of Housing concentrates resources on ensuring that growth will not be hindered by lack of housing; and the Ministry of Education pays special attention to technical institutes. The Government may itself give a lead by deciding to locate in the selected towns some Government departments, research institutes, or other facilities, including departments of the university, which do not have to be sited in the capital. A great deal is now known about the selection of industries for such towns; they have to be industries tied neither to markets (e.g. laundries) nor to the location of raw materials (e.g. smelters). The town will export (to the rest of the economy and abroad) about half its output, to pay for needed imports. The industries producing this exportable output (called 'basic industries') are not all in manufacturing—a town can live by exporting services. Roughly half the employment will be in basic industries, so if the planners find 30,000 basic jobs, total employment will be about 60,000 and total population about 170,000.

The major obstacle to this type of planning is not economic but political. Representatives of the towns which should be restricted oppose the policy; and so also do representatives of small towns which are not selected for special treatment. Hence this kind of policy cannot be adopted in countries where politics has not yet been subordinated to administration.

Towns selected for special treatment do not dispose of all the problems of choice, since resources will permit some investment in many other parts of the country, but not in every part. The planner's task is easier when it is a question of locating factories or harbours than when it is a question of hospitals or other public amenities. A factory has costs and revenues, and calculating whether these will be higher at site R or site S is a relatively simple matter. Politicians may argue for one site or the other in terms of local interest, but the planner knows exactly what he can contribute most usefully, viz: the relevant figures. When the issue is where to spend on public services, there are not always relevant figures. Every village ought to have a water supply; if funds over the next five years are enough only for a quarter of the villages, which villages shall be chosen?

Such decisions would be much easier if each village were left to decide for itself, for it could then have whatever it was prepared to pay for. The habit, common in Africa, of making the central Government responsible for all public services and utilities, instead of developing self-financing provincial and local authorities is a hangover from colonialism which involves the central Government in invidious decisions, burdens the budget, and makes tax-collecting difficult. For villagers would more willingly pay extra taxes for local services which they can see and control, than pay to a remote central authority, which can show no immediate connection between the taxes it collects from the village and what it spends there.[1] Decisions are also more arbitrary, being made so far from the villages. The Development Plan should allocate substantial capital sums to local authorities for matching with local finance or voluntary labour, leaving each community to decide for itself on what to spend the money.

From the economic point of view, securing the right regional balance raises no insuperable theoretical problems; resources should be spent where they contribute most to the national income (or most to the rate of growth of the national income, if that is the preferred objective). Measuring benefits and costs in different locations is not easy, but technicians can usually agree within reasonable limits. The intractable problems are political, and this explains why so much is said about regional imbalance, and so little is done to correct it. The planner's chief contribution is to produce as many as possible of the figures in the Development Plan on a regional basis, so that the debate may have real substance.[2]

Summary

1. Development funds should not be spread evenly all over the country; areas with the greatest growth potential should have priority.

2. The most developed areas are not necessarily those with the greatest potential; overdevelopment of such areas is common, owing to errors of economic policy.

3. A Plan should contain measures to restrict the further growth of cities with populations in excess of 500,000, and to develop a limited number of other urban centres.

4. Decentralization of public decision-making and public finance helps to secure a better regional balance of public expenditure.

5. Where possible the statistical tables required for development planning should be prepared with each region shown separately.

[1] See pages 103-4 below.
[2] See Chapter III, Tables XXXVII to XL.

5. UNEMPLOYMENT

Very high rates of unemployment are common in most under-developed countries. It is not unusual for the unemployment rate, strictly defined, in towns with populations of 10,000 and over, to exceed 10 per cent even in the best season of the year. Defining unemployment in rural areas is much more complicated; during the two or three weeks of the grain harvest it may sink practically to zero; at all other times it is likely to be high, even if one excludes farmers and their families.

Social Equilibrium
A high rate of unemployment is neither caused by nor an index of population pressure. Countries with high population pressure learn over the centuries how to provide some work for everybody. If farming operates on a small-scale basis the farms get smaller and smaller, and surplus labour stays on the farms, so everybody has a claim to income, even though he may not be fully occupied. This is not possible if agriculture is operated by large-scale capitalists who hire only as many labourers as it pays to hire at the current wage. The surplus is then driven into other sectors. Social custom imposes on the middle and upper classes the obligation to burden themselves with hordes of useless servants; having many servants becomes a status symbol which extends even deep down into the lower middle and upper working classes. If population pressure is severe, it becomes almost immoral for any man of status to do for himself what a servant could do for him, or to soil his hands with manual operations. Even entrepreneurs get caught up in this spirit, if they accept the social mores, and burden their businesses with large numbers of useless clerks, messengers and other hangers-on. Wages are low; barely adequate to keep body and soul together; not adequate for serious hard manual work; and more in the nature of charity than of payment for hard, serious labour, which is neither given nor expected. The rest of the surplus swarms into casual trades; markets are crowded with pedlers and stallholders, making occasional sales; and there is a vast reservoir of casual labourers, gardeners, dock workers, construction workers, and porters. Thus everybody has some sort of job, however great the pressure of population.

Unemployment is due to the breakdown of this social system

before it is fully replaced by another. When wages cease to be a form of charity, and start to rise sharply, jobs begin to be confined to those whose productivity meets the test of high wages. The economy divides into two sectors; a highly productive sector using capital and modern technology and paying high wages; and the rest of the economy. If these two sectors could be insulated from each other, there need still be no open unemployment, but this insulation is not possible. For wages in the traditional sector start to chase wages in the modern sector, helped perhaps by trade unions, as well as by normal human envy. If your cousin in the factory or mine is getting £6 a week for unskilled labour, you are not so willing to be a garden boy for 10s a week. The clerk's wife kept a servant when all this cost was 10s a week; but a maid demanding £3 a week is more likely to be replaced by an electric cooker, a refrigerator, a vacuum cleaner and a washing machine. The housewives get rid of their servants, and the businesses purge themselves of useless clerks and messengers. The farmers' relatives pour into the high wage areas, looking for casual work. Thus the disguised unemployment is converted into open unemployment.

At the same time, the high capital-intensity of the modern sector reduces its capacity to offer employment. Too low rates of interest and of foreign exchange combine with too high wages to make it profitable to substitute machinery for labour. For the same reasons capital is diverted into destroying handicraft industries, at the cost of widespread unemployment, instead of being confined to uses in which it would not merely substitute for labour. When one adds irrational preferences for spending lavishly on structures, for using the latest techniques, however capital-intensive, and for large rather than small units of operation, it is not difficult to see why in many underdeveloped countries employment has increased so little during the last fifteen years despite unusually high levels of investment. Given wasteful use of capital, the traditional sector throws out labour faster than the modern sector takes it up, and open unemployment increases steadily.

Wage Gap
Economists have usually expected wage rates in the modern sector to be about 50 per cent above the income of subsistence farmers. This brings the modern sector as much labour as it wants, with-

out at the same time attracting much more than it can handle. However, if this is to happen, wage rates in the modern sector must not rise with productivity in that sector, unless farm productivity is also rising; any differential increase in productivity must go to profits, or taxes or to the subsistence sector via improved terms of trade.

It seems that during the nineteenth century modern sectors expanded very considerably at constant real wage rates. Britain in the first half of the nineteenth century and Japan in the second half are often quoted as showing that the availability of a reservoir of labour in agriculture and other traditional sectors makes considerable expansion possible at a constant real wage rate.

This seems not to be possible in developing countries in the second half of the twentieth century. Three factors cause this difference. First, the rise of trade unions. Secondly, a more powerful social conscience among capitalists, which causes them to wish to share the fruits of progress with their workers, and to limit profit ratios. Thirdly, strongly nationalist Governments which support the claims of workers as against foreign capitalists. These three factors operate most spectacularly in countries with rich mines; it is not unusual for the mines to be paying unskilled labour a wage five times as high as the average income of a subsistence farmer. Manufacturing and plantation industries cannot afford such big differentials, but their wages too are under constant pressure to diverge more and more from the average farmer's income. Thus the rise of one new profitable industry, capable of paying very high wages, can have a devastating effect on employment throughout the economy, since, as wages elsewhere chase the leader, not only the traditional sector, but also existing industries in the modern sector, dispose of labour, and throw it into open unemployment in the labour market. Jamaica's case is classic; during the decade of the 1950's net investment averaged 18 per cent of national income, real output doubled, and 11 per cent of the labour force emigrated; yet open unemployment was as great at the end as at the beginning of the decade. Several countries of Latin America and Africa have had similar, if not so spectacular, experiences.

Unemployment of the Educated
In much the same way unemployment of the educated results

from the salaries of the educated getting out of line with the incomes of the uneducated. When economic development starts there is an acute shortage of persons with secondary and higher education, which results in an abnormally wide gap between their incomes and the incomes of the uneducated. The gap is especially wide if a large proportion of the educated have to be imported from developed countries, since this sets their salaries even higher than can be earned in developed countries. The educated acquire not merely incomes but also social status far in excess of those of other people of equal abilities, so ambitious young people and ambitious parents move towards the schools. Soon the output of educated persons exceeds what the economy can take at current prices. Ultimately an economy can absorb any number of educated persons, by cutting the salaries of the educated (absolutely or relatively), and by raising the qualifications for jobs requiring some training. Employers raise their demands, and the educated lower their sights. However, this takes time, and meanwhile the market may be flooded with unemployed young people who cannot find jobs of the sort to which they consider themselves entitled, or at the salaries which they had been expecting.

Unemployment among graduates of secondary schools and universities is a long-standing phenomenon in Asia and the Middle East. Recent years have seen the emergence of unemployment among the graduates of primary schools, in parts of Africa where schools have been multiplying in the countryside much faster than the opportunities for profitable employment, and faster than the expenditure on other amenities which would make the countryside attractive. After seven years of primary education, a boy cannot be so easily contained by three acres and a hoe as his father was; if his school was any good, his aspirations must have been raised above this level. Only a reformed agriculture, using modern technology to secure high yields per man, could attract him; but agriculture cannot be reformed as quickly as schools can be built. Furthermore, in a country where only 10 per cent of the children complete primary school, and less than 1 per cent enter secondary school, graduates of primary schools are in demand as clerks and teachers, and can earn several times as much as the average farmer. Primary school is thus established in young people's minds as the road to a well paid white-collar job. When, as a result of crash programmes, the number completing primary school is raised within a decade from 10 to 50 per cent of the age group, frustration is inevitable. Graduates of the rural primary schools stream into the towns, where they cannot find jobs; indeed, the simultaneous expansion of the output of secondary schools will mean even fewer white-collar jobs than before for primary school graduates. Blame is laid on the curricula of primary schools, but this is hardly relevant; young people's aspirations are determined by past market opportunities rather than by schoolbooks. The problem solves itself with the passage of the years. It becomes obvious that a primary education is no longer a passport to a clerical job in a town, and graduates of rural schools settle down to make the best of the opportunities available to them in the countryside. But they will still find it hard to remain in rural areas if the Government is spending most of its money on developing facilities in the larger towns, and neglecting the rural areas.

Explosion of Towns

The breakdown of the social mechanism results in the explosion of towns, which grow faster than they can offer employment, housing and other amenities; and which therefore become centres of squalor, delinquency and unrest. Men come streaming into the towns looking for work, and whether they get it or not, are held by the attractions which the town offers—bustle, anonymity, water out of a nearby tap, freedom from obligations to relatives and chiefs, schools, cinemas, hospitals, buses, and even in some cases the chance of assistance from social security agencies. The wider the gap between urban wages and rural incomes, the greater the flow.

The towns can usually offer a few days' work per week in casual trades. It is normal in an underdeveloped country for certain sectors to live by employing casual labour, most notably the docks, the building industry, some factories, some personal service trades, motor trucking (and in the countryside the mines and plantation agriculture). If hourly wages are high enough, a man can earn enough to live on with a few days of casual labour per month. As more men attach themselves to these trades, the number of days' work per man declines. Pressure develops for higher wages, which in turn attract still more, in a cumulative process.

Premature decasualization intensifies unemployment. Modern personnel theory is against casual labour. Men on the permanent staff feed better, work more effectively, have a higher morale, and cause less trouble. Unions also object to casual labour, because it is more difficult to organize. Decasualization does not increase the average level of unemployment, but it makes unemployment less supportable. If 100 men each work three days a week they can all live. When sixty work five days a week and forty become continuously unemployed, one faces a major social problem. High wages stimulate decasualization, since the employer seeks to get best value from those he employs; and also because high wages make him put in machines, which require him to train a staff and keep it.

We have already seen, in studying regional balance,[1] that it is desirable to restrict the growth of large towns even if their growth is not due to the unemployed coming in from elsewhere. If the countryside received its proper share of development expenditures, migrating to the towns would not be so much more attractive than remaining on the farm. Special attention should be paid to building in small country towns their due share of secondary schools, hospitals and other amenities, since people are more likely to remain in the countryside when amenities are reasonably close to where they live.

Population Policy

Now while it is true that population pressure by itself does not cause unemployment, it is nonetheless also true that, once the development process has started, the existence of population pressure makes it possible to have many more unemployed, and delays, perhaps by decades, the time when equilibrium can be attained. If a country is overpopulated, the reservoir of people in rural areas who can stream into the towns without substantially reducing the output of the farms can be quite large. So also is the proportion of domestic servants, clerks and messengers who get thrown onto the labour market as wages rise. In an underpopulated country the farms need all the labour they have, and the proportion of people in make-work jobs is also very much smaller. A high rate of growth of population has the same effect as does

[1] See above, page 73.

an initial state of over-population, since it makes it harder for the expansion of the modern sector to catch up with the supply of labour. A policy of population control is therefore a desirable part of any employment policy.

Population control is economically advantageous even in the absence of unemployment. Every extra pair of hands has to be provided with additional capital, in the form of housing, schools, hospitals, factories and other physical resources. Thus capital can be used either to raise the level of living of the existing population, or to provide for more people at the existing level of living. In the majority of underdeveloped countries domestic saving is barely adequate to keep up with population growth, leaving nothing towards raising income per head. Countries which are already overpopulated also face the difficulty that while capital can be created, land cannot; population can easily grow by 3 per cent per annum, while it is unusual for the fertility of land to grow for long periods at an average rate much above 1 per cent per annum; so it is quite easy for population to outrun food supply in an area where all the cultivable land is already occupied. Underpopulated countries do not need to bother about their food supply. An increase in their population brings some advantage, since it permits fuller utilization of some services: the cost per head of running roads, water pipes, electric cables or telephone lines through underpopulated areas can be extremely high. Population control is not urgent in underpopulated countries, but even here it is likely that capital will raise the standard of living of a constant population faster than that of a growing population.

The evidence shows that at present only a minority of adults (more women than men) are interested in family limitation, but this is not an obstacle; interest in this subject always starts with a minority and spreads; the minority is already much larger than can be helped by available facilities. The main obstacle to population control in poor countries has been the absence of a method which was simultaneously cheap, certain, safe to health, simple and inoffensive. Doctors now believe that the inter-uterine coil meets all these requirements. As soon as this is finally demonstrated, measures to facilitate family limitation should have the highest priority in every Development Plan. Given the growing gap between rural and urban incomes, and the high capital-intensity of investment which this occasions, unemployment will inevitably increase sharply in every underdeveloped country whose population grows by 3 per cent per annum.

Using the Unemployed

The remedies for unemployment are implicit in the analysis of its causes. The popular belief that unemployment is due to the absence of development, and will inevitably be reduced by development, is clearly without foundation. On the contrary, development is itself in a sense the primary cause of unemployment since it is development which opens up the gap between modern and traditional earnings, converts disguised into open unemployment, and accelerates population growth. Ultimately the gap will close if the modern sector expands rapidly enough to drain off all the surplus labour in disguised unemployment, but this cannot be ensured unless there is a deliberate policy for employment.

The most important ingredient in employment policy is to prevent too large a gap opening up between wages in the modern and earnings in the traditional sectors. So long as the traditional sector is not disturbed by a large incomes gap, it can hold and provide for all the people whom the modern sector is not yet ready to employ. This is discussed in the section of this book dealing with the distribution of income.

Other ingredients are: measures to prevent excessive capital intensity; avoidance of an overvalued currency; adequate expenditure on developing the countryside; curbing the growth of a few large towns, in favour of developing more numerous small urban centres; and a population policy. These have all been covered in previous discussion. Deliberate action to substitute labour for machinery, in accordance with shadow pricing, even if confined to the public sector would go a long way towards eliminating open unemployment.

Such unemployment as remains, whether open or disguised, can always be utilized by devising useful work for people to do. This does not necessarily involve diverting physical capital from other uses, since useful works (roads, water supplies, land reclamation, etc.) can be undertaken, as over the past scores of centuries, without much equipment; but it does involve using resources to finance such works, rather than to raise the consumption levels of the employed, or to purchase (or make) machinery and other capital goods for other purposes.

The most profitable way to use the unemployed, in countries which have empty land (as is common in Africa) is to settle them on the land, where they can produce extra consumer goods for themselves. The next best thing, in countries which have no idle cultivable land, but could make some, is to use unemployed people to prepare new land for cultivation, or to rehabilitate eroded lands—with reclamation, dams and conservation measures; this is next best because it, too, will increase consumer good output swiftly. Other measures for creating useful capital do not yield results so soon, and therefore involve a longer continued drain on the budget; making roads, building rural schools, hospitals or other public buildings; adding to rural water supplies—there is no shortage of ways of employing people usefully, whether in the towns or in the countryside, without having to find a lot of equipment for them to work with.

Much the same sort of work can be done by the partially employed, especially in the countryside. Tropical agriculture is normally confined to a few months, in which the rain is concentrated. Outside the agricultural season there is a vast reservoir of manpower which could usefully add to productive capacity. Efforts are being made in some countries, under the name of 'Community Development', to get the villagers to work voluntarily on projects which would improve their villages. This is obviously most desirable, since it puts little burden on the rest of the community; but the work is difficult to plan and organize, and succeeds only where enthusiastic leaders can be found. Also voluntary labour is available only for a limited range of projects of strictly local significance. Paid labour is more flexible.

In some parts of the world, organizing the unemployed to work on the land has become a problem. There are psychological difficulties in getting the unemployed in cities to return to agriculture or rural works. And there may be trouble with trade unions, demanding for such work wages two or three times as much as the unemployed would get if merely kept on relief. One way round these difficulties seems to be to organize the unemployed into a national corps, on semi-military lines, with semi-military titles of rank. The idea of using the unemployed on useful works of conservation and rehabilitation usually arouses a good deal of emotional enthusiasm, which helps to overcome psychological and institutional resistances.

UNEMPLOYMENT

While recognizing the value of the work the unemployed can do, Ministers of Finance nevertheless shrink from launching on employment works because of the burden on the budget, representing the transfer of consumer goods away from the rest of the community. The cost of Community Development is relatively low, and once its potentialities are grasped, finance is not allowed to stand in its way, but paid work is viewed differently. It is often suggested that such work be financed outside the budget, by creating new money; but however the work may be financed, the burden on the rest of the community remains the same, namely the transfer of consumer goods to the unemployed. Perhaps the rest of the community would otherwise merely consume more. Or perhaps it would save more and invest in productive capital; the comparison is then between the productivity of the works on which the unemployed would be engaged, and the productivity of the investments which would otherwise have been made. These two differ in their labour-intensity; money spent on the unemployed buys only labour, whereas money spent on other investments buys less labour and more machinery (which presumably makes more capital). They also differ in what they add to productive capacity, since money spend on the unemployed produces cultivable land and public service structures; while other investment is more likely to add to capacity in manufacturing, transportation and private service sectors.

Economists living in cities can easily underestimate the productivity of investments in the countryside. Forty per cent of Indian villages are more than five miles from a road. In the monsoon season they are cut off for months. People who live in such environments are almost out of this world. The potential effect of a small investment in broadening their experience, widening their horizons and releasing their energies is incalculable. A road is immediately followed by trucks. People move in and out to nearby urban centres, where they learn new ways of living. Traders, teachers, doctors and other professionals arrive, stimulating the desire to produce more. New crops are planted which could not meet heavy transportation costs. Small power mills are installed, to end the drudgery of grinding grain. Power leads to other new ideas: tubewells, domestic electricity supplies, small sawmills, and so on. Workshops and small factories make their appearance. Very small investments can revolutionize a countryside, turning what was stagnant and depressing into a source of development energy.

If the cost of maintaining the unemployed falls upon the savings rather than upon the consumption of the employed, and if the real capital made by the unemployed is less or adds less to output than the investments which might otherwise be made, then the cost of maintaining the unemployed is higher consumption now at the expense of a slower rate of growth of output in the future. Whether this is justified must depend on the condition of the unemployed. If they are in disguised unemployment, living contentedly on family farms, one can arguably leave them where they are, and concentrate on maximizing saving and the rate of growth of output; but if they are in open unemployment, rotting in the towns, the situation is quite different.

Most underdeveloped countries have no organized system of social insurance. The unemployed depend on occasional casual jobs, on irregular help from relations and patrons, on begging and on stealing. In most towns with a high unemployment rate burglary is one of the major industries, and the middle classes live in fear of waking up in the middle of the night to find a man with a knife or a gun. The unemployed are also the shock troops of political discontent, their presence intensifying all the social tensions which are endemic to new and rapidly growing communities. Prudence, no less than human charity, demands that employment now be given priority over employment at some time in the future.

Employment also makes its own contribution to productivity. One feature of countries with high unemployment rates is the high proportion of unemployability. Young people leave school because jobs are scarce anyway. A young man finds one day's work here; gets no work tomorrow; cadges a meal next day from his aunt; finds another job for a few hours; steals something while the owner is not looking; shares a meal with a friend; borrows a few cents from a patron; and so on. After one has lived this life for two or three years, one becomes unemployable, and could not do eight hours' work a day for five days a week even if it were offered—for psychological no less than physical reasons. It is not sensible deliberately to postpone to the future creating employment for people who will by then have become unemployable.

THE DISTRIBUTION OF INCOME

Summary

1. The chief cause of the increasing level of open unemployment is the growing gap between wages in the modern and earnings in the traditional sectors. This converts disguised into open unemployment. It also, along with the other factors causing excessive capital-intensity, reduces the amount of employment created by new investment.

2. Neglect of the countryside when allocating development expenditures contributes to the gap between urban and rural living, and attracts excessive numbers into a few large towns.

3. Where these forces are operating, high population growth increases the rate of growth of open unemployment.

4. Ingredients of an employment policy include a wages policy, measures to prevent excessive capital-intensity, avoidance of an overvalued currency, adequate expenditure in the countryside and especially in small towns, and a population policy.

5. If the fundamental causes cannot be checked, the unemployed can be used productively on land reclamation and public works. These will not always be as productive as alternative less labour-intensive investments, but can nevertheless be justified on social grounds.

6. THE DISTRIBUTION OF INCOME

Changes in the distribution of income are the most political part of the development process; provoke the most envy and the most unrest. Sensible policy-making is impossible without understanding why these changes occur, and what function they serve.

Growth Versus Distribution

Normally, in the early stages of development, when the rate of economic growth is accelerating, the distribution of income becomes more uneven; in the later stages distribution stabilizes, then tends to be less uneven.

Distribution becomes less even in the early stages, because acceleration of the rate of growth creates acute shortages of those factors of production which play the greatest part in bringing about growth. Entrepreneurs are scarce, and in a private enterprise system will remain scarce if profits are low. If growth is accelerating, profits are high; and since the modern sector is growing faster than the traditional, the relative share of profits in national income must increase even if the relative share of profits in the modern sector is constant. There is an acceleration in the demand for technicians, engineers, administrators, accountants and other educated persons, so middle class incomes rise. Incomes of skilled workers rise relatively to those of the unskilled for the same reason.

Most of these trends are reversed after a time. Most notably, the schools pour out graduates at all levels. The shortage of the educated is thereby diminished. Decisive proof of the narrowing of differentials between skilled and unskilled comes when the middle classes find that they can no longer afford to hire servants. The status of entrepreneurs is also changed. The developed economy no longer needs foreign entrepreneurs and foreign capital; it generates its own. The ratio of profits stabilizes, or may even diminish.

A change in distribution occurs because demand and supply are out of equilibrium; the supply of some resource is either too small (price rises) or too large (price falls). A rising price signals that supply is growing too slowly. But the movement is self-reversing. For the price increase encourages people to increase supply, to check the rise in price, and if it has been excessive, to bring the price down again.

Faced with a change in distribution, the policy maker may react in one of two conflicting ways. The easier and more popular is to control the price; the more difficult is to effect an increase in supply. The two conflict because the incentive to increase supply is reduced when the price is not allowed to rise.

In development planning the same conflict arises between the degree of change in the distribution of income which will minimize envy and unrest, and the degree of change which will maximize the rate of growth of income. What line a society takes depends on its power structure. The United States in the nineteenth century opted for the maximum rate of growth, leaving the distribution of income to take care of itself; the upshot is simultaneously the largest number of millionaire fortunes made in commerce, with the highest working class standard of living. European capitalist economies started on the same line, but because of their greater homogeneity and longer welfare traditions, were forced increasingly to substitute welfare for growth, by using the taxing power to redistribute income. The new nations of the second half of the twentieth century have been born into a welfare age. Though clamouring for economic growth, they face towering demands for welfare and for income redistribution which must almost certainly hold down the rate of growth.

The planner's contribution is to put major emphasis on increasing the supply of those resources whose scarcity is responsible for the uneven distribution of income. The conflict between distribution and growth arises only out of shortage of supply; if shortage can be eliminated, growth is possible without uneven distribution. However, shortage cannot be eliminated without incentives; so the planner has also to plead for that minimum of change in distribution without which supply cannot be adequately increased.

The most difficult areas are farm incomes, profits, differentials for skill, wage rates and profits. Each of these is considered below.

Farm Incomes

Development may raise or lower the farmers' incomes. Since farmers are more than half the population an increase in their real incomes is much to be desired: the main purpose of development is to raise the real incomes of the majority of the people.

Farmers' incomes fall if world prices move against them, or, in commodities insulated from world prices, if supply increases faster than demand. The former case is liable to damage the whole economy; the latter calls for more rapid development outside agriculture, which would increase the demand, and, at the same time through migration, reduce the supply.

The kind of increase in farm incomes which is required is not that which is due to food prices rising relatively to other domestic prices: this makes the farmers richer, but only at the expense of the rest of the population; and it may bring development to a stop by raising wages relatively to profits. The kind of increase in farm income which is required is that which is due to an increase in productivity (more output per head, or a switch to more valuable crops) or to an increase in exports or the prices of exports.

An increase in farm income, due to the right causes, helps not only the farmers but also the rest of the economy. In countries where development policies mainly make the rich richer, the market for local manufactures is limited, since the rich spend much of their surplus on luxury imports and foreign travel. By contrast, an increase in farm income widens the market for manufactures, and so stimulates industrialization; even the difference between a good harvest and a bad harvest can be observed in industrial output, once the limits of import substitution have been reached.

If the increase in farm income is due to increased productivity in growing food for the home market, some of this increase in productivity can be shared with industrial workers by means of lower food prices. Developing economies experience intense pressure to raise urban wages—whether because of trade unions, or because industries which can afford high wages exert an upward pull, or because of inflation. If farm productivity is constant, this pressure can damage the economy, since it increases the demand for food while the supply of food is constant. By contrast, increased productivity in food helps to contain the pressure; the urban standard of living can be raised; and the currency need not be devalued.

An increase in farm income also increases the resources available for development. Farmers save and invest more; borrow less from other sectors; or invest more in other sectors. They can also be taxed more heavily, the proceeds being used either to finance public services, or to finance increased capital formation. If the farmers save more, the economy is not so dependent on the savings of capitalists, and need not therefore be so tender towards profits.

Thus a sound agricultural policy is a necessary basis for policy towards all other incomes, including wages and profits; for rising farm productivity provides leeway which does not exist when agriculture is stagnant.[1]

Differentials for Skill

The range of wages and salaries is much greater in poor than in rich countries because of the relatively greater shortage of skills. This handicaps development, since it makes relatively expensive all services and industries which depend on skill, and these tend to be the sectors that should grow fastest in a developing economy.

The situation is currently worst in Africa, which has been importing not only university graduates, and high school gra-

[1] See pages 45–48 above.

duates, but also skilled artisans, and which has in consequence had to establish for these grades salaries higher than could be earned in Europe, whence personnel has been recruited. The ratio between the earnings of high school graduates and of unskilled workers is therefore fantastic, when compared with differentials in other continents.

This situation will reverse itself dramatically as the proportion of young people passing through secondary schools climbs to 10 per cent, and the university proportion to 1 per cent and more. The higher incomes may not fall in terms of money, but they must fall relatively, as unskilled wages rise faster than middle class salaries, and real income may even fall absolutely, as the opportunity of hiring servants cheaply diminishes. This will not happen without heartache. For those few Africans who currently enjoy higher than European standards will deeply resent their loss of status, if not also their loss of servants, and will make political trouble.

Wages

Politically the most difficult problem in new states is wages policy, since the trade unions have usually more power than either the middle classes or the farmers. Both the general level of wages, and the differentials between prosperous and less prosperous industries cause trouble.

From the point of view of trade unions (or labour-dominated Governments) the obvious policy to pursue is to raise wages highest in the industries which can pay most, and trust to the high wages there to pull up the low wages elsewhere. We have already seen the disastrous consequences this can have for employment. One industry can pay higher wages than another, whether because it can more easily pass wages on to the consumer (or the taxpayer) in higher prices (or taxes), or because it is using natural resources which it has obtained too cheaply (ores, fertile land) or because the opportunities for mechanization are specially good. Raising wages in such an industry may have little effect on investment there, but it pulls down investment in the rest of the economy, as wages are driven up there, or pulls down employment by turning investment in the labour-saving direction. If a country wants to achieve a high level of investment it is clearly undesirable that the general level of wages be determined by what the most prosperous industry can afford to pay. The appropriate way to treat industries with excess profits is not to raise their wages but to levy taxes on them (export taxes, excise duties, or royalties in the shape of special profits taxes) if they are producing for an export market, or to control their prices (directly or by lowering import duties) if they are producing for the home market under monopolistic conditions.

In the absence of trade union or Government pressure, the general level of wages would be determined by the level of agricultural incomes, since by paying something more than the average agricultural income, the towns could get all the labour they wanted. Urban wages will always exceed farm incomes, partly because the cost of living in towns is higher, partly because a more rapidly growing sector has to offer higher real earnings in order to attract labour, partly because working eight hours a day for five or six days a week throughout the year requires a greater input of food than working the farmer's year, and partly because working eight hours every day for wages in towns is less pleasant than working on one's farm, and therefore demands higher compensations. The equilibrium wage for unskilled workers is therefore normally about 50 per cent higher than the average agricultural income.

The practical question is whether the unskilled wage in the modern sector should rise *pari passu* with productivity in the modern sector, or should remain tied to the average agricultural income, irrespective of what happens to productivity in the modern sector.

Holding the wage level stable would not hold average earnings steady. For, as the modern sector expands, employing more persons at a wage 50 per cent higher than is earned in the traditional sector, average earnings automatically increase. This transfer of people from the traditional to the modern sector is one of the important ways by which the standard of living of the masses is raised, and the rate at which it proceeds is a function of the ratio of wages to profits in the modern sector. If agricultural productivity is increasing, real wages can be increased, through a fall in the cost of living, without eating into industrial profits.

Opposition to this policy comes both from workers already in full employment in the modern sector, and also from those who dislike what it might do to the profit ratio. For while it is true that widening the gap between earnings in the modern and earnings in the traditional sector is the major cause of unemployment, it is equally true that holding wages steady while productivity increases in the modern sector raises the share of profits.

Profit

Profit generates enterprise and saving. An economy can dispense with private enterprise if it possesses a capable and enterprising public service (which most underdeveloped countries do not), but it cannot in any case dispense with profit, since profit is the major source of saving in a developing economy, whether in private or public enterprise. Small farmers do a fair amount of saving in kind, using their own labour for physical improvement of their farms and houses; but they tend to look outside agriculture for funds to finance those agricultural investments which require a good deal of money, whether on the farms (cattle, buildings, conservation, water) or off the farms (roads, irrigation, processing, research). So the modern sector has sometimes to finance not only itself but some part of agriculture as well, unless the farmers are properly taxed. The working classes save very little, and what the salaried classes save goes mainly into housing and education. Profits (private and public, corporate and unincorporated) provide most of the saving for new investment in commerce and industry. They are also a major source of taxation. An economy will grow rapidly if profits are high, and will stagnate if profits are low.

In an economy depending mainly on public enterprise, the Government has no difficulty in seeing the close connection between the share of profits and the rate of growth, and in the early stages of its development programme, always throws its weight on the side of keeping down real wages. In a private enterprise economy dominated politically by capitalists, the same philosophy is effective. In a private enterprise economy whose Government is hostile to capitalists, the conflict between growth and distribution comes to a head.

However, even in this situation to raise wages is not the only way of eating into profit, since that can be done equally effectively merely by raising the rate of taxation of profits. Profits can be squeezed by the workers, for the benefit of personal consumption of the workers in the modern sector; or they can be squeezed by the Government for a much wider range of purposes—to spend on education, health, agriculture, etc.; to save and invest in physical resources either alternately or additionally to private investment; and to benefit the whole community rather than the small percentage who are wage earners. In some of the literature the problem is presented simply as a clash between employers and workers. This is a hangover from the nineteenth century, when Governments were dominated by capitalists, and spent very little on purposes which benefited the broad masses of the people. In the second half of the twentieth century, new Governments dominated by welfare philosophies are a third competitor, and the battle over profits is really between the Government and the workers, both of whom can see to it that the employer is left no more than is needed to keep him going.

This is already recognized in some of the new countries of Asia and Africa, where Governments have come to grips with the trade union movement, and have tried to keep trade union demands in check. Indeed, in many African countries the Government is the largest employer of labour, and the unions are most strongly organized in the public sector, so where the Government is anxious to expand the public service, and reluctant to tax the farmers more, a clash with the unions is inevitable.

Incomes Policy

If it were feasible to regard the level of profits as a matter mainly between the Government and the employers, in the sense that the Government will set tax rates or control prices at whatever gives the appropriate level of profits, then the desirable wages policy would be clear. There is no ethical or economic reason why unskilled labour should outdistance the farmers, at the cost of increased unemployment and reduced saving and investment. The main elements of an incomes policy would then be clear:

(1) raise agricultural productivity as quickly as possible;
(2) keep unskilled wages about 50 per cent above average agricultural incomes;
(3) accelerate the output from secondary schools, training schools and universities, so as to diminish the gap between middle class and working class earnings;

(4) in a private enterprise economy, tax profits as heavily as they can bear without reducing gross private investment below 15 per cent of national income.

This is not a wage freeze policy since, if agricultural productivity is rising, workers' and farmers' incomes will both rise in step. It is only a policy for the early stages of growth. If private investment exceeds 15 per cent, the modern sector must sooner or later absorb all the surplus farm labour, and the gap between wages and farm incomes will have to widen if the labour force of the modern sector is to continue its relative expansion. By that time wage earners will be so large in numbers relatively to farmers that their incomes will determine the farmers', rather than the other way round.

This formula is only one possible solution; it assumes that in a private enterprise economy profits are recognized as necessary to growth; that growth is given equal priority with distribution, and that as far as possible the fruits of growth should be enjoyed generally, rather than be concentrated on workers in some industries, or on special grades of skill. These assumptions are acceptable to most Governments, and even to some trade union leaders, but are difficult to sell to the rank and file. A *modus vivendi*, based on mutual confidence between political and trade union leaders, is one of the more important features of development strategy.

The chief condition for confidence between the Government and the workers is that the Plan should clearly be in the interest of the workers. The temptation to favour savings and growth excessively at the expense of consumption should be resisted; the Plan should provide for substantial increases in consumption.[1] The rate of growth of public discontent is a logarithmic function of the rate of growth of the ratio of domestic savings to national income. Special emphasis should be given to items of mass consumption, especially food and clothes, and a deliberate effort made to keep the cost of living index from rising. The Government should spend liberally on social services, especially education, health and welfare services, and take aggressive steps to improve working class housing; adequate opportunities for secondary education are especially valued because they give working class families the sense of an opening future. The employment aspects of the Plan should also receive special consideration; prestige expenditures should be cut, and the money used instead to create resources

[1] See also pages 161–64 below.

95

which will provide employment; capital-intensive schemes should give place to more productive labour-intensive enterprises; and useful relief projects should be started for all who are genuinely seeking work. This is hard medicine for some planners. Their test of success tends to be the growth of the aggregate called gross domestic product; the people's test is what is happening to food, clothes, education, health services, housing and employment. Gross domestic product may be rising rapidly without improving the people's level of living—or even at the cost of the people's level of living. No Plan is satisfactory which makes output its goal rather than consumption; or gives excessive weight to future consumption at the expense of current needs.

And finally, if Ministers seek restraint in others, they must first restrain themselves; in one underdeveloped country after another the workers are striking or rioting in protest against the personal extravagance of politicians in office. Men who waste public funds can hardly expect public co-operation.

Summary

1. An equal distribution of income is not compatible with economic growth.

2. An increase in agricultural productivity is fundamental to the solution of problems of distribution, since it makes possible simultaneous increases in mass consumption, saving and taxation.

3. The range of middle and working class incomes is abnormally wide in poor countries. The relatively high cost of skills impedes growth. Multiplication of skills through expansion of facilities for education and training is highly desirable.

4. Profit is the main incentive to private enterprise, and an important source of savings and taxes whether in private or public enterprise economies. Excessive taxation or control of profits will cause stagnation.

5. If unskilled wages rise substantially above farm incomes, unemployment gains rapidly. There is no moral or economic justification for paying unskilled workers substantially more than farmers can earn.

6. The remedy for excessive profit is not necessarily an increase in wages. An increase in taxation or a reduction in prices shares the benefit more widely.

7. Restraint is needed in wage demands, to prevent inflation,

control unemployment, and conserve resources for public services and capital formation. A wage freeze policy is not necessary if agricultural productivity is increasing, and if the planners avoid the temptation to seek excessively high rates of growth.

8. Implementation of a reasonable incomes policy depends on general consensus that the Government's objectives are in the public interest, and provide widening opportunities for the masses of the people.

7. PUBLIC EXPENDITURE

The attitude of development planners to the public services has passed through a number of phases. When planning began in underdeveloped countries, at the end of the Second World War, the emphasis was on the public services. This was defended by asserting that infrastructure is the key to economic development. After a while this assertion began to be doubted, as it was found that improving infrastructure burdened the budget without necessarily having a notable effect on other output. Governments were therefore advised to concentrate instead on measures designed to stimulate the private sector, with emphasis on exportable commodities. 'Production,' it was said (meaning 'commodities'), 'must come before consumption' (meaning 'services'). Development Plans which concentrated mainly on public service programmes fell into disrepute, yielding the place of honour to Plans which were full of arithmetical targets for industry and agriculture. Then came a counter-attack in which services were taken out of the category of consumption, and defended on the ground that they are 'investment in human resources', and just as productive as investment in physical resources. Ministers of Finance find this disputation not a little confusing.

Infrastructure

The argument about infrastructure has swung from one extreme to the other. At first it was insisted that infrastructure must precede development. Investors would not be attracted to a country if it lacked electric power, or transport facilities, or skilled labour. Hence the first priority was to create infrastructure, *after* which investment in other sectors would flow. This result did not always materialize; many examples exist of facilities built in

97

advance of demand which have not attracted users. So ten years ago the opposite case began to be argued. According to this, infrastructure may safely *follow* other investment. For example, if industrial investment increases, there will be pressure on electricity supplies and on transportation facilities. The men responsible for public facilities will notice the increase of demand, and, because business is good, will have no difficulty in raising funds to finance extensions to the system. Meanwhile, lower priorities (especially domestic consumer demands) will have been excluded by shortage of supplies, but major investments are not likely to have been held up.

Both generalizations are untrue. It is wrong to let infrastructure lag behind demand; but surplus infrastructure does not possess much power to attract investments. Here, as in other sectors, demand and supply should keep in step.

Lagging infrastructure is not likely to hold up major large-scale investments; the infrastructure they need is likely to be incorporated into their planning; or if it is not, and supplies are short, they are likely to get priority over other consumers. But economic growth depends as much or more on thousands of small investments, and these can be inhibited by shortage of basic facilities. Also, entrepreneurs who have a choice of locations, e.g. for factories, are not likely to choose sites where, by reputation or established policy, there is a chronic shortage of basic facilities. On the contrary, in order to attract footloose investments, an area must have adequate facilities, and create the impression that it intends always to be able to meet demand.

On the other hand, while it is necessary to have adequate facilities, surplus facilities have little attractive power, so there is no advantage in building significantly in advance of foreseeable demand. It is necessary to build in advance of current demand if the investment has to be built in large-scale lumps. For example, a port must be built with a certain capacity, which should allow for growth of demand. Investments in electric power, or water, or roads, are lumpy, and all such new installations have to be built with adequate excess capacity. However, their scale should be designed in line with foreseeable demand; to build beyond foreseeable need, in the hope of attracting footloose investment, is likely to result in frustration.

Services which sell their product for cash—e.g. ports, electricity, motor transport—tend to keep up with demand, partly because they raise out of their own revenues some or all of the money they need for investment, and partly because influential consumers see to it that they are not forgotten. The free public services are more easily neglected.

Take the departments concerned with discovering new resources, or discovering better ways of utilizing known resources, such as the departments of Survey, Geology, or Soil Survey. With few exceptions, the fastest growing underdeveloped countries are those which have discovered rich deposits of minerals, such as iron ore, bauxite, tin, copper or oil. A Development Plan should give the highest priority to geological survey and mineral prospecting. Yet, rather oddly, geological departments tend to be the most poorly staffed in the public service.

Apart from finding exportable minerals, geologists find useful building materials, including materials for making cement, pottery and glass. They may also find underground streams and lakes, or surface formations suitable for conversion into lakes, dams and reservoirs. Practically every tropical country—even the wettest— is short of water for a large part of every year, and nothing can revolutionize tropical agriculture more dramatically than finding, transporting, or discovering how to conserve water. Getting rid of water may be as important as finding water. Large areas can be brought into cultivation by drainage and reclamation. In many irrigated areas, the annual loss of land through salinity due to bad drainage is a formidable problem; some countries are losing more land for this reason than they are adding in new irrigation schemes. One simple test of the quality of a Development Plan is to see what it says about water.

The departments which find resources are basic. Equally important are those which study how to use known resources better —especially the agricultural department, and industrial and economic research. Agricultural departments have achieved spectacular results in selecting seed varieties, controlling pests and diseases, testing fertilizers, and improving processing, especially in the great export crops such as rubber, cocoa and cotton. Similar work on crops domestically consumed, such as yams, cassava, maize or plantains is still in its infancy (except in the case of rice), but could pay equal dividends. Economic research is growing in popularity, especially in the form of cost, marketing and feasibility studies. Frequently, the major obstacle to investment is ignorance; measures which increase knowledge of potentialities are an important way of raising the rate of economic growth. Indicative planning has itself been praised as a form of market research for all entrepreneurs taken together, which may increase investment by showing how much larger the market for each will be if each invests more.

A good Civil Service is a crucial part of the infrastructure, since the quality of all other public services will depend upon the quality of the Civil Service. This is even more important in underdeveloped than in developed countries, because of the difference in the amount of private enterprise. Over and above the normal Civil Service functions of running the public service, plus the regulatory duties which the management of an economic system now always requires, there falls upon the Civil Servants of underdeveloped countries most of the task of discovering new natural resources, investigating how they can best be exploited, finding investors for large-scale enterprises, teaching small producers how to improve their methods, creating and operating an infrastructure, and instituting and executing a wide range of institutional reforms. A good Civil Service is thus even to some extent a prerequisite of rapid growth. In this respect the record of underdeveloped countries is poor; failure to establish systems of recruitment and promotion based on merit leads to inefficiency; failure to pay competitive salaries leads to corruption; and failure to delineate the respective roles of professional administrators and of party politicians leads to confused decision-making. Development planning is hardly practicable until a country has established a Civil Service capable of implementing plans.

Social Services
Deciding how much to spend on the public service is more acute in relation to the social services (especially education, health, housing and welfare) than it is in regard to the administrative, judicial or economic services. Countries do not differ very widely in the proportions of national income which they spend on general and economic administration. Adding central and local authorities together, it is unusual for recurrent expenditure on these items to be less than 5 or more than 7 per cent of national

income.[1] Curiously, the proportion spent by the less developed tends, if they are ambitious, to exceed the proportion spent by the more developed. The latter have better administrative services, and relatively more people engaged in the public service. But in the less developed economies, because of the shortage of educated persons, the ratio of the salary of a Civil Servant to *per capita* national income is higher than in the more developed. As countries grow richer, they employ relatively more Civil Servants, but the percentage of national income which a Civil Servant receives diminishes, so the proportion of national income spent on general and economic administration stays within a narrow range. The social services are more flexible. The degree of development of these services varies so widely that the percentage of national income spent on them also varies widely.

The social services still face a lingering prejudice because they produce services, rather than commodities which can be exported. This reasoning is fallacious. As national income grows, demand grows for both services and commodities; hence more of both should be produced. If income is increased by producing more commodities only, there will be a shortage of services; if by producing more services only, there will be a shortage of commodities. Critics of early development planning who opposed the concentration on expanding the public service were right; but to concentrate on expanding commodities only would be just as wrong. Balanced growth, in the proportions dictated by demand, is the right path.

However, the adjustment mechanism is such that it is more dangerous to concentrate on services only than to concentrate on commodities only. If income is increased by producing commodities, the demand for services will grow; but, the elasticity of supply of services being high, the demand will be met. There is no such assurance that the supply of commodities will respond to an increased demand generated by an increase in the production of services. The elasticity of supply of commodities being low, an increased demand is more likely to be met by imports, with a balance of payments deficit resulting. This is the sense in which it is more important to plan commodities than to plan servic

[1] See W. A. Lewis and Alison Martin, 'Patterns of Public Revenue and Expenditure', *Manchester School of Economic and Social Studies*, September 1956.

the output of services can 'look after itself', while the output of commodities cannot; but what should be done is to plan them both in balanced proportions.

In any case, this kind of analysis applies only to services supplied by the private sector, or to public services financed by inflation. If the Government expands its services and takes in as much in taxation, imports of commodities remain unaffected. Personal income increases by the value of the additional services, but personal income after payment of taxes remains as before. Hence there is no balance of payments limitation on the expansion of public services financed by taxes; the only financial limitation is the unwillingness of the public to pay more taxes.

The balance of payments is an unreal bogey, so long as the social services are financed out of taxes and not by inflation; but it is still necessary to compare programmes for expanding the social services with alternative ways of using resources. The lingering prejudice against services, in favour of commodities, has impelled some advocates of the social services to defend them on the ground that they represent 'investment' rather than 'consumption'. This seems hardly necessary; if the question is whether to produce more education and public health, or more radios and bicycles, it is not obvious that the commodities are superior to the services. The social services are desirable in their own right, as a form of consumption, capable of competing with all other forms of consumption, and do not need to be defended as 'investment'. This defence, in any case, does not work, since in most cases, notably education and health, the quantity of service which the public seems to want is significantly greater than can be justified in the language of investment. As we shall see later, when examining each service separately, at the margin the social services are consumption rather than investment. This cannot be held against them; there is no general presumption in favour of investment rather than consumption. Such a presumption would be odd, since the purpose of production is consumption; an item of expenditure does not have to be 'investment' in order to be justified.

Controlling Demand

The main problem in planning the public services is deciding how much of the consumer's demand to meet. Planning the services demanded by industry and agriculture is not a major problem, since everyone agrees that services which help to increase other output should have priority. The real problem with water or electricity or telephones is not how much industry wants, but how many villages to add to the system, for the sake of the domestic consumer, when all the villages want to be included and the money suffices only to finance a few. Similarly the real problem in education is not how many jobs require training, but how far to continue expanding the system when there is already serious unemployment among school leavers.

This problem tends to be compounded in new states by a deliberate flouting of two of the maxims of public administration. The public services can be divided roughly into those which meet the needs of the individual customer (e.g. electricity, water) and those which provide for society as a whole (e.g. defence, internal security). When dealing with the former, the decision how much to produce is made easier if one of two principles is followed. Either the consumer should pay the cost of what he uses, or else the service should be financed by an authority so close to him that he can see clearly the connection between the amount he uses and the taxes he pays. When the service is financed by the central budget, without any charge for use, the connection between demand and taxes is tenuous; nobody wants to pay taxes to a distant central Government, whose use of them is neither known nor approved, but the demand for installation of services is unlimited. Governments are then saddled with insoluble problems. If 10,000 villages want the service, but there is money only for 1,000, which 9,000 shall be excluded? These problems are evaded if one puts a price on any service which is sold directly to the consumer (e.g. electricity). Or, if this is held to violate egalitarian principles, and the service is 'free' (e.g. water), financial responsibility should be delegated as far down the line as is consistent with economies of scale; the federal Government does nothing that the states could do as well; the states do nothing that the counties could do as well; and the counties do nothing that the municipalities or the village authorities could do as well. The obvious link between use and taxes not merely keeps use in check; but usually makes people more willing to pay more taxes in order to have services which they value. The central Government can impose such standardization as is necessary by administrative regulation; it does not have to operate or finance the service in order to standardize it.

If the central Government delegates authority, it relieves itself of much awkward decision-making, but does not altogether escape the obligation to provide finance, whether in the form of subsidy or in the form of loans for capital investment. Strong provincial and local authorities will succeed in getting substantial sums from the Plan, and may not even have to show in detail in the Plan whether they will choose to spend the money on roads or water or clinics. Weaker authorities get less, and have to be more specific. This is one of the points where the machinery of planning may make a significant difference to the outcome. Plans which are made in the capital city without a regionally balanced network of committees tend to spend most of the money on the capital; this cannot happen when private citizens from all over are allowed to participate in drawing up the Plan.

Education

Poor countries cannot afford to pay for as much education as richer countries. They have therefore to establish priorities in terms both of quality and quantity.

The cost of education is higher in poor countries, for two reasons. First, because of the higher birth rate, the school age population is relatively larger. The proportion of the population aged five to fourteen is only 15 per cent in Great Britain, but it is 25 per cent in the typical underdeveloped country. Secondly, because of the relative scarcity of educated people, the ratio of a teacher's salary to *per capita* national income is much higher in poor countries—two to three times as high. For these two reasons, whereas universal primary education costs a rich country rather less than 1 per cent of national income, it would cost a poor country from 2 to 4 per cent of national income.

The cost of university education is particularly high in Africa, since at present more than two-thirds of the teachers have to be imported from Western Europe and America. Inducement allowances, plus the cost of transporting them and their families to and fro and on leave, makes the cost per student 50 to 100 per cent higher than the cost of maintaining universities in Western Europe. Since tuition fees in Europe are very low, an African Government can send two or three students to Europe on scholarships for what it costs to maintain one student in a university at home, even without bringing the high capital cost of the universities into the account. Africa needs her own universities to do research into her own problems but (except where foreign Governments or foundations pay the cost of the universities) it is good strategy to tailor the size of the local university to the size of staff required for local research, and send abroad as many additional students as can be placed at low cost. Whatever may be the special advantages of going to college in one's own country, from the social point of view if the choice is between educating one at home or two abroad, the latter is more useful.

Asia's situation is different. There the cost of university education is low, partly because the salaries of university teachers are low, and partly because student/staff ratios are abnormally high. Many Asian universities have exploded in numbers of students, at the expense of standards, and are producing a flood of poorly trained graduates greatly in excess of the current market demand.

In rich countries the core of educational planning is the use of Census figures and vital statistics to estimate how many children will need places over the next twenty years. In poor countries such exercises are secondary, since one knows in advance that the number of children will exceed the number of places that can be afforded. The strategy is rather to begin by estimating the demand for skills, and to try to provide at least as many places as are required to meet the demand for persons with different levels of schooling. The techniques of doing this exercise are illustrated in the next chapter.

What always emerges from such calculations, even in countries which have a surplus of high school and university graduates, is a shortage of persons with technical skills; at the university level, of engineers, scientists, agronomists and doctors; at the secondary level, of technicians, agricultural assistants, nurses, teachers, competent secretaries and supervisors; and at the primary level, of skilled workers. A vast multiplication of the facilities for technical training requires priority in every Development Plan. These need not always be institutional; facilities for apprenticeship and in-service training are just as important.

Calculating the demand for skills will give the minimum number who should be trained if the demand substantially exceeds the number of skilled persons likely to be produced; but ceases to help when the number of places has caught up, as happens easily in respect of general education. Such calculations are based on employers' current practices in hiring staff, but these practices are themselves partly derived from the current market situation. What qualifications employers expect when hiring will depend partly on what the market has to offer. If there is a shortage of secondary school graduates, they will hire primary school graduates to be stenographers. Expectations are also conditioned by relative prices. If the salaries of secondary school graduates were lower relatively to those of primary school graduates, employers would prefer to hire secondary school graduates for jobs as sales clerks. Employers' expectations are therefore elastic. Since the continual upgrading of the requirements for jobs is one of the more important reasons why productivity increases, one should always train more skills than current estimates of demand would indicate; but how many more cannot be stated, and hardly matters in terms of productivity, since education is desired for its own sake, irrespective of productivity.

If educational requirements and relative prices were a simple function of the level of economic development, one would get a good correlation between economic structure and education. This relationship has been tested by comparing countries in respect of the proportion of the male population aged twenty-five and over which has received four years of secondary education, and the proportion of the occupied population engaged in agriculture.[1] The result (with rather low correlation) was

$$x = 26.1 - 0.37a$$

where x = percentage of males aged twenty-five and over who left secondary school after reaching age fifteen

a = percentage of the occupied population engaged in agriculture.

This formula was subject to the restriction that x should not be less than 3.0. The formula relates to the stock of educated people in existence. Annual enrolment is a function both of wastage, and of changes in the desirable level of the stock resulting from changes in the proportion of the occupied population engaged in

---

[1] W. A. Lewis, 'Secondary Education and Economic Structure', *Economic and Social Studies*, June 1964. In the article the population aged fifteen and over is used instead of the occupied population. Conversion is made here by multiplying by 0.55.

agriculture. A series of further assumptions (detailed in the same article) suggested the enrolment percentages shown in Table I below, for each level of economic development, taking boys and girls together.

TABLE I. *Required School Enrolments*

Per cent of Occupied in Agriculture	Per cent Completing Secondary School	Per cent Completing Higher Education
70	6	0.8
60	9	1.1
50	13	1.6
40	18	2.3
30	21	2.6

These suggestions are highly tentative. The original statistics are rather shaky, and do not fall into a neat pattern. Several countries had many more (apart from the USA and Canada) and several had many less persons with secondary education than such a formula would require. Departures from the formula were not obviously associated with productivity. What emerged was that commerce serves as a reservoir for the products of secondary schools. If a liberal education policy is pursued, the proportion of sales clerks who have had secondary education is high, while the proportion is low where opportunities for secondary education are restricted. There is no obvious correlation between productivity and the extent to which sales clerks have received a secondary education.

The main conclusion of attempts to link education with economic structure is that a country can absorb almost any number of educated persons by varying the qualifications for jobs, and adjusting relative earnings. The demand for various skills serves as a target for the educational planner while he is still in the stage that demand exceeds places; but as soon as the number of places catches up, he has to look behind employers' demands to more fundamental factors.

Recently American economists have tried to measure the productivity of education on an economy-wide basis for the US economy, by correlating income statistics with educational attainments.[1]

---

[1] For a summary see a paper by a leading pioneer, T. W. Schultz, 'Investment in Human Capital', *American Economic Review*, March 1961.

The results of such efforts can hardly be applied to underdeveloped countries, for three main reasons. First, the assumption that the pattern of earnings reflects differences in productivity seems rather doubtful; in Jamaica an unskilled labourer earns three times as much in the bauxite industry as in the sugar industry; such 'anomalies' are too numerous in underdeveloped countries for earnings to be accepted as a guide to productivity. Secondly, even where earnings reflect productivity, education is so correlated with other causes of high productivity (especially intelligence, patience, persistence and ability to persuade) that one would have to be able to distinguish these other factors before deciding how much of differential earnings was due to education; this is not easy. Having regard to the irrelevance of what is taught in schools (even at the college level, not more than 30 per cent are trained in scientific or technological skills) employers probably pay more for arts graduates not because of what they have learnt in school, but because ability to survive the tests imposed by schooling is as good a test as any of the kind of personal qualities which employers are seeking. Thirdly, this kind of correlation would not be useful in underdeveloped countries because of the big difference between average and marginal earnings. In most of Asia, where there is acute unemployment of educated persons, a correlation between education and marginal income might well lead to the conclusion that the marginal productivity of higher education is negative. When making such calculations in the United States one can assume that the economy can quickly absorb any number of educated, because the kinds of industries and services which the United States has are capable of taking people from the educational system and building on whatever the educational system may have given them. This is not the case in underdeveloped countries, where the absorptive capacity is strictly limited by the fact that more than half the people are in a backward agricultural sector. That raising a country's educational level increases its productive capacity is clear; but education is not effectively utilized if it outpaces changes in economic environment.

It is more useful to try to determine the effect of education on one occupation at a time than to plunge into economy-wide calculations. The effect of education on efficiency is under constant review by those who have the responsibility for determining professional qualifications, as well as by educational planners and by employers or their associations. This is the main reason why the educational requirements for most jobs (e.g. nurses, teachers, engineers) are raised continually. The most important unanswered question is how much difference universal primary education would make to agricultural productivity. That literate farmers would produce more than illiterate farmers cannot be doubted, since the problems of agricultural extension would be simplified. The difficulty is to make the transition; one does not produce literate farmers simply by building schools in rural areas. For if the agricultural system cannot provide young literates with the sort of income they expect, they drift into the towns. They can be attracted by a modernized agriculture, but not by three acres and a hoe. Thus the rate at which agriculture can absorb primary school boys depends upon the rate at which it is modernized. If the schools are producing the youngsters faster than this, frustration is inevitable.[1] This is not a case for restricting the intake of primary schools; it is rather a case for tackling agricultural modernization vigorously, a line of policy which is in any case desirable on every ground. However, given the time and money which agricultural modernization takes, on the one hand, and the high cost of primary education on the other hand, some African Governments are reaching the conclusion that it is better to give themselves twenty or thirty years to get all the children into school rather than, as was previously intended, to try to do it in ten years. Allowing for some absorption into farming, and for the expansion of non-agricultural employment, a developing economy needs to have at least 50 per cent of its children in primary schools, so this is a priority target. Progress beyond this depends on resources and on the rate of modernization. Such a policy needs to be rounded out by a considerable programme of adult education in rural areas, including adult literacy campaigns. Adult education can have remarkable effects on agricultural productivity, at low cost, as well as ensuring that the whole population is reached by modern ideas.

The practical problem can therefore be summed up as follows. It is fairly easy to estimate what the demand for the educated will be, at current prices. It is also fairly easy, using the Census and birth and death statistics, to estimate how many children there will be at different ages, and using one's knowledge of trends, to

---

[1] See pages 79–80 above.

estimate how many of these will be demanding education. If the demand by employers exceeds the supply, priority should be given to expansion of educational facilities. However (except for secondary and higher education in Africa), most developing countries have passed or are passing into the stage where the number demanding education exceeds the foreseeable number of jobs, and their problem is how far to go in satisfying this demand.

This question the economist cannot answer. He can calculate the likely number of jobs. He can point out that a surplus of educated persons can only be a temporary phenomenon, since any economy can ultimately absorb any number of educated by reducing the premium for education and raising the educational qualifications for jobs. He can stress that a wide educational base is needed to find the best brains, which may make the crucial difference. He may welcome the fact that education raises aspirations, because low aspirations are one of the causes of low achievement. He can add that any kind of education must have some productivity, since it stretches the mind; but he cannot demonstrate that the marginal product of expenditure on education is bound to exceed that of other investments. Finally, he can remind the Government that education does not have to be productive in order to justify itself; it is valuable for its own sake, and, when compared with other consumption expenditures, giving young people more education is just as valuable as giving them gramophones. In the end, each Government must set its own pace, having regard to how much store its people set by having greater opportunities for education, and how much increase in taxation they are willing to face for the purpose.

Health

Expenditure on health is productive in three ways: first it increases the number of man-hours of work that can be performed; secondly it improves the quality of work; and thirdly, by clearing otherwise uninhabitable areas, it makes possible the use of natural resources which would not otherwise be utilized.

One cannot rest the case for medical expenditure in underdeveloped countries primarily on the economic value of the increased number of man-hours which it will provide, since most of them already have as many man-hours as they can cope with. Extra man-hours of work mean more income for the individual, but in conditions of unemployment, if one man falls ill, another takes his place. Extra man-hours due to the survival of more people are also not of economic interest, except in the unlikely case where an increase in population would raise output per head (but they may have social value for other reasons, including sentiment). The man-hours which raise output per head are those which result from less sickness of a constant population in full employment. These are very important in the calculations of developed countries, which have conquered unemployment; but they are less relevant in underdeveloped countries. The latter reduce sickness because they value health for its own sake, rather than because more man-hours would increase national income per head.

The two other sources of increased productivity are more important in calculating the economic return on medical expenditure. Better health enables people to use existing resources more productively, by reducing lethargy and inattentiveness. Here one has in mind those diseases which remain in the body, not preventing work, but diminishing effort; most notably malaria, sleeping sickness and bilharzia. Finally, one must add diseases which make land uninhabitable. To get rid of these adds physical resources, as well as man-hours and attentiveness, so this type of health expenditure is the most productive of all.

There is a vast difference between the productivity of public health measures and the productivity of curative medicine. The spectacular fall in the death rate over the past hundred years owes very little to curative medicine. The great killers have been wiped out at relatively small cost, using the services of only a handful of doctors, either by improvements in the water supply—which have curbed cholera, typhoid and dysentery—or by environmental sanitation—which has materially reduced the incidence of malaria, yellow fever and tuberculosis—or by vaccination—which has nearly eliminated smallpox, diphtheria and poliomyelitis. One can see this by comparing statistics for developed and underdeveloped countries. The death rate is now about the same in Jamaica as in the United States. But the United States has four times as many doctors per thousand as Jamaica. A country needs a minimum number of doctors to provide a good public health service. Beyond this number, extra doctors add to the comfort and convenience of patients, but do not add a great deal to health.

In underdeveloped countries how much to spend on public health is not the problem at issue. Most Governments realize the productivity of this type of expenditure, and this is why death rates are falling so rapidly towards the levels of advanced countries. The real problem is how much to spend on curative medicine, especially on hospitals and on clinics. This is the part of the medical service with which the public comes most into contact; this is what the public wants most; it costs most, and achieves least, in terms of productivity.

Productivity analysis is not a helpful approach—the modern tendency to defend services only in terms of productivity must be rejected. Men value health for its own sake, as they value consumer goods. They value it above most other goods or services, often being willing to mortgage all they possess in search of health. They value medical attention even when it does not bring health, and so spend much money on the chronically ill, including those who will never again be able to work. If a Government is trying to give people what they want, it seems right to conclude that they want health more than they want anything else.

The practical problem is the burden of loading on to the budget the expense of the general practitioners' service. The budget can bear the cost of public health measures quite easily. Hospitals are more of a strain, but their use can be controlled, and if finance is decentralized to municipalities and provinces, the clear link between cost and taxes will keep the demand for hospital facilities in check. The demand for general practitioners, however, is virtually unlimited. Countries which now have one to 20,000 of population could easily use twenty times as many as they have now, if there were uncontrolled access at zero price.

The developed countries are moving one after another towards a 'free' medical service, borne completely by the budget. Poor countries cannot as yet afford this. They have to make some provision for the poorest classes, and encourage the rest to enter voluntary insurance schemes for the time being. Here, as in education, the fundamental limit is how much the public is willing to pay in taxes for this purpose.

Housing
No aspect of public policy causes more frustration than housing;

almost everywhere the gap between intention and achievement is wide.

The first source of trouble is the expense of building houses. Nobody has discovered how to build a small but acceptable urban working class family house or apartment out of wood, brick or cement, to cost less than $1,000 without land. The annual cost of such a house is about $100. If a worker paid 10 per cent of his income in rent, he would need an income of $1,000 a year. Even if he paid 20 per cent he would need $500 a year. And the percentage of workers who earn $500 a year in Asia or Africa is small.

Rural houses cost much less because lower standards are accepted. The density of rural houses per acres is low, even in villages, and houses built of local clays at low density are accepted. Densities are much higher in towns; suitable clays are not so easily available; and even if available, are more likely to be regarded as an eyesore by those who make public opinion. Housing is therefore an urgent problem of towns, rather than of villages; and this is a blessing, since dealing with the towns is hard enough without taking on the villages as well.

Since labour is half the cost of a cheap house, self-help building schemes appeal to the administrator. These are arrangements under which a team of, say, six men collaborates in building six houses under supervision. When the houses are built the men draw lots, and over twenty years each repays his share of the cost of materials and supervision. Some schemes are doing well, but they are tiresome to organize, and not so appealing to Ministers who want to build publicly owned working class houses.

To approach housing policy in terms of public housing is bound to cause frustration, since the number of houses the Government can afford to build is a drop in the bucket when compared to need. The required housing can be supplied only by encouraging private persons to build houses, whether for owner-occupation or for rent. Government policies, on the contrary, normally discourage private building for rent, whether by the application of rent controls at uneconomic levels, or else by building enough Government houses at subsidized rents to make private building unattractive, but not enough to meet the demand.

The best housing policy is to encourage private building. This is done by preparing suitable sites, by subsidizing interest rates (e.g., by making the income from houses tax-free), and by guaranteeing mortgages. The test of a successful housing policy is not how many houses the Government has built, but how many houses have been built by the Government and private persons taken together.

The housing problem is insoluble if the Government insists on wanting people to live in more expensive houses than they can afford, while not itself having the money to meet the difference in cost. Too much emphasis is put on the house itself, and too little on its environment. A town of well-spaced houses, built in local clays, and washed in different colours, is very attractive. Governments should do more to provide sites where workers can build their own houses cheaply; control the spacing of buildings; and look after lighting, water supplies and garbage disposal. What makes slums is not that houses are built of clay, but the overcrowding of sites and the absence of utilities.

Welfare Services
Even the poorest Governments cannot escape a growing network of welfare services, for children, the handicapped, the old and the unemployed. In traditional societies such persons belong to extended families, which look after them. Economic development destroys the extended family, and sends hundreds of thousands to live in new, impersonal towns, where they have to fend for themselves. The growth of stark poverty through the explosion of towns and the breakdown of the extended family system is one of the most terrible features of economic development.

Here, too, one can attempt to measure productivity, but this should not be necessary. The purpose of economic development is to create a good society. No society should give priority to future growth over current misery.

Summary
1. Infrastructure should be planned to keep slightly ahead of expected development. Investors will not necessarily be attracted merely because infrastructure has been built well in excess of expected demand.

2. The departments which find new natural resources, or study how to use existing resources better—especially Surveys, Geology, Agriculture, and Research—should be given the highest priority.

3. Good planning cannot be done without an efficient civil service.

4. It is not necessary to demonstrate that the social services are an 'investment' in order to justify their expansion.

5. The public would understand the cost of demanding more public services more easily, and would regulate its demand more intelligently, if the control and financing of those services which cater to individual needs were decentralized to the lowest administrative levels consistent with enjoying economies of scale. The central Government can impose necessary standardization without operating or financing the service.

6. The relatively high cost of education precludes universal education in this decade. Given current requirements for occupations, and the current salary differentials, the capacity of underdeveloped countries to absorb educated persons is relatively small; but the number educated need not be limited to current absorptive capacity, since this capacity changes as supplies increase. Skills should be created in excess of current demand, but there is no objective way of testing how large the excess should be.

7. Relatively small expenditures on public health reduce death and sickness rates spectacularly. Expenditures on individual care and on hospital service are not so effective, but the public demand is insatiable.

8. Since the number of houses which the Government has the capital to build is insignificant, measures to encourage private building of houses are much more important than programmes for public housing.

9. The need for rapidly increasing welfare expenditures is one of the inevitable by-products of economic development.

8. TAXES AND SAVINGS

The quantity and quality of Government activity which underdeveloped countries now demand for themselves cannot be provided (taking central and local Governments together) for less than 20 per cent of gross domestic product, even when defence and debt charges are excluded. Recurrent expenditure on general and economic administration takes, say, 6 per cent, education 3 per cent, health 2 per cent, welfare services 2 per cent, capital expenditure on public works (including roads, schools and hospitals) 3 per cent, and at least 4 per cent is required for capital expenditure either by enterprises in the public sector (water, transport, ports, housing, etc.) or by the Government's financial corporations which lend to the private sector (industrial bank, agricultural credit or mortgage finance)[1].

The contribution to capital formation is heavy. Ideology apart, it results partly from the low level of private saving; partly from the fact that, in the absence of a capital market, what little private savers do not invest directly in their own firms, farms or houses goes most safely into Government bonds or savings banks; and partly from the fact that the Government is the principal channel for foreign loans and gifts. How much of this 20 per cent the Government has to raise in taxes and other current revenues will depend on how much it can borrow at home, or raise abroad in loans and grants. However its total need from revenue is not likely to fall below 17 per cent, excluding defence and debt charges.

The figure of 17 per cent assumes current expenditure amounting to 13 per cent of national income. This estimate is what current expenditure would cost in Africa, given current aspirations. The cost would be lower in Latin America, for about the same aspirations, since there is not such a wide gap between *per capita* national income and the average cost of a civil servant. The cost would be still lower in Asia, for the same reason; perhaps recurrent expenditure would cost only 10 per cent, excluding defence. However, both Latin America and Asia spend much more on armies than Africa; nearly as much more as eats up the difference. Hence the 17 per cent target for revenue applies equally to them, in so far as such rough indications have value.

The most important way to ensure an automatic increase in the ratio of government revenues to gross domestic product is to have a tax structure such that the marginal tax ratio exceeds the average ratio. This is the situation in developed countries; their average ratio of taxes to income may only be 30 per cent, but 40 per cent or more of all increases in income accrue as taxes. Hence every year, in the absence of increases in military expenditures, the Minister of Finance finds revenue tending to increase faster than current commitments, and can if he wishes announce a tax cut. Underdeveloped countries are in the opposite situation, mainly

[1] See W. A. Lewis and Alison Martin, *op. cit.*

because they are not well protected against price increases. Too many taxes are fixed in absolute sums, instead of as relatives (e.g., an import duty of x cents per pound, instead of x per cent of value), and they are slow to adjust upwards prices of public utilities, postage, rents of Government houses and so on, as prices rise. The result is that the Minister of Finance has every year to announce increases in tax rates merely to keep his share of gross national product. In the review of some of the more important sources of revenue, which follows, this aspect will be kept in mind.

Private Saving

If people would save more, the government could tax less. The reverse is also true, but since the proportion of a tax cut which is saved is small, the sum of private and public saving is not increased by reducing taxes. On the contrary, a deficiency of private saving makes necessary an increase in taxation.

Private saving is the chief source of finance for capital formation; usually it finances not only the whole of private investment, but (via purchase of government securities) a substantial proportion of government investment as well. Measures to increase the rate of private saving therefore deserve high priority.

Several factors determine people's willingness to save. Most saving is done for a specific purpose. The people who save the largest proportions of their incomes tend to be those who need capital for their work—business men and farmers. People also save to buy furniture and other durable goods, to buy a house, to educate their children, to provide for such contingencies as births, weddings and funerals, and also to provide income during sickness and old age. Propaganda for savings now highlights the purposes for which the money can be used, rather than the act of saving itself. The Victorians urged people to save because prudence is a virtue; Puritans urge them to save because abstinence is good for the soul; bankers urge them to save for the sake of interest payments, which if also saved, will make them rich; and contemporary nationalist politicians urge them to save for the good of their country. Probably the most effective propaganda for saving is paradoxically that which concentrates on the enjoyment which the saver will in due course derive from spending the money. That some of these anticipated expenditures imply consumption (e.g. provision for old age) rather than investment does not matter, since much of this consumption would take place in any case. And once the savings habit catches on, the increase in saving even for such purposes is likely to exceed the increase in expenditure.

People save more if it is easy to save than if it is not. It is therefore desirable to create a countrywide network of savings institutions of various kinds—postal savings, co-operative credit unions, building societies, insurance companies and so on. Automatic savings plans also help; such as a plan under which a wage-earner authorizes a weekly deduction from his wages, or a farmer a constant percentage deduction from his marketings—subject to cancellation at any time. The amount saved is a function of the effort put into promoting saving; some public agency should concern itself specifically with making saving easy.

Many people borrow first and save afterwards to repay the loan. Hence the rate of saving depends on the opportunities for borrowing as well as on the opportunities for saving. Saving is stimulated by creating institutions which lend money to small business men, to farmers, to house purchasers, to students and other sound borrowers. Lending small sums is both costly and risky, but is worth while, given careful supervision.

Willingness to put one's savings into financial institutions depends on confidence in their integrity. All such institutions—banks, credit unions, insurance companies, building societies and so on—should be regulated by law, and required to submit annual returns. In the USA bank deposits are insured by the Federal Government. The governments of underdeveloped countries cannot afford to insure all the sums entrusted to financial institutions, but should not fail to control strictly the operations of all savings institutions.

The effect of the rate of interest on the rate of saving is a disputed point. Very few people save mainly for the interest which they could get on bonds; therefore it is deduced that, within the range of, say, 2 per cent to 6 per cent, the elasticity of savings is low. On the other hand it is also observed that the people who save the largest proportion of their incomes are those who can invest in their own businesses, expecting rates of return (from 10 per cent upwards) significantly above what can be earned on government bonds. It does not follow that they save more because of the higher rate of return; they may save more rather because success in their business (which brings power and prestige as well as money) requires them to have capital of their own. Nevertheless some governments are experimenting with offering fairly high interest rates to small lenders, in order to stimulate small savings.

Much saving is dissipated by expenditure on consumption to meet emergencies for which insurance would be more appropriate. Births, weddings and funerals come to every family, in statistically determinate proportions; for a family to be bankrupted by such foreseeable events does not make sense. Unemployment comes regularly to wage earners. Farmers face a regular succession of droughts, floods, hurricanes and crop epidemics. People save to meet these eventualities, and have to consume their savings with the event. If they were insured against these risks, they would probably save nearly as much, and net saving would increase. As communities develop they widen the range of risks against which there is compulsory insurance. Thus unemployment, sickness, old age, accident, widow's compensation, and funeral payments are now common in industrial societies; and many farming communities have insurance against hurricanes and various animal diseases. Wider extension of compulsory insurance would increase net saving.

Since agriculture produces half the national income of poor countries, an increase of farmers' savings is much to be desired whether it be invested in farm improvement or in off-farm activities. The need here is not for propaganda—the riskiness of their occupation makes farmers thrifty by nature—but for suitable institutions. Extension of the insurance principle to farmers is much to be desired, since it would diminish the dissipation of farm savings. Farmers would also save more if they could borrow more; hence an adequate system of agricultural credit is a first priority. In many countries the chief obstacle has been the inability of farmers to pledge land, whether because the land belongs to landlords, or because it is held on communal tenures and cannot be alienated, or because boundaries and titles are uncertain. The crop lien then becomes the principal collateral, and the marketing institution (e.g. the co-operative) becomes the most convenient source of loans. However, there are also countries where the propensity of farmers to borrow from moneylenders has proved excessive, to the detriment of their incentive to produce, and measures to control farm borrowing have become necessary.[1]

Urban wage earners save very little, partly because they too are plagued by insurable risks, which eat up their savings. Compulsory social insurance against unemployment, sickness, old age and funerals thus releases savings for other purposes, as well as meeting an important need. After these needs are met, the next most important reasons for working class saving are to purchase houses, durable consumer goods, and education. The first tends to be frustrated by a government preference for building working class houses for rental rather than for sale; and the second by recurrent measures to control hire purchase finance, inspired as much by the puritanism of middle class administrations as by the balance of payments arguments with which they defend their restrictions. Given adequate institutions and policies, there could be a welcome flow of working class savings into education and housing (especially self-help building).

The salaried middle classes put their savings mainly into education, housing and insurance. In poor countries the amount the middle classes save is less than the amount they invest in housing; there is great scope for developing building societies and life insurance. The more prosperous members of this class are willing to invest in mortgages and residential property. A good mortgage market is essential to them, as also to the insurance companies. Uncertainty of titles handicaps this business. Clarification of the customary law relating to titles, and easy registration of titles and mortgages stimulate the flow of housing finance. As income grows the number of persons able and willing to invest in bonds and equities increases; organization of a stock exchange increases liquidity, by reducing the margin between buying and selling prices. This increases the attractiveness of portfolio investment.

When all this is said it must be recognized that the net contribution of the farmers, the wage earners and the salaried middle classes to the supply of savings will be small—hardly enough to finance agriculture and housing. Everything should be done to increase this contribution. But the main source of private saving is the profits of business enterprises, corporate and unincorporated, distributed and undistributed. Most countries now design their

---

[1] See my *The Theory of Economic Growth*, pages 127-9. That volume also contains a much more extended treatment of the sources of private saving (pages 225-244) than is feasible in this introductory work.

tax laws to encourage reinvestment of profits rather than distribution of dividends. The main reason why the rate of saving is low in underdeveloped countries is that business enterprise accounts for a relatively small part of their national income. The savings ratio will grow automatically as the modern business sector expands relatively to the rest of the economy. Since this inevitably takes time, the rate of private saving cannot be increased sharply in a short period. This is why so much emphasis is now placed on the importance of raising the rate of public saving (government revenue minus expenditure on current account) in countries seeking to accelerate their growth.

Taxes on Commodities
The biggest yielders of revenue in underdeveloped countries are the taxes on commodities—import, export and excise duties. These are easiest to collect, administratively, when commodities pass through the hands of a few wholesalers in a small number of places. This is why the countries which raise the most in taxes are those which depend most on foreign trade. When trade is 40 per cent of gross domestic product an average import duty of 20 per cent will bring in 8 per cent of gross domestic product. When, as in India, trade is only about 7 per cent of gross domestic product, the same average rate brings in $1\frac{1}{2}$ per cent.

Unfortunately it is no longer possible to hide behind this explanation. Since the amount of revenue needed is not a function of the extent of foreign trade, it is not satisfactory to have a tax structure which makes the amount of revenue collected a function of the extent of foreign trade. There is also no escape from having to collect a substantial amount of revenue by the taxation of commodities, since it is not possible to raise 17 per cent of gross domestic product in poor countries without getting something of the order of 6 to 8 per cent from the taxation of commodities. What import and export taxes cannot do must be done by excise taxes.

The principal obstacle is that commodities other than food and beverages account (at retail price) only for about 25 per cent of national income. A number of countries have imposed sales or turnover taxes, of the order of 2 or 3 per cent; these help, but even allowing for double taxation as goods pass from wholesaler to retailer to consumer, 2 per cent on 25 per cent will not bring in much. This is the chief reason why Ministers of Finance rely not so much on taxing a wide range of commodities at a low rate, but rather on selecting a few commodities for taxation at rates of 50 or 100 per cent or more (alcoholic beverages, cigarettes, motor cars, refrigerators, etc.).

To qualify for this special status a commodity should have three characteristics. First, it should be produced or imported by a relatively small number of persons, or in strictly licensed premises, so that evasion can be controlled. Secondly the price elasticity of demand should be low, so that demand is not choked off very much by high taxation. Thirdly, it is preferable but not essential that its demand grow more rapidly than income. It is certainly easier administratively to tax imports and exports than to tax commodities produced for home consumption, when the number of producers is potentially large. But the necessary revenue can be levied on commodities even in the absence of foreign trade. The chief obstacle is not administrative but psychological; Ministers of Finance are accustomed to levying import duties at around 10 to 20 per cent. The idea of levying a number of 100 or 150 per cent taxes seems at first sight outrageous. One of the world's oddities is that, as a general rule, luxuries are cheapest in the poorest countries!

Export taxes are unpopular with economists because they discriminate against exports. How effectively they do this depends on the alternatives open to producers, which should also be taken into account when deciding upon the amount of the tax. An export tax is most justifiable when the price of the commodity is much in excess of costs. For example, if the price of a commodity rises, and this commodity can be produced only in a small part of the country (for reasons of soil and climate), farmers in that part of the country receive a windfall gain, which is justifiably taxed. In other words, an export tax can be used as a substitute for land rent or royalty, in recognition that farmers in different areas have differential advantages: this is the real theoretical justification of cocoa taxes in West Africa or cotton taxes in Uganda—though whether the tax rate is too high or too low in any of these cases is always open to argument. Exactly the same result would be achieved by a land tax or a personal income tax, if these were based on capacity to pay. Hence an export tax is justified in the absence of other means of discriminating between farmers on more favoured and farmers on less favoured lands. If the village has a tax system (land or personal tax) based on capacity to pay, an export tax is inferior, since it discourages exports—unless it is specially desired to reduce the export of some commodity in which the country is thought to be overspecialized.

Even those countries which have a large foreign trade must increase their excise taxes on production for the home market as development takes place. For import substitution reduces the proportion of consumer goods in imports, and therefore tends to reduce automatically the ratio of import duties to national income. Policy makers tend to think of assisting import substitution industries by relieving them of as many taxes as possible. This is ruinous to the budget, even though it is true that import substitution generates additional incomes which pay personal and property taxes. The need for taxes increases so sharply with development that it is necessary to use the growth of production for home consumption as a base for levying more in excise taxes.

One of the weaker spots in the budget is the losses of state enterprises. Such enterprises contribute significantly to taxes and savings in socialist countries, but in mixed economies they more usually make losses. In developed countries this is because the Government tends to take over unprofitable industries, and 'basic' services whose prices are kept down by consumer pressure. To these reasons underdeveloped countries add the fact that the Government tends to establish enterprises which it is not competent to manage. Running state enterprises at a loss diminishes the resources available for economic development. Ministers should give priority attention to eliminating this drag on the economy.

In a few cases these losses are deliberate. A number of Governments, in pursuit of welfare policies, have decided to supply many services free, or at subsidized rates—water, electricity, transport, housing, even food. A policy of taxing the rich to supply free services to the poor is appropriate to rich countries. However, poor countries have relatively few rich, and the taxes they pay do not come up to 17 per cent of gross domestic product (GDP). Governments of underdeveloped countries cannot raise the revenue they need without their tax systems reaching down to the lowest economic class, the small peasant farmers. Public utilities should be made to pay their way. What is more, wherever possible, public enterprises should yield a net profit as a contribution either to taxes or to new investment. Profit is the major source of taxes and of savings in modern economies.

Capital expenditures which raise the market value of private lands (urban improvements, land settlements, irrigation and other betterments) should also be fully recovered.

Income Taxes

Most underdeveloped countries have now brought their tax rates on the profits of corporations (including personal income taxes on dividends) close to those which obtain in developed countries. The main reason why these taxes raise so much less (typically less than 2 per cent of GDP in underdeveloped areas as compared with more than 6 per cent of GDP in developed countries, except in mining areas) is that their corporate activity is relatively so much smaller. The yield of these taxes is also menaced by the modern tendency to allow long periods of tax exemption (ranging from five to fifteen years) to new enterprises. How much effect this has on the total flow of international investment to underdeveloped countries is doubtful. Companies working under double taxation agreements gain little from such exemptions since remittances which are not taxed abroad are taxed at home, unless there are special laws to the contrary. An investor's first concern is to get back his investment without loss; thereafter, if profits are made, they can be shared with the tax collector. This objective is obtained by granting accelerated depreciation, stipulating that no tax is payable until profits earned equal the sum invested (after which there is no further allowance for depreciation). This would probably be nearly as effective as tax exemptions, and not so damaging to the revenue.

It must be remembered that the high rate of corporation taxes is one of the reasons why the marginal rate of taxation exceeds the average in developed countries. Underdeveloped countries need the same device.

The personal income tax also yields much less in underdeveloped areas. Many underdeveloped countries tax high personal incomes at the same rate as such incomes are taxed in developed countries, but they have more exemptions, and lower rates on the smaller incomes, so the number of persons liable to pay income tax is very much smaller, typically less than 3 per cent of the occupied population compared with 50 per cent in developed economies.

The exemptions are usually unjustified. Most of these countries levy no income tax on a family man with an income of US $1,000. Now a man with that income is far up the scale in his own country —probably 90 per cent of his compatriots earn less than he does. Since the indirect tax system is usually regressive, he is paying a smaller portion of his income in taxes than people with half his income. This is particularly unfair since he benefits more from Government services than people in other classes. His children go to secondary school, and use the hospitals, unlike the children of the villagers, who are paying relatively more. His town is kept free of mosquitoes, and supplied with light and running water. The rich do not use the Government schools or the Government doctors, and neither do most of the poor; it is the $1,000 a year man whom both income extremes are subsidizing.

The low starting rates also make the system expensive to administer. The lowest tax rate in the United States is 14 per cent, but starting rates of 2 or 3 or 5 per cent can still be found in less developed countries. This means that a very large number of taxpayers become liable for some such sum as five dollars, which is hardly worth collecting by the methods used by the central Government's tax collectors.

For years income tax reformers have concentrated on the upper end of the scale. The time has come to look at the bottom end of the scale, in the interest of revenue as well as social justice. Rates should be increased at the bottom end, and the exemptions reduced.

Since people hate paying direct taxes, it is worth asking whether countries which now exempt nearly everybody from paying an income tax should go to the trouble of trying to extend it over a wider section of the population. The USSR for example, manages with very little taxation of personal incomes, and is committed to abolishing the system. Absolute abolition need not be considered, since it is fairly easy to collect personal taxes on the top 5 per cent of incomes, but the system might be confined, for example to incomes in excess of $1,500.

Whether this is feasible depends on the alternative taxes available. The Government cannot raise 17 per cent of national income if people with less than $1,500 pay no taxes whatever. The comparison is therefore between levying direct and levying indirect taxes on this class. One of the tests is equity. Indirect taxes can pass this test if their structure is progressive; such that the rates on the commodities on which the $1,000 a year man spends most are higher than the rates on those on which the $300 a year man spends most. This, though seldom done in underdeveloped countries, is not difficult to achieve.

Another test is adequacy. Indirect taxes meet this test in countries with a large foreign trade. Countries with a small foreign trade have greater difficulty in raising all they need through indirect taxes, since excise taxes are more difficult to administer than import taxes. Such countries have to levy some form of direct tax on small incomes, whether a personal tax or a land tax.

Beyond these considerations of equity and adequacy lies the political desirability of making everybody pay some amount, however small, in direct taxes. Paying a tax has in the past been a symbol of allegiance on the one hand (and this is important in new states where the legitimacy of the Government is not always accepted), and a symbol of full-fledged citizenship with rights on the other hand. More important perhaps, in these days when the demand for Government services expands so rapidly, and so much faster than potential supply, it is good for the citizens to pay taxes directly to their local Governments, and to see the connection between the services they want and the taxes they pay. Therefore, while there is a case for the central Government not taxing incomes below $1,500, there is also a strong case for local authorities to levy some form of direct tax on low incomes.

Taxing Villagers

Whereas the land tax is the traditional village tax in Asia, some form of income tax, usually a poll tax, is the traditional tax in Africa. Some African administrations have reformed this tax, and put it on a roughly proportional or even progressive basis. Much of the difficulty of administering an income tax arises out of the desire to achieve precision in calculating the tax payable down to the last dollar. This is worth while when dealing with incomes of $30,000 a year, but not when dealing with $300 a year. For low incomes a simple scale would be appropriate, e.g.,

Under $300   pay $15
$300–$399   pay $25
$400–$499   pay $35

and so on. Exemptions are unnecessary. A man with fifteen children has more commitments than a man with one child, but he also uses up fifteen times as many places in school, and visits the doctor fifteen times as often, so it is not unfair to ask him to pay the same $25.

Such taxes can be administered at low cost. In the village everybody knows everybody else's business; if assessment is carried out by a committee of village elders (with the possibility of appeal on production of documents) evasion is unlikely, and rough justice is done. Even the small traders, traditionally hard to tax, cannot evade their neighbour's knowledge of how much business they do. (Large traders can be forced to keep records for the central income tax authorities.)

In Asia the land tax is the traditional tax on the villagers However, since the Second World War most Asian countries have failed to raise this tax proportionately with prices, so its significance is now sadly diminished.

Most of what we have said about the income tax on low incomes applies equally to the land tax. Excellent papers have been written on this tax showing its endless variety, the numerous anomalies which exist, and ways in which it could be simplified. As with the personal tax, rough justice is not difficult to achieve—by classifying land into broad categories of fertility, and by adjusting the rates to changing circumstances. However the basic problem is not administrative but political: the reluctance of modern democratic Governments to levy the tax, and the unwillingness of the villagers to pay.

As has been said before, unwillingness to pay is associated with not knowing to what purposes the proceeds of the tax will be put. At village level, direct taxation, whether by way of a land tax or by way of a personal tax, is not suitable for financing central Government services, but it is quite suitable for financing services under the control of village or county authorities. Given such control, the villagers could pay 10 per cent of their incomes (from 3 to 5 per cent of national income) in direct taxes without hardship. But it would then be necessary to transfer more services to rural authorities, away from operation by the central Government. Central Governments are reluctant to release their hold on services, but will be forced in this direction by the need for revenue.

Conclusion

A few of the developing countries receive a large tax income from mining industries, and a few others from taxes on exports whose prices have increased abnormally. The majority are not so fortunate.

However, even without such special sources of revenue, raising 17 per cent of gross domestic product for local and central Governments together is within the reach of most countries. A possible pattern for a country with a low foreign trade ratio would be:

1.	Fees, licenses and miscellaneous	2
2.	Personal income tax (incomes over $1,500, including landlords)	3
3.	Social insurance taxes	1
4.	Local taxes on land, urban property and small incomes	3
5.	Corporate income tax	2
6.	Import and export duties and excise	6
		––
		17

The items are listed in order of their variability. The first three are fairly standard. The fourth can yield the amount indicated, but its yield has fallen back over the last twenty years. The yield of the fifth varies widely from one country to another, according to the share of corporate enterprise; the figure given here assumes the absence of profitable mines and plantations. Revenues from the last item also vary widely, being greater in some countries with a high ratio of foreign trade, and generally much smaller in countries with a low ratio of foreign trade. It is countries in the latter category that have most to do in order to bring their tax revenues up to a reasonable proportion of gross domestic product.

Countries now raising less than 17 per cent of GDP cannot get there in one jump. Time is needed to persuade the public to pay more taxes. Essentially this requires that people, now just emerging to sovereignty, should learn the connection between the public services for which they are clamouring and the taxes which they pay. We have already suggested that decentralization of the financing and operation of some services is one of the best ways of achieving this. Another way is to tie the proceeds of a new tax to a new service, e.g., a tax on wages to a social security scheme, or a tax on beer to an extension of the education service. Anglo-

American fiscal experts frown on such ties because they reduce fiscal flexibility; but at this stage an increased willingness to pay taxes is more important than flexibility. By the time this major objective has been achieved it will not be difficult to explain why flexibility requires that the practice be discontinued. Teaching the people to pay taxes for the services they want is the chief fiscal problem of underdeveloped countries.

The effect of taxation on incentives must also be remembered. Economic growth will occur only if people make more productive decisions, and this they will do only if they get benefits for themselves. Taxation can take only a portion of the increase. Let us suppose that the practical limit is one-quarter, that taxes are taking 12 per cent of gross domestic product, and that *per capita* income increases by 2 per cent per annum; then it takes thirteen years for revenue to rise from 12 to 15 per cent of gross domestic product.

Hopes of a swift increase in taxation are usually based on the possibility of putting heavy taxes on rich landlords or capitalists, without detriment to production or savings. There are still countries where this is possible, though by now the number is greatly diminished. Most underdeveloped countries already have taxes on corporate profits up to between 40 and 50 per cent; some further levy on distributed profits can be justified in terms of social justice, but will not bring in much money. In part of Asia and of Latin America there are still some rich landlords who escape the tax net. Such countries can have a swift once-for-all increase in taxation, but in most underdeveloped countries the growth of the ratio of taxes to national income must take time. The test of a good tax structure is whether it is succeeding in raising the tax ratio at an adequate and steady pace.

Summary
1. Most underdeveloped countries need to raise at least 17 per cent of gross domestic product in taxes and other Government revenues, taking central and local authorities together.

2. This is relatively easy for countries with a high ratio of foreign trade, since it is easy to collect large sums as taxes on foreign trade. Countries with a low ratio must develop more internal taxes.

3. The income tax structure should be reformed to catch the top

5 per cent of the occupied population, and to increase the amounts taken at the bottom of the scale.

4. Incomes below the top 5 per cent should be taxed by local authorities, using either a personal or a land tax, assessed by local committees. With greater local taxation should go greater local responsibility for services which can be decentralized.

5. State-owned enterprises should operate at a profit.

6. The marginal rate of taxation should exceed the average; this is achieved partly by greater reliance on progressive personal taxes, and partly by levying the highest rates of import and excise taxes on those commodities for which the demand is growing most rapidly.

7. The ratio of Government revenue to national income must be raised gradually, so as not to kill incentives.

9. INFLATION

Governments are tempted to obtain resources by printing money or creating credit, because of the political resistance which they encounter if they raise taxes instead. The results depend on how much money is created, how long inflation continues, what the money is used for, how people react, and how well the economy is managed.

Matching Resources

An increase in the supply of money will not raise prices if it is limited to matching an increase in output or in the demand for money. There are two cases where a limited increase in the supply of money will not raise prices.

First, the amount of goods and services to be exchanged against money increases continuously. Population is increasing; productivity is increasing; and the monetized sector of the economy is increasing at the expense of the subsistence sector. For these reasons alone the supply of money could increase by, say, 30 to 40 per cent in a decade without prices increasing.

Secondly, an increase in the quantity of money will not raise prices if there are idle resources capable of producing increased amounts of the kinds of goods on which the money would be spent. Idle labour is not enough; there must also be idle factories and idle land capable of producing more consumer goods in immediate response to demand. This is the situation in industrial countries during a trade depression. It is not the case in underdeveloped countries, and is not therefore relevant to their problems.

In several underdeveloped countries (especially in Asia and the Middle East) unemployed labour exists which could be used productively without any significant drain on other currently used resources. It could not work in factories, because there are no idle factories; or produce agricultural products, because there is very little idle cultivable land. But it could be used to build roads, to drain swamps, to dig irrigation canals, to rehabilitate eroded lands, to build houses with local woods or clays, and in other useful ways which require no machines and employ only locally available materials. (Ever since the Pharaohs we have known that construction requires very little physical capital.) Such works can increase the productive capacity of the country, especially by making it possible to cultivate more land. The obstacle is that the workers, when paid for their labour, spend most of the money on consumer goods. They produce capital goods, but demand consumer goods. Hence the prices of consumer goods tend to rise. If they were producing consumer goods of the kind they demand there would be no increase in prices, but the resources required for producing more of such goods (industrial equipment, cultivable land) do not exist.

The effect of inflation in these circumstances is to redistribute consumer goods; the previously employed get less while the previously unemployed get more. Inflation is thus a substitute for taxation, used to finance investment in the absence of voluntary savings.

Effect on Investment

Some writers seem to deny that inflation can increase investment, but this position is not tenable. To analyse the problem correctly one must distinguish between the primary objective of inflation and its secondary consequences. The primary objective is normally achieved; if money is created for expenditure on investment projects, investment increases. What these writers are denying is that, if money is created for other primary purposes, investment will increase as a secondary consequence.

Most inflations occur in wartime, to enable the Government to get more resources for making war. This purpose is achieved. The normal purpose of peacetime inflations is to enable the Government to have more civil servants or soldiers than it could pay out of the proceeds of taxes alone. This objective also is normally achieved. Very rarely has a Government used inflation to create productive capacity—to build factories or to reclaim agricultural land, for example. (The USSR in the 1930s is one such case.) On the other hand, it is quite common for commercial banks to create credit to finance investment by private capitalists. There is no reason to doubt that if the purpose of creating money is to spend it on creating productive capacity, this purpose will be achieved.

Money which is created for other purposes does not have the primary effect of increasing investment. Does it have this secondary effect? It will if the increase in prices redistributes income in favour of people who are particularly prone to save and invest; otherwise it will not. The argument about the secondary effects on investment therefore turns on analyzing the effect of rising prices on income distribution.

The immediate effect of an inflation is to increase profits, since prices rise faster than costs. This is not necessarily the ultimate effect. Wage earners and consumers resent the price increase, and take steps to try to keep their money incomes rising as fast as prices. They may succeed, or they may not. If they fail, the share of profits in the national income increases. This is normally expected to increase investment, but whether it does so depends on the psychology of those who get the profits. The capitalists who save and invest in plant and equipment tend to follow conservative price policies, under the influence of cost accountants. A large part of inflationary profits goes to get-rich-quick capitalists, and are used rather for speculation in commodities and in foreign exchange. Hence inflation need not result in any large increase in investment if this was not its primary purpose.

Inflation will normally have some positive effect on investment, since the expectation of rising prices makes it profitable to acquire durable assets. But the pattern of investment may be grossly distorted in response to distortion of prices. An inflation raises domestic prices relatively to world prices. This discourages exports and import substitution. Thus investment is diverted from these important sectors into lines which are not affected by world competition. Investment of the kinds which could ease the balance of payments diminishes, in favour of investment in commercial and luxury building. To avoid this consequence requires either increasingly elaborate controls and subsidies to exports, or else frequent devaluation of the currency.

Effect on Prices

Suppose the Government prints money, and uses it to finance capital formation: how long will the inflation continue? Prices cease to rise in one of two circumstances. Either, if the inflation changes the distribution of income in such a way that the Government is able to continue financing capital formation without printing more money; or, if as a result of the capital formation, an extra output of consumer goods begins to keep pace with the extra flow of money.

The effect on the distribution of income depends on the public's reaction. At the start, the prices of consumer goods rise faster than wages, in favour of profits. Take first the simplest case: suppose that the public accepts the change; i.e., suppose that the distribution of income is altered permanently in favour of profits. Part of the profits will flow to the Government automatically through the income tax. If the profit-makers also use the rest of their profits to buy newly-issued Government bonds, prices will cease to rise, since the Government can finance continued capital formation, merely by issuing more bonds, and without printing any more money. This simple outcome is unlikely. The profit-makers will use only part of their net profits to buy Government bonds, so the Government will have to issue some more money. And in any case, the public will not simply accept an increase of prices, without trying to secure higher incomes; so wages will start to chase prices in a cumulative spiral.

The course of the inflation also depends on how quickly the new capital becomes productive, and how productive it is. If the money has been used to reclaim land and settle farmers on it, their increased output will check the rise of prices when it reaches the market. Also, the public is more likely to accept an unfavourable change in distribution which is offset by an increase in real consumption per head. This is a most important difference between the creation of money, say, to pay Government employees, and the use of such money to finance the creation of new resources which will increase commodity output.

Theoretically, an inflation can peter out either because of a permanent shift to taxes and savings, which flow to the original investors and so enable the new investment level to be held without additional new money; or because there is an increased flow of consumer good output which catches up with the increased money supply. If neither of these does the trick, prices will continue to rise. The reaction of the public then depends on the length of time during which this goes on. If the monetary tap is turned on for a couple of years, to finance some particular project, and then turned off again, prices may have ceased to rise before the public is sufficiently well organized to take protective measures. This is what happens in inflations caused by the creation of bank credit to finance private investment; the tap is turned on for two or three years, but before the public gets a chance to believe that prices will now rise continuously, the monetary authorities step in and turn it off again.

If the tap is not turned off, and prices continue to rise, the reaction of the public will also be influenced by the effectiveness of the Government in moderating the more obvious consequences of the inflation. Prices of goods which enter into the cost of living of the general population are more crucial than others; if these prices can be controlled, wage demands can be moderated. The increase in prices creates a shortage of foreign exchange; if the use of foreign exchange can be controlled effectively, and evasion avoided, priority needs can be met. Investment is distorted; export industries are discouraged; instead funds are put where prices are expected to rise most, including into stocks and real estate. An effective licensing of investment is difficult, but becomes necessary if the pattern of the economy is not to be grossly distorted. Governments differ in the efficiency with which they can operate such administrative controls, and populations vary widely in ther willingness to co-operate.

Spiral Inflation

No matter how efficient the Government may be, if the inflation is large enough (the rise in prices exceeding, say, 5 per cent per annum) and goes on for long enough (say, more than four years) it is likely to spiral. The public tumbles to what is happening and insists on taking protective measures. Wage and salary earners arrange for their incomes to rise as fast as prices. Each price increase is followed by an increase in wages; this raises costs, so prices increase again; and so on. This process can go on indefinitely, if the rate of inflation is held steady; some countries have had price increases averaging 20 per cent per annum for more than 50 years.

However, an 'equilibrium' inflation of this kind serves no useful purpose. An inflation is useful only so long as the cost of living rises faster than the average expenditure on consumption, for this gap is what permits an increase in capital formation. Once the stage is reached where wages and prices are rising at the same rate, the inflation ceases to be useful. If the Government persists in trying to transfer resources through monetary expansion, it will have to expand the money supply at an accelerating rate, with prices rising faster and faster. This is the way of hyper-inflation. This cannot go on for very long, since no population will tolerate it for long.

Spiral inflations are not only useless, but are also difficult to stop. Wage and salary earners have grown accustomed to getting regular pay increases to catch up with price increases. At any point in time that a decision to stop the inflation is taken, some incomes are due for a rise. If they do not get it, there is unrest; whereas if they do get it, but employers are prohibited from passing on the increase, there will be some unemployment. Investors have grown used to profits accruing from a continuously augmented supply of money. Once the monetary supply is stabilized, a number of enterprises cease to be profitable, and employment is cut. Hence an inflation cannot be stopped without a temporary crisis in investment and employment. The crisis need not be long; six to eighteen months is normal. But those who will lose oppose the adoption of measures which would stop the inflation, and if they are sufficiently powerful, they can prevent a Government from putting an end to inflation. Some Latin American countries have had persistent inflation for so many decades that they are now probably incapable of living in any other way, unless there are major changes in the balance of political forces.

Alternative to Taxes

Thus the course and effects of an inflation cannot be predicted without knowing its circumstances; what the money is being used for; whether a permanent shift to profits is possible; whether the Government can maintain effective controls; and how public opinion will react. One can say at once that most underdeveloped countries would be unwise to launch upon an inflationary course because they could not control it. But one cannot rule out the possibility that some of the better organized societies can safely finance some capital formation by the creation of money.

Given the desire to accelerate capital formation, the practical alternative to the creation of money is the levying of higher taxes. This too is likely to have some inflationary effects. For any attempt to reduce the share of consumption in national income, or to redistribute consumption at the expense of large groups, is certain to be unpopular whether it is done by increasing the supply of money or by increasing taxes. Inflation and an increase in indirect taxation both have the same immediate effect: an increase in prices; and direct taxes tend to be even more unpopular. Whatever the method of financing, the public will most probably react by demanding higher wages or income, so any method is capable of starting a price-wage spiral.

The fact is that an increase in the ratio of capital formation to national income is almost always accompanied by some increase in prices, however it may be financed. Even if the increase is financed by genuine savings, a rise in wages in profitable industries may provoke sympathetic increases in prices throughout the economy; or expansion may come up against crucial bottlenecks. If the increase in capital formation is financed from taxes, the public may resist changes in consumption patterns and start a cost-push spiral. It is not true that an increase in the price level always accelerates capital formation; but it is true that in most economies where the ratio of capital formation is accelerating, prices will be found to be rising. (Whether the ratio is high or low is not the point; the emphasis is on acceleration.)

Though taxation may also raise prices, it is nevertheless from the economic point of view greatly superior to inflation as a source of finance for capital formation. First, its effect on prices is likely to be much smaller. Secondly, the discipline of controlling the money supply is easier to maintain if the Government is not committed to using inflation as a means of acquiring resources. Once the tradition of monetary discipline is lost, Governments take to inflation like ducks to water, and financial control disappears. Thirdly, the incidence of taxation can be controlled more fairly and efficiently than the incidence of inflation. And fourthly, inflation is not so dangerous to the balance of payments, or so distorting to the pattern of investment. Continuous price inflation, moving domestic costs out of line with world prices, can be a major source of economic stagnation.

The idea that it is politically easier to mobilize resources through inflation than through taxation is probably spurious. For a Government which is capable of using inflation intelligently is probably equally capable of mobilizing resources through taxation; since if it is courageous, popular and efficient enough to enforce the measures which control inflation (and to stop it before it spirals) it is presumably equally capable of levying and collecting the necessary taxes. The situation may well be that countries which could use inflation safely do not need it; and those which need it cannot use it without getting into more trouble than it is worth; but political analysts may find some marginal cases.

Summary

1. The supply of money can be increased as fast as the supply of goods without raising prices. An increase in the monetary relatively to the subsistence sector also makes possible an increased supply of money to match increased demand.

2. An increase in the supply of money will immediately stimulate a greater output of consumer goods in an industrial country suffering from a trade depression. It will not generally have this effect in an underdeveloped country.

3. If the primary purpose of creating money is to finance increased capital formation, this purpose is likely to be achieved. The secondary effects of inflation on investment cannot be predicted with certainty. Some net increase is probable; considerable distortion is also probable, since inflation discourages investment in export industries and import substituting industries, and favours sectors not subject to world competition, such as luxury construction.

4. The degree of inflation will depend on the willingness of the general public to accept the redistribution of income which inflation causes; if the public is not willing, the inflation may spiral. The longer the inflation continues, the more effective the public becomes in evading its consequences, and therefore the greater the chance of its spiralling.

5. The degree of inflation also depends on the purpose of the

inflation. If its purpose is to create quick-yielding productive capacity, the resulting flow of consumer goods holds prices in check; the public is also more likely to accept an unfavourable change in distribution which is offset by an increase in real consumption per head.

6. In an underdeveloped country inflation is merely a substitute for taxation. From the economic point of view it is an inferior substitute.

7. It may be easier politically to start an inflation than to tax; but the measures which control inflation, maximize its usefulness and minimize its disadvantages are no easier to adopt or administer than would be an increase in taxation.

10. FOREIGN AID

Foreign aid now comes in many different forms, from many different sources. Originally the term was used only for Government to Government grants. Then it was extended to include borrowing by Governments. More recently it has been extended further to include all transfers, private or public, loan or grant, thus bringing in all foreign investment. In this chapter it is confined to loans and grants to Governments.

Foreign aid may take the form of men, money or goods. Men may come as advisers, or to do executive jobs; to consult for a few days or weeks, or on assignments running into years. Grants and loans in kind may involve anything from goods or tractors to a complete steel plant. Loans may be short, medium or long; tied to purchases from the lender's country or freely convertible; repayable in the borrower's currency (soft) or in convertible currency (hard); at low interest or at market rates; with interest or repayment commencing immediately or deferred. If the country providing the aid is amenable, there is no lack of room for negotiation of terms.

There is a similar variety of sources. Governments are the biggest suppliers of aid, then international agencies, then private foundations and individuals. There is little co-ordination. Even when dealing with a single Government one can sometimes obtain from one agency aid which is denied by another. The international agencies have different standards of toughness, as well as different objectives, and one will do what another will not. The foundations control very small sums, in comparison with Governments and international agencies, but they are more willing to experiment, and therefore do vital pioneering work. Knowing the habits of the various sources is a full-time occupation. No country can hope to exploit fully its opportunities for foreign aid unless it appoints some person or persons who will specialize on this work.

Conditions of Aid

Use of foreign aid costs something, even where no repayment is required. Agencies which send men will pay their basic salaries, and may pay their travel costs to and from the country, but the recipient country will normally be expected to pay subsistence allowances and travel costs inside the country. If the local salaries are low by international standards, these untaxed subsistence, housing and car allowances may exceed what it would cost to employ a local man, if one were available. They may be large enough to strain the budget of a small department.

Normally, agencies will not pay the entire cost of a project. Subsistence allowances apart, they expect the Government to pay a sum which is seldom less than half. This often takes the form of a stipulation that the agency will pay the 'foreign exchange' costs, but the Government must pay all sums that are disbursed in local currency. This mumbo-jumbo has no economic significance, since sums disbursed in local currency give rise to imports which have to be paid for in foreign currency. Its real purpose is to ensure that the Government is as interested in the success of the project as the agency, by requiring that it has just as much money at stake. This requirement bothers Governments whose financial programmes are not well co-ordinated, but is of no significance to those which have good financial control. To the latter it matters little whether an agency meets the entire cost of five projects or half the cost of ten. Other restrictions exist; some agencies finance only the cost of foreign operating personnel, and will make no contribution towards buildings. Some finance machinery, but not personnel. Some finance building, but only to the extent of the required outlays on imported materials, which may be small. Generally speaking it is easiest to get aid for personnel and equipment, and difficult to find money for construction.

Continuing costs also raise problems. An agency may finance construction, but leave the Government to meet recurrent costs.

Since over a five year period recurrent costs may come to much more than capital costs, a lot of calculation has to be done before deciding to accept even a capital gift. Agencies send men only for limited periods, and tend to taper off their commitments; Governments are usually required to undertake to carry on where the agency leaves off.

Because foreign aid is costly to the recipient, even when it comes as a grant, the financial authorities have to be in full control of acceptances. It cannot be left to each Government department to make its own aid commitments, without prior permission from the financial authorities. Normally all aid requests should go through a single channel, and the aid programme as a whole should be considered along with the rest of Government finances. This irks active Ministers and departmental chiefs, who like to visit the agencies when they go abroad, and are angry if offers of aid which they triumphantly bring back are turned down. But the agencies do not want to put their money into a project unless assured that full financial support will be forthcoming from the Government, so they welcome a single aid channel, with which they can deal authoritatively. Unfortunately, many Governments are still at the stage where the financial authorities are too jealous of their powers to welcome enthusiastic departmental chiefs who go out and find offers of foreign aid, but not competent enough to exploit all the aid sources by themselves.

Use of Aid

Borrowing is surrounded by myths. It is not true that a country should borrow abroad only for investments which will yield exportable commodities. What matters is the whole balance of payments situation. If imports are already tending to outrun exports, a country should beware of taking on new commitments; but if exports are buoyant, there is no reason to avoid using additional foreign exchange earnings to meet the debt charges on, say, the money invested in a water supply, rather than on importing more motor cars. Neither is it true that Governments should borrow (whether at home or abroad) only for 'self-liquidating projects', i.e., those which produce a service or commodity which is sold to the public. Again it is the entire revenue situation of the Government which matters; if expenditures are out-running taxes, it will hesitate to take on commitments involving more taxes. But if the taxes are buoyant (e.g., because the mines are expanding), there is no reason not to use the proceeds to meet the debt charges on school buildings. In the nineteenth century, Governments borrowed on the general security of their revenues, without having to tie a loan too closely to a particular investment. The modern tendency to tie loans to projects helps to make Governments act more responsibly; this rather than financial affinity between types of projects and loans, is its real justification.

When the lending Government not merely ties a loan to a particular project, but also insists that the money be spent on goods from the lending country, the borrower's ability to bargain when purchasing supplies is diminished. In some cases these stipulations force him to buy from a single seller, or small group of sellers acting together, and he may have to pay prices considerably higher than if he had been free to buy wherever he chose. This limitation would not be so severe if the lending Government did not confine itself to financing the direct foreign exchange requirements of the project; these may be small if the country makes its own building materials, and if the project needs little imported machinery (e.g., a road); while the indirect foreign exchange requirement for consumer goods, flowing from the income generated in hiring construction workers, may be large and varied. Nearly all Governments now tie the use of their grants and loans to purchases from their country; but recognizing the disadvantage to the borrower of the further restriction to the direct foreign exchange required for particular projects, some are now willing to make general loans or grants in support of a development programme taken as a whole.

Long-term money is hard to borrow; short-term money is over-abundant. The capital cities of new states are full of foreign financiers offering to lend millions of dollars at 6 or 7 per cent for five years to finance imports of industrial equipment. A number of Governments have fallen for this, and have loaded themselves up with such obligations. Unless one hopes to borrow from Peter to pay Paul, a loan which has to be repaid in five years is of small help to development planning. On the one side is the advantage of having more money at the start of the Plan; on the other, the disadvantage of having 20 per cent less (the interest and handling charges) five years later.

Most of this short-term money is guaranteed by the Governments of industrial countries as part of their efforts to export machinery; this is why so much is available. This kind of money appeals to those Governments of underdeveloped countries which give high priority to building factories for operation as state enterprises. The machinery salesmen can act without inhibition; they can sell plants for which no economic justification exists, knowing that their money is guaranteed. Thus unsophisticated Governments acquire enterprises whose annual losses are a drain on the budget, and whose amortization repayments are a drain on the balance of payments. Within five years of starting on this path, the Government is bankrupt.

There has been such a regular procession of Governments along this path, that the road is now well marked. The increasing interest and amortization payments make it necessary to restrict imports to a minimum, with adverse consequences for output and consumption. When the foreign exchange reserves are exhausted, the Government can default on its payments, or seek a moratorium. Open default is unwise, since it diminishes the prospect of future assistance. If the British or American Governments have political reasons for wanting to prop up the country, one or other may agree to convert the short-term obligations into long-term loans. In other cases the Government is told to seek help from the International Monetary Fund. This Fund will lend money to tide the country over its difficulties, but will normally do this only if the Government undertakes to cut its expenditures, to control credit creation by its banks, and not to repeat the performance which has caused the trouble. Thus the country swings from boom to depression. Some Governments give these undertakings, but do not have the will or courage to carry them out.

In a world where Governments are encouraged to borrow excessively on short term, and are not effectively disciplined when they do so, a regular procession of Governments along this path is to be expected. Though such behaviour may increase a country's capacity to invest for some time, it is hardly to be recommended, even on strictly economic grounds. Undisciplined borrowers tend also to be undisciplined spenders: the projects into which the money goes tend to be uneconomic and badly managed. Also whether a succession of booms and setbacks accompanied by recurrent foreign exchange crises and bouts of restrictive licensing creates a good atmosphere for continuous investment and growth, is to be doubted.

Qualifying for Aid
The current flow of new loans and grants to the Governments of underdeveloped countries is equivalent (excluding military support) to about 4 per cent of their gross domestic products. The distribution between countries is very uneven. Nevertheless, any Government which receives less than this can consider itself to be challenged.

Aid from one Government to another has a large political element, of which nothing can usefully be said here. However, not all Government to Government aid is political, and most of the aid from international agencies and foundations is not. Something can be said about the conditions for receiving favoured treatment for non-political aid.

Non-political aid is dispensed by professional administrators who judge their success and are judged by whether the people to whom they give or lend money spend it well. The fact that the administrators are not handling their own money makes them specially strict, not only to satisfy those to whom they are answerable, but also to satisfy their consciences. The best insurance they have that they are choosing wisely, is to give money to people whom they trust. Choosing projects is not as satisfying as choosing people. Projects are words and drawings and figures on paper; interpreting them requires expert engineering and other knowledge which the administrator does not possess. Even if the project proposal is excellent, things go wrong, and whether they are then put right will depend on the kind of people in charge. If the people are all right, it is all right to give them money; if not, they should be denied, however wonderful their projects may look on paper.

It follows that the way to be chosen as a recipient of aid is to make an impression on the people who administer aid agencies. The man whom the Government sends to look after this business must be the kind of man aid administrators admire; this means that he should resemble their own image of themselves—highly intelligent, well-balanced, cultivated, good at figures, reasonable, well-informed, a good mixer and a good conversationalist. It should be remembered that the aid administrator is just as likely to make his decision in the course of a Sunday afternoon picnic (even though no business is discussed there), as in Monday morning's office.

However, even the most likeable representative will fail if he is not served properly by those whom he represents; if the documents arrive late, are badly prepared and do not contain all the necessary information; or if the agency, on making on the spot investigations, finds that the people who will be responsible for the project are incompetent or irresponsible. The best way to get more aid is to spend wisely and promptly the aid one has already received. Agencies are not impressed when asked for money for a fourth project, if expenditure on the first project is still running two years behind schedule. The potential amount of foreign aid is large; special care should be taken in selecting those who will manage projects financed by foreign aid, since they help to make the country's image abroad.

Personnel apart, aid administrators are guided increasingly by the amount of progress which a country is making towards standing on its own feet. The simplest test of this is the proportion of its output going into personal consumption. If one assumes a 3:1 capital-output ratio, a country needs to spend about 30 per cent of GDP on gross capital formation and recurrent Government expenditure, taken together, to achieve a growth rate between 4 and 5 per cent per annum; it should therefore be consuming only about 70 per cent of its GDP. Part of the case for foreign aid is that it takes time for a country to reduce consumption from, say, 80 to 70 per cent of GDP. This requires at least twenty years of rapid growth. In so far as the long time needed for this adjustment is part of the case for aid, it is fair to judge countries by performance: those who are reducing consumption towards 70 per cent are clearly using aid for the purpose for which it is given, whereas those who are not becoming any less dependent than before are clearly misusing aid.

Political ties still count for more than anything else in determining which countries get most aid, but aid administrators learn from experience, and become more sophisticated with the passing years. Development Plans are not so impressive as they used to be, because of the painful gap between promise and performance. Even among political allies, more attention is being paid to performance, and especially to levels of domestic saving and taxation, actual performance in land reform, expenditures on health and education, and whether the opportunity presented by rising *per capita* income is being used to reduce the ratio of personal consumption to GDP. Self-respecting countries do not shape their policies in order to please foreigners; it is therefore fortunate when what pleases aid administrators and what produces economic independence happen to coincide.

Summary

1. The types and sources of aid are very varied. A Government needs high grade specialists in this subject.

2. Requests for aid should be channeled through a single agency, especially as it is often necessary to spend considerable sums as a condition of receiving aid.

3. Short-term credit is available in almost unlimited quantity, but should be used only with discretion. Unlimited use leads to bankruptcy.

4. Political considerations play the largest role in determining who receives aid. Professional aid administrators tend to favour the countries which seem to be most effective in planning development.

FOR FURTHER READING: CHAPTER II

Anderson, C. A., and Bowman, M. J. (Editors). *Education and Economic Development*. Chicago, 1965.

Baer, W., and Kerstenetzky, I. (Eds.) *Inflation and Growth in Latin America*. Homewood, Ill., 1964.

Benham, F. *Economic Aid to Underdeveloped Countries*. London, 1961.

Bird, R., and Oldman, O. (Eds.) *Readings on Taxation in Developing Countries*. Baltimore, 1964.

Chandler, L. V. *Central Banking and Economic Development*. Bombay, 1962.

Chenery, H. B. 'Comparative Advantage and Development Policy', *American Economic Review*, March 1961.

'The Interdependence of Investment Decisions', in *The Allocation of Economic Resources*, by M. Abramovitz and others; Stanford, 1959.

'Patterns of Industrial Growth', *American Economic Review*, September 1960.

Diamond, W. *Development Banks*. Baltimore, 1957.

Due, J. F. *Taxation and Economic Development in Tropical Africa*. Cambridge, 1963.

Eicher, C. K., and Witt, L. W. (Eds.) *Agriculture in Economic Development*. New York, 1964.

Galenson, W. (Editor). *Labour and Economic Development*. New York, 1959.

Hapgood, D., and Millikan, M., *Policies for Promoting Agricultural Growth*. MIT, Cambridge, Mass., 1965.

Harbison, F., and Myers, C. A. *Education, Manpower and Economic Growth*. New York, 1963.

Hicks, U. K. *Development from Below*. London, 1961.

Hirschman, A. O. *Journeys Toward Progress: Studies of Policy-Making in Latin America*. New York, 1963.

Meyer, J. 'Regional Economics: A Survey', *American Economic Review*, March 1963.

Prest, A. R. *Public Finance in Underdeveloped Countries*. London, 1962.

Nevin, E. *Capital Funds in Underdeveloped Countries*. New York, 1961.

Ranis, G., and Fei, J. C. H. 'Innovation, Capital Accumulation and Economic Development', *American Economic Review*, June 1963.

Reynolds, L. G. 'Wages and Employment in the Labour Surplus Economy', *American Economic Review*, March 1965.

Schultz, T. W. *Transforming Traditional Agriculture*. New Haven, 1964.

Scitovsky, T. 'Two Concepts of External Economies', *Journal of Political Economy*, April 1954.

Sen, A. K. *Choice of Techniques*. Oxford, 1960.

United Nations, Department of Economic and Social Affairs. *Processes and Problems of Industrialization in Underdeveloped Countries*. New York, 1955.

Wald, H. P. *Taxation of Agricultural Land in Underdeveloped Countries*. Cambridge, Mass., 1959.

CHAPTER III

The Arithmetic of Planning

The making of the Plan should begin simultaneously at its two ends; at the individual project level, and at the macroeconomic level. Then the results of these two are adjusted to one another.

Work on each project involves both technological and economic investigations. The technologist is concerned with the methods of production, with costings, and with blueprints; the economist with the choice among different methods, with potential markets, with the assessment of indirect benefits and interrelationships, and with the appropriate scale and location of output. This work is time-consuming; is, indeed, the major reason why it takes two whole years to prepare a Plan properly. Since one is predicting the future, the work is subject to much error; its quality depends more on flair and judgement than it does on technical arithmetic.

The purpose of the macroeconomic exercise is to help to ensure that the Plan is internally self-consistent; that the resource requirements of the proposed increases in private consumption, public services and investment do not add up to more than is available; that the expected increases in output of individual sectors are consistent with the expected increases in inputs; that demand and supply will balance, in the sense that what people will demand is what the system will produce; that imports will not grow faster than exports; that the expected rate of growth will be consistent with available skilled manpower and capital; and so on. One has only to read the average Development Plan now being issued to see how useful this exercise could be; most published Plans are riddled with inconsistencies of the kind referred to in this paragraph, which could not have survived the construction of a macroeconomic framework. On the other hand, such a framework cannot be better than the statistics available for making it, and it must be fully recognized that the majority of underdeveloped countries do not as yet have good enough statistics for reliable calculations of this sort.

The technique of this exercise is to project what the national income will be, sector by sector, at the end of the Plan period; this is compared with national income at the beginning, and, in the more elaborate models, with national income in each intervening year. These projections are used to compare demand and supply in as many markets as possible: required investment with likely savings; demand and supply of each commodity; imports and exports; and so on.

To illustrate the technique we shall make such a projection in this chapter for an imaginary country. This will be done at a very elementary level, because this volume is intended as an introduction to development planning for people learning the elements of the subject, and not as a technical treatise for experts. One simplification will be to deal in a small number of sectors, so as to keep the arithmetic simple. Working with twenty to forty times as many sectors, as Planning Agencies do in large countries, may give much greater accuracy, but does not involve any change of principles.

I. THE PLAN PERIOD

Plans come in three sizes, short, medium and long. The short is the Annual Plan. The medium range between three and seven years, with five years as the most popular choice. The long range upwards from ten years to twenty years.

The Annual Plan is not a substitute for the others. This is the controlling Plan, in the sense that this is the only document which, when passed by Parliament (normally in the form of an annual capital budget) authorizes Ministers to spend money; a Five or Ten Year Plan is not an authorising document, but merely a statement of intentions. The Annual Plan is also the controlling Plan in the sense that it is this which year by year matches resources to possible achievements. It is governed by the medium or long term Plan, which sets its direction, but the Annual Plan is the operative document.

The first Development Plan should be a Ten Year Plan: this for three reasons.

First, the making of the first Development Plan requires an assessment of long term perspectives. To formulate the portion of the Plan dealing with roads one must look ahead at least ten years. The school authorities should also be looking at least ten years ahead, since teachers are not produced overnight. The Ministry of Agriculture is going to be called upon to build up an extension service; training will take many years, and results will take still more. One of the more important uses of planning is that it forces decision-makers to stop and think; to formulate long-range goals, and to bring immediate actions into line with longer perspectives.

Secondly, what is true of policy-making in individual industries is also true for the economy as a whole. The main purpose of development planning is to move towards 'self-sustaining' growth; i.e., to create a cadre of trained manpower, to raise the percentage of national income saved domestically, to increase knowledge of natural resources and their effective utilization, and to create institutions which favour enterprise and investment. All this takes time. Development planning is a long-term business.

The third advantage of long-term planning is purely political. When the call goes out for projects, every area and every interest puts in its claim. The result is a demand for public services far in excess of available resources. In order to retain support, the Government will be anxious to show that it recognizes the legitimate needs of all the people. It cannot put everything into the Plan, but it can put more than twice as much into a Ten Year Plan as into a Five Year Plan (since resources should be larger in the second five years than in the first five years), and so it can provide twice as much pleasure. The importance of such political considerations must not be underestimated, since the people are more likely to acquiesce in the payment of the high taxes which development requires if they see that their needs are recognized, than if the Plan does not mention schemes which they value, or mentions them only to put them aside.

These arguments for a Ten Year Plan support even more strongly a Fifteen or Twenty Year Plan. These longer-term plans (called 'perspective plans') are sometimes made, whether for some sectors only, or for the whole economy, but are seldom published. They serve as guides to decision-makers, by showing up bottlenecks which will emerge as the economy expands, if anticipatory action is not taken well in advance. They are not published because a document looking fifteen to twenty years ahead is largely guesswork; and also because much of what it contains is irrelevant to immediate decision-making. The main purpose of the published Development Plan is to serve as a framework for preparation of the Annual Plan, and for this purpose one needs a narrower horizon than fifteen or twenty years.

To start with a Ten Year Plan may avoid one of the chief defects of Five Year Plans, which is their overcrowding. Too much is expected in too short a time. Publication of the Ten Year Plan is an earnest of good intentions. However, a Ten Year Plan soon gets out of date. By the end of the second year work should start on a new Five Year Plan, to come into effect say at the end of the fourth year, when the existing Ten Year Plan will be superceded. Five years is a good plan period, though it is not immensely superior to three, four, six or seven years, which are also popular numbers.

Summary
There should be an Annual Plan, a medium term Plan, and a long term perspective Plan. The first published Plan should cover about ten years; this should be superceded by Plans for shorter periods.

2. THE RATE OF GROWTH

The commonest error in development planning is to project an impossibly high rate of growth. The rate of growth of an economy cannot be immensely different at the end of a five year period from what it was at the beginning, except in countries recovering from disaster. This is so because the rate of growth is constrained by fundamental factors which are not easily changed in five years. When one reads in a Development Plan that an economy, now growing at 3 per cent per annum is 'planned' to grow at an average rate of 6 per cent per annum over the next five years, one knows at once that the document cannot be taken seriously, since it will be planning to dispose of output, taxes and savings in quantities which will not be there.

Excessive Projections
Governments fall into this error for one or other of three reasons. First, they may be publishing a Plan merely as a propaganda

exercise, without intending to be bound by it. Secondly, their Plan may list what the country needs, rather than what the country is capable of producing. Thirdly, it may be thought that the amount of resources likely to be available is itself a function of the size of the Plan.

It may seem strange for a Government to publish a Development Plan which it does not intend to implement. This may happen for several reasons. The Plan may have been made by the wrong people. For example, the Minister of Development may be keen to have a Plan, while the Prime Minister is lukewarm. The Cabinet agrees to set up the machinery for making the Plan; foreign experts are hired; and prodigies of arithmetic are performed. The Plan is accepted, published, and acclaimed. The Minister of Development moves on to some other office, and this is the end of the Plan.

Even if the right people make the Plan, they may have their tongues in their cheeks. One may publish a Plan to please the public, or to please foreign aid administrators, without ever intending implementation.

Every political party publishes a party programme, as a way of attracting votes, but only the unsophisticated expect political parties to adhere to their programmes. When a Government publishes a Development Plan the same sort of ritual is involved. Whether the Plan is meant seriously or not, its publication is an important occasion. The Plan fortifies the nation's consciousness of itself. In this it is at least on a par with such other occasions as the celebration of the King's Birthday, or the playing of the World Series, or the lining of the streets to wave to a visiting President. The fact that a Development Plan is not an authorizing document permits Governments to exploit it for political purposes.

A Government newly in office is especially prone to publish an inflated Plan. While in opposition it has made innumerable promises, which it must now recognize. Actually, one need not overload a Five Year Plan beyond the capacity for implementation, merely to recognize commitments. All that is necessary is to issue instead a Ten Year Plan: since resources grow, one can commit more than twice as much in a Ten Year as in a Five Year Plan.

The second source of error is to base a Plan on 'needs' rather than on resources. Assessment of resources may indicate a possible 4 per cent rate of growth. This is judged to be too low. The country 'needs' 6 or 7 per cent. So a high figure is assumed; capital needs are calculated on this base; and the Plan comes out with a long list of projects which there is no hope of implementing. Alternatively, one calculates how much investment it would take to eliminate unemployment, and programmes accordingly, without regard to available resources.

This again raises the question of intent. If the purpose of a Plan is to control the use of resources, it must be based on available resources. Needs are unlimited; a Plan based on needs is an advertisement rather than an instrument of control.

This brings us to the third reason for excessive Plans, which is that an advertisement may bring replies; more specifically, the amount of money available may itself be a function of the size of the Plan. This is obvious in relation to the search for foreign aid. If one presents to the foreign aid administrators a Plan for which all the required resources are already available, no role is left for them. But if one can point to a large number of useful and feasible projects which lack finance, they may begin to give serious consideration. The demands of foreign aid administrators have now become one of the most important reasons for making Development Plans, and have indeed helped to improve the quality of Plans.

The Plan also helps to increase the amount of domestic finance. When development planning begins, the idea is new to the public, and suggestions that taxes be raised or savings increased to finance it are not taken seriously. But if the Plan lists a number of projects which seem desirable to the public, and then year by year the Plan is falling behind for lack of resources, the public may well educate itself into being willing to make a larger contribution.

However, the legitimate desire to plan in such a way as to attract more resources is easily met by having first and second priorities. A first list shows what can be done with the financial resources likely to be available, while a second list shows additional projects which are feasible and desirable, but for which finance is not yet in sight. Thus the Plan is made realistic by giving a range of possibilities.

To publish a Plan which cannot be implemented because it is excessively large negates the principal purpose of planning, which is to guide policy. When too many projects are listed, those which get carried out are not those with the highest priority, but just those which happen to get off the board before the money runs out. The Plan misleads all who take it seriously. It tells civil servants how much they should prepare to spend; if the money is not there, such preparations are wasted. To the private sector it indicates how much foreign and domestic finance the Government thinks will be available, and therefore what its foreign exchange and lending policies will be; if these expectations are excessive, private decision-makers are led astray. In 'indicative planning' the matrix of interrelated demands is intended to guide producers as to the probable size of their markets; if the figures are set deliberately high, they will cause frustration. If the Plan bears little relation to what is likely to happen, it is not merely useless for control; it is also dangerous to anybody who takes it seriously. In practice, unrealistic Plans are not taken seriously by alert decision-makers. The document is not consulted, because it is irrelevant. The planning authorities are unable to exercise influence. And foreign aid administrators take note that the Government is not serious about development planning.

One reason for the increasing popularity of macroeconomic exercises with professional planners is that these exercises do impose upon politicians the burden of consistency. If the Plan as a whole is too large, consistency is not of much help. But if one can get the Prime Minister to agree to fixing a reasonable total, then a macroeconomic exercise works wonders in eliminating proposals from individual Ministers which are inconsistent with balance in other sectors. On the other hand, determined politicians are not defeated by arithmetic; if they have to accept consistency, they merely work for a Plan which is consistent but excessive. Many Development Plans are now published which meet every test of consistency, but which are nevertheless obviously excessive.

Constraints on Growth

Development planning starts with assessing what the economy can do, rather than by asking what it would have to do to meet some desirable end, such as increasing output by 50 per cent or halving the unemployment rate. The four fundamental constraints on the rate of growth are: natural resources, skilled manpower, the physical capacity of the capital goods industries, and finance.

DEVELOPMENT PLANNING

The planner's first task is to pinpoint the new resources or techniques whose exploitation is going to carry the economy upwards. This is done in co-operation with the geologists, the agronomists, the industrial promoters and all the other specialists who are studying outlets for new investment or new knowledge.

In practice the overall rate of growth achievable in an underdeveloped economy depends primarily on what happens to its agriculture. In the typical African or Asian economy, agriculture produces something like 50 per cent of gross domestic product (GDP), services account for 35 per cent, and industry for only 15 per cent. Dreams of rapid growth usually centre on the manufacturing sector. However, this sector is so small that even if it expands at an extraordinary rate, its influence on the growth rate of the economy as a whole is relatively small. The main determinant of growth of the economy as a whole is the growth rate of agriculture.

This is easily illustrated statistically. Between 1950 and 1960 manufacturing industry grew at an annual rate of 3.3 per cent in Britain, 6.5 per cent in India and 9.2 per cent in Brazil. Let us assume that an underdeveloped country achieved the extraordinarily high rate of 10 per cent. Let us also assume that its agriculture grows at a rate of 3 per cent p.a., which is also higher than most underdeveloped countries achieve. The output of services (including transportation) usually grows a little faster than the output of commodities, in real terms. (In money terms services grow much faster than national income; productivity increases faster in commodities, so service prices rise relatively to other prices.) We then get the following result:

TABLE II. *Growth Rate Averages*

	GDP Year 0	Growth Rate	Absolute Increase
Agriculture	50	3.0	1.5
Manufactures	15	10.0	1.5
Services	35	4.9	1.7
	100		4.7

The resulting increase of 4.7 per cent is very high. Most underdeveloped countries are not in a position to achieve a growth rate of 5 per cent, not because they cannot step up manufacturing activity, but because they have not found the secret of getting their farmers to increase agricultural output by more than 3 per cent per annum. Many of these countries claim to be growing at rates of 6, 7 or even 8 per cent. Most of these claims can be dismissed summarily. A rate of 5 per cent per annum can be exceeded only in the following circumstances:

(1) if agriculture is growing rapidly because new lands are being opened up, or massive investment in irrigation is paying off, or the peasants have become enthusiastic about fertilizers, new varieties, or new crops; or

(2) if the development of the economy is already well advanced, so that the importance of agriculture in the total has already diminished significantly; or

(3) if there is a rapidly expanding mining industry.

In most underdeveloped countries none of these conditions holds. An annual rate of increase of 5 per cent must then be regarded as a remarkably high achievement, and claims in excess of this must be treated with suspicion.

The moral of this arithmetic is not that Development Plans should normally accept 4 per cent as their target, but that they should normally give priority to trying to raise agricultural output faster than by 3 per cent per annum. In the absence of mining, high rates of growth are impossible unless there is a breakthrough in agriculture. A few underdeveloped countries are getting rates of agricultural growth as high as 4 and 5 per cent per annum, over a decade. Most of the others could do as well, if they tried.

Manpower

The second constraint on growth which may make 5 per cent hard to achieve is a shortage of skilled manpower. This may show itself in any sector. One may be able to build schools or hospitals, but not to man them with teachers or nurses. Industry needs skilled artisans, foremen and supervisors. The agricultural programme may lag for lack of extension agents, and so on. Two of the more important manpower bottlenecks are in the Government's administrative service and in the construction industry. These two are so important that if they are set targets beyond their capacity the result is not merely a shortfall, but may well be that less is achieved than would be possible if the targets were lower.

This may occur because the Plan consists of hundreds of individual projects, each of which must itself be planned. If buildings are required, they must be designed, put out to tender and watched. Machinery must be imported. Skilled labour must be trained and hired. The capacity of the administrative service is limited. If it tries to do more than it can do efficiently, mistakes multiply rapidly. Buildings are not properly designed; equipment is not ordered in time, or chosen with care; training plans are delayed. The result is waste. If one has resources capable of yielding results worth one million and tries to get from them one and a half million of results, one may end up with a product worth only three-quarters of a million. It is unquestionably a mistake to load on to the administrative service a bigger programme than it can efficiently execute. If what can be done seems small, the correct remedy is to begin by strengthening the administration.

Administrative capacity is strengthened in the long run by educating more people, especially at secondary and higher levels: this is an essential part of any Plan. In the short run administrative capacity can be strengthened by importing skills. A shortage of engineers or architects need not hold up the preparation of projects, since it is possible to hire the services of consulting engineers and architects. A shortage of entrepreneurs can be met by using foreign entrepreneurship, alone, or in association with domestic enterprise (whether private or public). Thanks to bilateral and multilateral technical assistance programmes, high-level manpower is available at relatively low cost. Intermediate skills are more difficult (nurses, teachers, secretaries, technicians), since the numbers required are large, and the cost of importing them high. But these, on the other hand, are fairly easily multiplied by establishing facilities for training. High-level manpower is therefore no longer such a bottleneck as it was fifteen years ago.

Capital Formation

Most new projects require capital formation, hence the capacity to create new capital is one of the constraints on growth. About two-thirds of capital formation goes into construction, and about one-third into equipment. The nature of the constraints is different in these two sectors.

In construction the main constraint would be skilled manpower, since more than half the workers in this industry are artisans who must have at least a year of training to acquire proficiency. How much more work one can load on this industry therefore depends on how much slack there is. After a period of stagnation the industry can probably take as much extra work as can be financed; but if the industry is already working near capacity, a decision to accelerate capital formation rapidly may come up against the constraint of building capacity. The construction industry will then expand rapidly with unskilled labour, but owing to inadequate supervision and poor training the work is done badly and at high cost. Contractors take the opportunity to double and treble their profit margins. Many refuse to quote a fixed price, and insist on cost-plus contracts. Almost inevitably, what was planned to cost a million costs one and a half million or even two million. The moral is that one should look closely at the capacity of the construction industry when beginning to plan, and should include in the Plan itself measures for increasing capacity. Proposals that the amount invested should grow by more than 10 per cent per annum should normally be resisted.

The existing capacity to produce machinery is a constraint in a closed economy, but not in an open economy which can convert savings into foreign exchange. In a closed economy, acceleration of growth requires heavy investment in the machine-producing industries, to the extent permitted by the rate of saving. An open economy need not produce its own machines, and does not therefore have to start by expanding its heavy industries. If savings can be converted into foreign exchange, the decision whether to import machines or to make them at home turns on simple considerations of cost and convenience.

An increase in saving is converted into foreign exchange because it causes a reduction in the imports of consumer goods, or a reduction in the demand for domestic resources, whose product is then exported. The factors which make this easy or difficult were examined when we considered the related possibility that the rate of growth of exports could be a brake on the rate of growth of output.[1] In the textbook economy saving is the only constraint on investment; foreign exchange does not constitute a separate constraint since saving can always be converted into foreign exchange. In the real world, this conversion can be difficult. Imported machinery then becomes more expensive in real terms

[1] See page 39.

than it is in money terms, and it pays to produce rather more machinery at home than would otherwise be the case. Then, the more dependent the country is on its own machinery supplies, the more important the capacity to produce machines will loom as a separate constraint on the possible rate of growth of the economy.

Most countries begin their industrialization by investing in light consumer good industries rather than in heavy capital good industries. This is partly because many capital good industries require advanced skills, and partly because the market for such goods is relatively small when compared with the scale at which their production is economic. A large country like India, which is relatively well equipped with skills, iron ore and coal, has a comparative advantage in the production of iron and steel, and of some machinery. Small countries, not similarly endowed, will find it more profitable to start with consumer goods and to move into capital goods, via repair services, only as the home market expands and skills accumulate.

Finance

The fourth constraint on the rate of growth is money. Economic growth requires large expenditures on the public services and also on capital formation. The annual recurrent budget must allocate large sums to such services as research and surveys, road maintenance, agricultural extension, education and public health; there is no fixed ratio, but less than 10 per cent of GDP (excluding defence expenditures and social security transfers) is not likely to be adequate. Again there is no specific figure for capital formation; but adopting for the moment an incremental capital output ratio (ICOR) of 3 to 1, it would follow that an annual rate of growth of 5 per cent requires annual net investment amounting to 15 per cent of GDP. This sum exceeds the current savings ratios of most underdeveloped countries. If these countries had to depend only on their own resources, very few would have a 4 per cent growth rate.

Capital-Output Ratio

ICOR's can vary widely. In the first place, only a small proportion of investment goes directly into the production of commodities (agriculture, mining and manufacturing); usually well under half. About a sixth goes into housing, and the rest into public utilities (transportation, power, water) and public services (e.g. schools, hospitals, roads). The proportions can be varied. One can temporarily get a very low ICOR if the existing public utilities and services have excess capacity (one reason for rapid recovery rates after a war). One may also distinguish between that capital which is required to produce the growth of commodity output, and other capital which is wanted for services which are demanded because growth has taken place. One cannot postpone investment which is wanted for growth, without impeding growth; but it is possible to postpone investment which merely facilitates consumption, e.g. housing, hospitals or entertainment services (as the USSR did in its earlier Five Year Plans). However, this can only be temporary; for sooner or later the expansion of commodity output will create irresistible demands for increased expenditure on housing, utilities and services.

Secondly, even in the commodity-producing sector, the ICOR depends on technology, and on the commodity mix. Is the development mostly in heavy industry, or in light industry? Does agricultural expansion require heavy investment in irrigation or reclamation, or is it merely a question of using fertilizers and planting better varieties or more profitable crops? Development planning offers much leeway for the use of scarce capital resources in ways which keep the ICOR low.

Thirdly, the ICOR is a function of the rate of investment itself. New investment and new technology go together; hence, the faster capital grows, the greater the proportion of new technology embodied in the capital stock. A country which has doubled its capital in twelve years will have a higher output per unit of capital than a country which (*ceteris paribus*) has doubled in twenty-four years, because the technology of the last twelve years is embodied in half the capital in the first case, but only in perhaps a third of the capital in the second case. It may be true that growth owes more to technology than to capital; but in practice those who invest most will also improve technology fastest.

Fourthly, the ICOR depends on how easily the country can accommodate population growth. If plenty of empty cultivable land exists, a growing population can be accommodated in the countryside for an investment not notably different from the existing ratio of the capital stock to output (usually between 1.0

and 1.5), since tools and housing are simple, and the supply of utilities (power, buses, water) and services (schools, hospitals, roads) is rudimentary. Not so if the population increase is swelling the towns, with their more elaborate infrastructure, and more capitalistic methods of production. Here and here only is it plausible to speak of an ICOR without distinguishing whether income is increasing because of population growth or because of increased productivity.

On the other hand, given the population, the ICOR is higher in sparsely populated than in densely populated countries. This is because the cost of running water pipes, electric cables, roads, telephone wires and railway lines is primarily a function of the area served, and only secondarily a function of the traffic carried. (The cost of such services per head is much greater if there are fifty persons per square mile than if there are 500 persons per square mile.) For the same reason, the cost of infrastructure may fall with development, since, as population increases, the cost of extending the system is proportionately smaller than the original cost of building it.

Finally, the ICOR depends on employment policy. If land is abundant, as in West Africa, and most of the people live in the countryside, and the towns have not yet become a magnet, there will be little unemployment. Capital can then be used in ways which maximize the rate of growth of income, without bothering about effects on employment. But if the country is overpopulated, and unemployment in the towns substantial, and large numbers live in intolerable misery, humanitarianism (not to speak of the fear of revolution) demands that immediate relief measures take precedence over future growth. A large part of available resources will then go into public works, using very little equipment, in order to create as much employment as possible. Well chosen works will increase productive capacity (e.g. water works, reclamation, erosion controls, roads, schools, hospitals, and even houses) but it is quite conceivable that if the same resources were invested instead in commodity-producing industries using more equipment and less labour, the ICOR would be smaller.

Increasing Domestic Resources
However one trims the ICOR, the basic difficulty will remain: domestic resources available for public expenditure and capital

formation will not suffice for the rate of growth which the Government wishes to achieve. These resources can be supplemented by foreign aid, whether investment by foreign companies, or loans or grants. Here again the variations are wide, and in a few cases the sum of domestic resources and foreign aid is adequate. But in most cases resources still do not add up to what is needed for achievement of the desired rate of growth. Sometimes the gap in resources can be plugged by an increase in taxation, but often it is too wide for this. How hard it is to mobilize domestic finance is best illustrated by an arithmetical example.

Assume that the ICOR is $3:1$, and the desired rate of growth 4 per cent, making desired net investment 12 per cent of GDP. Assume that depreciation accounts for 4 per cent. Further assume that the Government's current expenditure requires 10 per cent (its capital expenditure is included in investment). It follows that gross investment and public expenditure require 26 per cent of GNP, and the amount of resources available for private consumption will be 74 per cent of GDP. Now assume that private savings and public revenue presently come to 18 per cent of GDP, and that private consumption is therefore 82 per cent of GDP. Self-sustaining growth, defined to exclude any need for foreign aid, requires that private consumption must fall from 82 to 74 per cent of GDP.

In the theory of national income accounting all that one need do to reduce private consumption from 82 to 74 per cent is to levy additional taxes amounting to 8 per cent of GDP, but in practice this is obviously impossible. Any Government which tried to reduce consumption from 82 to 74 *in one swoop* would have a revolution on its hands, except in some dire emergency such as a war. If the purpose is only economic development, one may assume that an *absolute* fall in consumption is out of the question, since very few people are willing to have their consumption forcibly reduced this year in return for an uncertain promise of an increase in 'GDP' next year, expecially as the distribution of the increase in 'GDP' is certain to be very uneven. Attempts to bring about an absolute fall in consumption, whether through taxation or through inflation, always result in strikes, and often in riots, and they ultimately fail because people insist on raising their money incomes sufficiently to offset increased taxes. The only practicable way of reducing the share of consumption from 82 to

74 per cent without violent strife is to increase GDP faster than consumption. It is not feasible even to hold the absolute amount of *per capita* consumption constant, since GDP can be increased only by offering inducements. Workers must move to higher-paid occupations; farmers must adopt more profitable methods; and as the incomes of some groups rise, incomes of other mobile or powerful groups will also rise, even though their *per capita* output is not increasing—especially in the rapidly growing service industries, where wages keep pace with industry but productivity lags. An increase in *per capita* output unaccompanied by an increase in *per capita* consumption is therefore inconceivable, at least in a free society.

It is not merely inconceivable, but also undesirable. Economic growth creates very disturbing tensions in society, which can be resolved only if some of the increased output is used to secure more equitable distribution. Men migrate from villages where they have been sustained in time of want by the obligations of extended family systems. In the towns they fall sick, or become unemployed, and it falls to the public authorities to look after their welfare. Other men are deprived of their living by technological changes which make them poor but others rich. Some are by-passed by opportunity, but are made envious by the good fortune of neighbours or relatives, and join with others in unions or other societies in an attempt to obtain a share of the obvious increase in national riches. The early stages of economic development are always a time of tension and unrest. Narrowly conceived, economic interests may seem to require that consumption be held down as long as possible; but the creation of a healthy society with tensions and injustices mitigated requires that welfare be given equal priority with growth right from the beginning.

Economists have written many articles in search of an optimal rate of saving. By making simple assumptions relating the growth of output to saving, one can calculate the rate of saving which would maximize the absolute level of consumption in n years' time, or the sum of consumption over the next n years, or the present value of the sum of consumption over the next n years. One can also add constraints, such as that consumption cannot fall below its starting level, or that *per capita* consumption must grow from one year to the next by at least r per cent. The number of possibilities is infinite.

For example, assume that income grows by 1.0 per cent per year for every 3.0 per cent invested. Then one can calculate what rate of saving will maximize consumption in ten years' time. Consumption in the tenth year is

$$(1-s)\,(1+\tfrac{s}{3})^{10}$$

where s is the rate of saving. This is maximized when s is 0.64. Thus, out of an income of 100, consumption must now be cut to 36, but will rise in ten years to 249. Such a cut is obviously not feasible. Suppose instead that we assume that the current rate of saving is 9 per cent, and that the absolute amount saved grows at a constant rate. Then consumption in the tenth year is

$$1+.03\,\frac{(1+r)^{10}-1}{r}-.09\,(1+r)^{10}$$

where the second term is the increase in national income over ten years (one-third the sum of ten years' savings), and the third term is the amount saved in the tenth year. This is maximized when the absolute amount saved grows by 13 per cent, making saving in the tenth year 20 per cent of income. In this case consumption increases every year; but this rate of acceleration of savings is still not feasible, and also not worthwhile, since the increase in consumption in the later years does not make up for the restraint on consumption in earlier years. Such formulae can be multiplied *ad infinitum*.

The most plausible approach to this problem is to recognize that the rate of growth of output depends not only on saving but also on consumption. Since growth requires inducements, it will not occur unless consumption is allowed to increase. One can devise a rule of thumb by assuming that the minimum allowable growth of consumption is tied to the rate of growth of output itself. Suppose that at least 50 per cent of the *per capita* increase in (gross) output must go into private consumption, and that consumption is currently 75 per cent of output. Then if *per capita* output grows by 1.0 per cent per annum, the ratio of consumption to output will fall in ten years to 72.6. If the *per capita* growth is 2.0 per cent, the ratio falls in ten years to 70.5; if 3.0 per cent, the ratio falls to 68.6. In practice the less developed countries have difficulty in raising their *per capita* output faster than 2.0 per cent per annum, partly because of the obstinacy of their subsistence agriculture, and partly because of high population growth. Hence one can practically rule out a fall in the ratio of consumption to output by more than five points over ten years. There are half a dozen countries where *per capita* output is growing by more than 2 per cent per annum; these can make swift transitions. Elsewhere, attempts at reducing the share of consumption by more than a half of 1 per cent per annum are likely to be frustrated by strikes, riots, inflation, or political action, and also to diminish growth by diminishing incentives. Precision is not claimed, but rules of thumb are often useful in practical affairs.

Assessment of financial resources, and of the possible rate of growth, therefore calls for moderation; the deficiencies of centuries cannot be made good in a single decade. At the same time, even a moderate assessment demands bold action. For while many underdeveloped countries have had a 2 per cent *per capita* increase in output over the last ten years, very few indeed have reduced the share of consumption by one half of 1 per cent per year. The majority have held the share of consumption constant, thus making no progress towards self-sustaining growth. If foreign aid ever comes to be given on the basis of self-help, the rate of change of the ratio of consumption to output will be a good index of self-help.

Summary

1. A Plan should be based not on 'need', but on resources and their development potential. If expenditures are planned in excess of resources, the Plan cannot serve as an instrument of control and will either mislead decision-makers and cause waste, or else be ignored by them.

2. The overall rate of growth of an underdeveloped economy depends primarily on the rate of growth of its agriculture. Manufacturing industry is such a small sector that its rate of growth makes little difference to the overall rate. Unless a breakthrough is expected in agriculture or mining, it is unrealistic to assume a growth rate of 5 per cent.

3. Manpower imposes constraints on the rate of growth; especially administrative capacity, and also skilled manpower in the construction industry. It is normally uneconomic to increase investment as fast as 10 per cent per annum.

4. The capacity of the machine-making industries is not a constraint on the rate of growth of an open economy.

5. The incremental capital-output ratio varies considerably as between economies, partly because of differences in natural resources, industries, technology and population density; and partly because it is possible to postpone some service investments temporarily, without diminishing the rate of growth.

6. The ratio of domestic savings (including the budget surplus) to output must be increased if self-sustaining growth is to be attained; but cannot be increased rapidly. Unless the economy is growing rapidly, it is unrealistic to expect the ratio of consumption to output to fall by more than one half of 1 per cent per annum.

3. PROJECTING FINANCIAL RESOURCES

Having studied the structural and financial constraints on the growth of the national income, the planners pick the highest growth rate which seems plausible for the period which is to be planned. The feasibility of this figure must then be tested. Each industry has to be examined separately to see whether it can grow at a rate corresponding to the proposed overall rate: does the sum of the parts add to what is projected for the whole? Can the required interrelations between industries be sustained? Will there be enough savings to finance the postulated rate of growth? Can exports and foreign aid keep pace with the demands which growing income will make on imports? Will the necessary skilled manpower be available? And so on. The main purpose of the macroeconomic framework is to show up and check the implications of the postulated rate of growth.

In this section we begin by testing for financial consistency. On the one side, the rate of growth determines capital requirements. On the other side, the capital available consists of private savings, public savings, and the capital (including grants, loans and private investment) obtained from abroad. By projecting national income at the postulated rate of growth, we can see whether the capital required and the capital available will keep up with each other. It will be necessary to make a separate projection for each year of the Plan period, since the output of the last year depends on the sum of the investments of previous years. However, to simplify calculations, we start by projecting the figures for the last year of the Plan period; it is then not difficult to interpolate the intervening years and check their consistency with what is required of the period as a whole.

Another simplification is used in the treatment of uncertainty. In estimating the size of some sector five years ahead one normally comes up not with a single figure (e.g. '538') but with a range (e.g. 'lying probably between 530 and 550'). However, since the procedure which is followed is to make a set of interlocking tables, it would be awkward to work with ranges; hence one uses instead the most probable figure. The appropriate way to take account of the uncertainty of the estimates is to make a complete set of tables for each different set of assumptions. Since the number of assumptions is large, and each can be assigned upper and lower limits, as well as a most probable quantity, the number of complete sets of tables could run into thousands if all possible combinations were worked out. At later stages of planning, when studying particular possibilities, such as savings or the balance of payments, the statistician will reconstruct the same table several times over, utilizing different assumptions. But at this preliminary stage, where he is only building a rough framework, he is content to work in each case with the figure he thinks most probable.

For projections of national income, we shall assume that a set of national accounts exists, which gives all the figures required for year zero. Actually, the first work on the Plan is being done in Year −2, or even −3, so the figures for Year 0 are themselves projections. We shall assume that these figures are given, and will not, for the purpose of the calculations in this chapter, be questioning their accuracy. In practice, of course, many of these figures may not be available, and when available may not be reliable. But the purpose of this chapter is not to assess the reliability of national income statistics, but merely to illustrate how such statistics are used.

Projections are usually calculated in constant prices, and this involves constant terms of trade. Prices will change over five years, and the terms of trade may improve or deteriorate. Speculation about price movements does not help much at this stage of planning. Changes in prices will be taken into account in the Annual Plan.

PROJECTING FINANCIAL RESOURCES

First Trial

We will begin by assuming that the Government makes over-enthusiastic demands, and see how the national income projection helps to spotlight inconsistencies. Let us assume that it issues the following instructions to the Planning Agency:

1. The Plan period is five years.
2. By the end of the fifth year, GDP is to be growing at an annual rate of 6 per cent. The current rate is 3 per cent, and to allow time for acceleration the average over the five years is to be 5 per cent per annum.
3. Government expenditure on goods and services on current account, now 8 per cent of GDP is to rise to 10 per cent.

For its preliminary projection the Planning Agency makes the following further assumptions:

4. The rate of growth of agriculture (including mining), currently 2.5 per cent p.a., might reach 3 per cent in five years, with an average of 2.75.
5. The rate of growth of industry (including construction), which is currently 4 per cent, might average 5.5 per cent.

If GDP is to grow by an average of 5.0 per cent p.a., it follows residually that services must grow by 7.5 per cent p.a.

The results of these assumptions are shown in Table III below, which projects gross domestic product. In this and subsequent tables GDP is shown at factor cost (i.e. exclusive of indirect taxes and subsidies). Figures are expressed in millions of units of the national currency. As can be seen from the structure of the GDP in the first column, we are assuming a country in which some development has occurred (industry, including construction, contributes 18 per cent of GDP), but *per capita* output is still low (agriculture contributes 47 per cent), say, about 100 US dollars per head.

TABLE III. *Projected Sectoral Growth, I*

	Year 0	Year 5
Agriculture	470	538
Industry	180	235
Services	350	503
GDP	1,000	1,276

The first warning light is flashed in Table III. GDP grows by 5.0 per cent per annum, commodity output by 3.5 per cent, and the supply of services by 7.5 per cent p.a. Normally the margin between the growth rates of services and of commodities is less than 10 per cent (e.g. commodities 3.50, services 3.84). If we have GDP growing so much faster than the output of commodities, the demand for commodities is likely to exceed the supply, and inflation and a balance of payments deficit will result. The growth rate of services is tied to that of commodities except in one or other of two cases. If the services are for export (e.g. tourism), the proceeds of the exports can be spent on importing commodities. Or if the Government is expanding its services, *and increasing taxation by the same amount to pay for them,* the taxes will reduce the demand for commodities to the available supply. If neither of these is the case, the Planning Agency should stop right here. The growth of services should be cut back to only slightly more than that of commodities (say, to 3.7 per cent), thus admitting that, in view of the obstinacy of agriculture, the 5.0 per cent target for output as a whole is unattainable in five years. However, let us proceed in search of further danger signals.

The next step is to project the total resources available and their use. This is done in Table IV. Resources available are shown on the left. This is the sum of GDP and the net amount obtained from abroad (the difference between imports of goods and services and exports of goods and services, which we here abbreviate as 'Surplus'). On the right hand side of the Table the use of resources is grouped under capital formation, use by the Government on current account (excluding transfers) and private consumption. The Agency makes the following assumptions:

6. The surplus from abroad, though only 0.2 per cent of GDP in Year 0, can be raised to 3 per cent by Year 5.

7. The ICOR (excluding stocks) will be 3 : 1. (This is only a preliminary tentative assumption. The actual ICOR will depend on the individual projects which are finally chosen, and will not therefore emerge until the Plan is complete.)

8. Depreciation, now 4.5 per cent of GDP, will rise to 5.0 per cent.

9. Net increase in stocks, now 0.8, will rise to 1.0 per cent of GDP.

The three assumptions relating to capital raise the requirement in Year 5 to 24 per cent of GDP (since the 6 per cent rate of growth requires 18 per cent for net investment). The increase in Government use of resources to 10 per cent was among the original instructions.

When all these calculations are completed, one space remains blank in the Table: consumption in Year 5. This item is then obtained by difference. The essence of our procedure is to make reasonable assumptions for all but one of the items in the account; this last item is obtained residually; in each of the tables it will be marked with an 'R'. We then check whether the answer so obtained is reasonable. If it is not, then the preceding assumptions are inconsistent; a new trial must be made with more reasonable assumptions. The student reader is invited to construct each of these tables for himself with pencil and paper as we go along, to make sure that he understands the procedure.

TABLE IV. *Resources and Their Use, I*

	Year 0	Year 5		Year 0	Year 5
GDP	1,000	1,276	Capital	143	306
Surplus	2	38	Government	80	128
			Consumption	779	880 R
	1,002	1,314		1,002	1,314

Another danger signal is flashed in Table IV: the residual item, consumption, is unreasonably low. It falls from 77.9 per cent of GDP to 69.0 per cent in five years, as against the rule-of-thumb that it should not fall by more than half of 1 per cent per annum. Achievement of this result would demand an enormous increase in taxation, partly to finance capital formation. Let us then see how capital formation is to be financed.

This is shown in Table V. The left shows capital requirements, which are the same as in the previous table. On the right are the sources of finance, domestic and foreign. Capital available from abroad (here abbreviated to 'Foreign') exceeds the Surplus shown in the preceding table, because part of what comes in has to be paid out in profits and debt charges. (Both sides of this table include the non-monetary investment done by subsistence farmers; this is not normally a large item, except where the farmers are putting in irrigation ditches, or planting tree crops.) The Agency now makes the following further assumptions:

10. Corporate profits, taxes and savings will rise at the same rate as industrial output. (This is given by assumption 5 as 5.5 per cent per annum.)

11. Private savings (including unincorporated enterprises) will rise from 5.0 to 5.5 per cent of GDP.

Depreciation is given by assumption 8. The residual item is then Government saving (excess of revenue over expenditure on current account). The table brings out what a large increase would be required.

TABLE V. *Capital Account, I*

	Year 0	Year 5		Year 0	Year 5
Fixed Inv.	135	293	Foreign	3	50
Stocks	8	13	Depreciation	45	64
			Corporate S.	20	26
			Private S.	50	70
			Govt. S.	25	96 R
	143	306		143	306

Finally we look at the Government's account to see what the programme involves in taxation. (Government here means the aggregate of central, provincial and local authority budgets.) Government expenditure on goods and services comes from Table IV; required savings from Table V; and corporate taxes from assumption 10. Government transfer payments will increase, partly to provide welfare services, and partly to make payments on some of the heavy borrowing from overseas. So the Agency assumes:

12. Government transfer payments will rise from 1.0 to 1.2 per cent of GDP.

The residual item is 'other revenue'. Table VI shows that this more than doubles over five years.

TABLE VI. *Government Current Account, I*

	Year 0	Year 5		Year 0	Year 5
Expenditure	80	128	Corporate Taxes	20	26
Transfers	10	15	Other Revenue	95	213 R
Savings	25	96			
	115	239		115	239

These tables have thus produced three warnings that the proposed rate of growth is not feasible:

    a. It involves an excessive rate of growth of services (Table III).

    b. It involves an excessive rate of decline in the ratio of private consumption (Table IV).

    c. It involves an excessive increase in taxation (Table VI).

The third of these warnings followed from assuming reasonable contributions by private savings and by foreign capital, thus making public saving the residual item. Either of the other two could have been residual. Reasonable tax assumptions would have produced residually either an excessive marginal domestic savings rate, or an excessive deficit in the balance of payments.

Second Trial

It follows that if this is a serious Plan, and not a propaganda document, the Government must revise its original instructions. The rate of growth cannot be raised from 3.0 to 5.0 per cent in five years. Let us assume that we are dealing with a reasonable Government, which issues a new set of feasible instructions:

    13. The Plan period will be ten years instead of five. This enables the Government to recognize various commitments.

    14. The terminal rate of growth is to be 4.5 per cent.

    15. The share of Government revenues in GDP will rise over ten years from 11.5 to 15.0 per cent.

The Agency now adjusts some of its earlier assumptions to these changes. It further assumes:

    16. The rate of growth of agriculture will rise to 3.0 per cent, averaging 2.8 per cent p.a. over the period.

    17. The rate of growth of industry will rise to 8.0 per cent, averaging 7.0 per cent p.a.

    18. GDP will be growing by about 4.5 per cent p.a. at the end of the period, but owing to the time acceleration takes, will average only about 4.2 per cent p.a. over the ten years.

These assumptions produce the figures in Table VII. The residual item, services, is increasing only a little faster than the output of commodities.

In the trial run we made taxation the residual item. Since taxation is now given by assumption 15, either domestic saving or the foreign balance must now be the residual. We shall keep to reasonable assumptions for domestic savings, and see whether

TABLE VII. *Projected Sectoral Growth, II*

	Year 0	Year 10
Agriculture	470	620
Industry	180	354
Services	350	536 R
GDP	1,000	1,510

the resulting foreign balance is reasonable. Thus we now start with the Government's account, and work forward to the foreign balance and private consumption.

In Table VIII, the total revenue of the Government is given by assumption 15, and corporate taxes by assumption 10; other revenue is therefore derived by difference. On the left side of the account, expenditure on goods and services is given by assumption 3 (which the Government now confirms). For Government transfers the Agency makes a new assumption:

19. Transfers will grow from 1.0 to 2.0 per cent of GDP.

The residual item is Government saving, which we transfer to the Capital Account.

TABLE VIII. *Government Current Account, II*

	Year 0	Year 10		Year 0	Year 10
Expenditure	80	151	Corporate Taxes	20	39
Transfers	10	31	Other Revenue	95	188
R Savings	25	45			
	115	227		115	227

Capital requirements continue as in assumptions 7, 8 and 9; but with the lower rate of growth the terminal requirement is only 19.5 per cent of GDP. Depreciation, corporate saving and private saving are given by assumptions 8, 10 and 11 respectively. Government saving comes from Table VIII. The residual item is the contribution from abroad.

The required foreign contribution comes to about 3.3 per cent of GDP. This is not impossibly high; even the higher rate assumed for intermediate years (Table XXXIII) is compatible with the current level of foreign aid programmes. But, of course, if the country is to get this much, it will have to pursue policies attractive to foreign investors and aid administrators.

TABLE IX. *Capital Account, II*

	Year 0	Year 10		Year 0	Year 10
Fixed Inv.	135	279	Foreign	3	51 R
Stocks	8	15	Depreciation	45	76
			Corporate S.	20	39
			Private S.	50	83
			Govt. S.	25	45
	143	294		143	294

As we have already noted, this sum is not all available to add to resources. From it must be deducted profits and debt charges. This could nearly swallow it all up. As Table XXXIII will show, total external aid over ten years will come to 444. If this were all loans, to be amortised over twenty years, amortisation alone would be 22, and interest might bring the total cost to over 40. Borrowing is only a temporary (and expensive) way of increasing resources, since interest and repayments soon catch up with new lending. The Agency estimates optimistically that it can obtain a high proportion of grants and soft loans, and also counts on foreign investors largely reinvesting their depreciation quotas, so interest, profit and amortisation are estimated at an extra 20.

To estimate the Surplus of goods and services, which is required for the table showing Resources and their Uses, the Agency must make a balance of payments forecast. This is done in Table X. Loans and grants come from Table IX. The new assumptions are:

20. Receipts from tourism will treble.

21. Debt charges will rise from 1 to 21.

22. Payments on services will double.

The residual item is the Trade Deficit.

TABLE X. *Balance of Payments*

	Year 0	Year 10		Year 0	Year 10
R Trade Deficit	3	36	Tourism	4	12
Services	3	6	Loans and Grants	3	51
Debt Charges	1	21			
	7	63		7	63

The Surplus (excess of imports over exports) is the sum of Trade Deficit plus Services minus Tourism; this comes to 30 in Year 10, and is entered in Table XI. The GDP comes from Table VII, Government use of resources from Table VIII, and capital from Table IX. The residual item is personal consumption.

TABLE XI. *Resources and Their Use, II*

	Year 0	Year 10		Year 0	Year 10
GDP	1,000	1,510	Capital	143	294
Surplus	2	30	Government	80	151
			Consumption	779	1,095 R
	1,002	1,540		1,002	1,540

We now have all the information required for calculating what personal income will be, and how it will be spent. On the left side of Table XII we enter the sources of income: GDP plus transfers minus various items which do not enter into the domestic personal income. On the right we show how personal income is used. Since all these figures come from previous tables, the fact that both sides add to the same total serves as a check that we have not made arithmetical errors.

TABLE XII. *Personal Income*

	Year 0	Year 10		Year 0	Year 10
GDP	1,000	1,510	Private Saving	50	83
Transfers	10	31	Pers. Taxes	95	188
			Consumption	779	1,095
	1,010	1,541			
Less Depreciation	45	76			
,, Corporate S.	20	39			
,, Corporate Taxes	20	39			
,, Debt Charges	1	21			
Personal Income	924	1,366		924	1,366

Now we have the final check on whether what is proposed is reasonable. Consumption is required to fall from 77.9 to 72.5 per cent of GDP over ten years. This is on the very edge of the tolerable limits. The tax burden is particularly heavy. In marginal terms, of every 100 by which GDP is to increase, taxation is to take 22. The real significance of this can be seen only when the figures are put in terms of increases per head. Suppose that population is increasing by 2.3 per cent per annum, or by 25.6 per cent over ten years. Then the marginal rate of taxation on GDP per head is 32.5 per cent. The Government is straining the economy to its limits by demanding simultaneously a big increase in investment and a big increase in the public services. This is feasible if the Government is efficient, and its objectives are widely understood and popular; but in many underdeveloped countries this programme would not be feasible. The Agency would have to return to the Government for new instructions involving less taxation. Either investment and the rate of growth must be cut, or else the rate of growth of the public services must be further restrained.

The usefulness of this kind of arithmetic is already clear; it brings out the problems inherent in even modest goals—for a growth rate of 4.5 per cent is not excessively ambitious. Many of the target growth rates which appear in published Development Plans could not survive careful arithmetic of this kind.

Summary

1. The rates of growth of the outputs of commodities and of services must be in step with each other. An excessive growth rate of services will produce inflation and a balance of payments deficit.

2. By projecting capital requirements on the one hand, and private savings, the budget surplus and the foreign balance on the other hand, one can check whether the required funds are likely to be available to finance the postulated rate of growth.

3. The same projection will check whether the assumptions would permit a sufficiently high rate of growth of personal consumption, which is one of the incentives for growth; or demand a level of taxation which would not be feasible.

4. OVERALL COMMODITY BALANCE

If the programme so far outlined is deemed to be feasible financially, it must next be tested for balance in the commodities market. We noted in the preceding section that if services are planned to grow much faster than commodity output, the demand for commodities may exceed the supply, with inflation and a balance of payments deficit resulting. We adopted a temporary solution; now this must be checked.

Technical Prelude

Before continuing, we must clear two procedural points out of the way. The first concerns the grouping of commodities. It is not feasible to make separate calculations for every commodity, since the number of separate commodities is extremely large, if every difference is taken into account (e.g. if each book is a separate commodity). Commodities have therefore to be grouped into 'industries'. The number of groupings can be large or small. It is normally convenient to work with anything from fifty to one hundred 'industries', and hardly worthwhile to work with less than fifteen to twenty. In this section we shall begin by reducing all commodities to seven groups. The list could easily be lengthened, but we should then frustrate one of the major purposes of this book, which is to enable the student reader to work everything out for himself, with pencil and paper, whenever he is in doubt as to how a result was obtained. In input-output analysis and linear programming the number of calculations multiplies formidably as the number of commodities increases. If we lengthened the list of commodities the tables would look much more realistic, but the reader would be deprived of the opportunity of testing his understanding of methods. The groups used here are foodcrops, livestock products, raw materials (including both mineral and agricultural materials), 'local' manufactures, 'processed' manufactures, 'other' manufactures, and construction. The first three explain themselves. 'Local' manufactures are those which use mainly raw materials produced locally, such as cement, pottery or furniture; and 'processed' manufactures are industries using light imported raw materials, such as textiles, cigarettes, or shoes. This distinction is adopted because it will be useful in analysing the potentialities of foreign trade. It is not precise, and it does not matter which commodities go under which title, so long as they stay there consistently.

The second procedural matter is the choice of a set of uniform prices in which to work. Since imports have to be added to domestic production, and exports subtracted, commodities must be valued on a consistent basis—at factory cost, or wholesale prices, or retail prices, or import or export or any other set of prices. Which basis one uses does not matter much.

For our input-output tables we have opted to use 'ex-service prices'. The ex-service price is the price of a commodity less any transportation, wholesaling, retailing or other service costs. It embodies only value added in one or more commodity-producing industries, plus imported materials. To exclude service costs after the commodity leaves the factory or farm gate is easy; but one must also exclude services which enter into cost during production, such as the cost of transporting raw materials into the factory, and this requires a little manipulation of the input-output table.

The advantage of using ex-service prices for our purpose is that the sum of commodities available is then simply the sum of value added in producing commodities, plus the net import of commodities, appropriately valued. Raw materials produced at home and other intermediate goods cancel out. Hence, once the value added in commodity industries has been determined, as in Table VII, and the trade deficit calculated, as in Table X, the total value of available commodities is determined. This reduces the total amount of arithmetic. For, if one uses any price wichh includes services, the total value of available commodities cannot then be determined until the proportions in which the different commodities are to be produced has been determined, since services enter into different commodities in different proportions. This is not an insuperable objection to working with prices which include services. For it only means that if one works with such prices, extra trial runs will become necessary. (The figures for Year 10 in Table III will only be provisional until one reaches Table XXII, whereupon the whole exercise must be redone if the total assumed for services in the former proves different from the total reached in the latter.) The work can be done with whichever set of prices is most convenient—ex-service, factory value, wholesale, retail or foreign trade. All that matters is that one should use the same set consistently.

Since we have opted to use ex-service prices, foreign trade has now to be revalued so that the commodities in foreign trade have the same average price as the ex-service price of similar commodities produced at home; thus addition or subtraction will change quantities and values in exactly the same ratios. This operation reduces export prices (probably by about 20 per cent) and may either increase or reduce import prices, according to how much lower import prices are than the cost of producing the same goods at home. In the tables which follow it is assumed that the net effect on the trade deficit is to increase it by 10 per cent.

Overall Balance

The first step is to check whether the demand for commodities and the supply of commodities will be in overall balance. This is done in Table XIII, which shows the supply of commodities on the left, and the various demands for commodities on the right.

TABLE XIII. *Availability of Commodities*

	Year 0	Year 10		Year 0	Year 10
Value Added in			Construction	85	163
Agriculture	470	620	Equipment	35	83
Industry	180	354	Stocks	8	14
Net Imports	4	40	Government	20	38
			Services	58	85
			Consumption	448	631 R
	654	1,014		654	1,014

The supply side is easy. Since we are working in ex-service prices, supply is simply value added in producing commodities, plus net imports of commodities. Value added is brought forward from Table VII. Net imports comes from the trade deficit in Table X, with 10 per cent added, as already explained, to convert to ex-service prices.

The demand side is more complicated. Construction, equipment and stocks come from Table IX, with some adjustment on the way. The 'fixed investment' shown in Table IX has to be divided into construction and equipment. It is assumed that the national income accounts show equipment to be 30 per cent of fixed investment in Year 0, and is further assumed that this proportion will rise to 35 per cent in Year 10. Each of the components of investment is then reduced to ex-service prices by making a deduction for the service element: stocks by a deduction of 5 per cent, construction by 10 per cent, and equipment by 15 per cent.

The national income accounts should also show what proportion of the Government's expenditure (Table XI) is spent on services, and what proportion on commodities. It is here assumed that the proportion on commodities is 25 per cent. The other services also use up commodities. The amount of these services is the figure given in Table VII, less 75 per cent of the figure shown for Government in Table XI. It is assumed that 20 per cent of this is spent on commodities. Thus in Year 0 other service is 350—60=290, and the amount of commodities used is .2×290=58.

Consumption is the residual item. What we now have to test is whether the supply of commodities which will be available for personal consumption, shown as 631 in Year 10, will be greater or less than the demand. According to Table XII, consumption of goods and services together will be 1,095 in Year 10; it is held to this figure by the assumptions made about the rate of growth of the national income, savings, taxes and so on. If total consumption expenditure is 1,095, will this break down roughly into 631 on commodities and 464 on services? If the proportion spent on commodities is too high, there will be inflation and a larger foreign exchange deficit than has been anticipated; if too small, there will be deflation.

The answer depends on whether the balance between commodities and services was projected correctly in Table VII; it is not enough to project a growth rate for the economy as a whole; the distribution between sectors must also be right.

Consumer Demand

The next step is therefore to project the demand for each commodity separately, and see whether the total for Year 10 will come to 631. This is done in Table XIV, the first column of which shows how the 448 for Year 0 (in Table XIII) was divided among the various commodities. Although we are assuming that the national income accounts contain all the figures required for Year 0, it takes a little ingenuity to prepare this table, partly because the national income accounts will not use quite the same breakdown as one needs for analysing output, and partly because the national income figures will have to be converted from retail to ex-service prices.

To project the demand for any commodity we must multiply consumption in Year 0 by a factor for population increase, then

TABLE XIV. *Personal Consumption of Commodities. Ex-Service Prices*

	Year 0	Income Elasticity	Year 10
Food Crops	200	0.5	266
Livestock Products	100	1.2	144
Local Manufactures	30	1.1	43
Processed Manufactures	70	1.2	101
Other Manufactures	48	1.5	71
	448		625

by a factor for increase in *per capita* income, and then by a third factor for changes in taste.

(a) Population is assumed to be increasing by 2.3 per cent per annum, so, over ten years, the population factor is 1.256.

(b) Consumers' expenditure (including services) rises from 799 to 1,095 (Table XI). The *per capita* increase is therefore 11.9 per cent. To this must be applied the income elasticity (more strictly expenditure elasticity) of demand for each of the commodities. Some typical elasticities are assumed in the second column of Table XIV. They average less than 1.0 because as income rises the consumer spends relatively more on services (transportation, distribution, entertainment, etc.). The use of such elasticities depends on the assumption that the distribution of personal income will remain unchanged. Since changes in the distribution of personal spending are not likely to be large over the Plan period (certainly not as large as changes in the distribution of income and savings) we ignore this element in the first round.

(c) The third multiplier is for movements in the trend of demand not due to changes in population or *per capita* income. Fashions change; new commodities establish themselves; old commodities are displaced by rivals. Unravelling what is due to changes in trend and what to changes in *per capita* income is not easy. In practice one tends to begin by projecting trends, and then adjusting for expected changes in *per capita* income.

For the purpose of constructing Table XIV the trend factor has been left out, since, when demand is consolidated into so few groups, the results of competition between commodities which are close rivals cancel out. Putting the population and income factors together we get, for example for food crops, that demand in Year 10 is:

$$(200)\,(1.256)\,(1.0+0.119\times0.5)=266.$$

The calculation in Table XIV brings the demand for Year 10 to 625, as against the 631 available according to Table XIII. This is a difference of 1 per cent. Most Development Plans err by producing a greater demand for commodities than can be met by the supply; our error is on the other side. It is not easy to plan this balance correctly at the stage of constructing Table VII, since commodities go into so many other uses besides personal consumption, and are supplemented by net imports. But, as usual, there is an effective rule of thumb. If Government service and tourism are expected to increase massively their shares in GDP (as in this case), then services should grow annually up to 15 per cent faster than commodities; but if there is no such explosion of the demand for services, and no explosion of net imports, the annual rate of growth of services should not exceed that of commodities by more than 5 per cent. In our projection in Table VII the output of commodities grew by 4.1 per cent and the output of services by 4.35 per cent. The student reader should rework the exercise for himself from the beginning to verify that demand would have equalled supply exactly if we had assumed that services would grow at an annual rate of 4.54 per cent.

If the difference between demand and supply had proved to be large, it would have been necessary to start again from scratch, with a different projection of the rate of growth, that is, if one really attached importance to projecting the output of each industry separately. (If not, the rule of thumb would suffice: it would be enough to make sure that the growth of services does not exceed that of commodities by less than 5 or more than 15 per cent.) For our exercise commodity projections are required, but since the difference between demand and supply has come out at less than 1 per cent, it can be ignored. We merely add a little to each of the commodities, bringing the total to 631, and proceed. The result is seen in column P of Table XVI.

Summary

In planning the growth of the economy, it is important to get the right balance between commodities and services, since, if the service sector is too large, the demand for commodities will exceed the supply, and inflation and a balance of payments deficit will result. This is checked by projecting separately the demand for commodities and the supply of commodities.

5. INDUSTRIAL BALANCES

From projecting the overall balance for commodities, we turn to the individual industries or groups of industries. This is not always necessary. We examined in Chapter I the arguments for and against projecting the output of individual industries, and will not repeat that discussion here. In this Chapter we assume that it is desired to make such projections, and confine our attention to techniques.

What the planners are trying to ensure is that in each industry home demand plus imports shall equal home supply minus exports, within the context that the sum of outputs and the sum of the foreign balance are already fixed. In this process it is implied that consumer demand is sacrosanct, given the level of consumer purchasing power; if any industry is out of balance, adjustment must be made by altering output, imports or exports, but not by altering demand. The alternative assumption would make the exercise unnecessary, or at least much simpler; for if demand were too high, one could simply tax or ration the commodity, or if demand were too low, subsidize or advertise the commodity. This, in effect, has been the path taken by planners in the USSR, and also by most other countries in wartime. In what follows we assume that the main purpose of the economic system is to provide consumers with what they want; adjustments are therefore made to output, imports or exports, but not to consumption.

Input-Output Table

The tool used for this piece of analysis is an input-output table. Readers who have never heard of an input-output table will not be able to follow this analysis; they should skip the remainder of this section. Readers who are completely expert in the subject should also skip. The pages which follow are for the student who knows the basic principles of input-output analysis, but needs some practice in using this tool as a part of development planning.

The input-output table for Year o is shown in Table XV. As usual, columns (reading vertically) show the items entering into

TABLE XV. *Input-Output, Year* 0   'Ex-Service' Prices

	A Food	B Livestock	C Raw Mat.	D Local Man.	E Processed	F Other Man.	G Construction	H TOTAL	J Intermediate	K Fixed Inv.	L Stocks	M Government	N Services	P Consumption	Q Imports	R Exports
A. Foodcrops	16	32	—	13	—	—	—	400	61	—	2	4	—	200	20	153
B. Livestock	—	—	—	—	—	—	—	80	—	—	1	4	—	100	25	—
C. Raw Materials	16	4	11	3	11	22	3	110	70	—	2	2	25	—	20	30
D. Local Manufactures	16	—	—	—	—	—	14	75	30	—	2	4	5	30	—	4
E. Processed	—	—	—	—	—	—	—	55	—	5	2	3	10	70	40	5
F. Other Manufactures	12	4	9	6	4	—	9	50	44	30	1	3	18	48	97	5
G. Construction	—	—	—	3	—	3	—	91	6	85	—	3	—	—	—	—
H. Value Added	340	40	90	50	40	25	65			120	8	20	58	448	202	198
J. Total	400	80	110	75	55	50	91									

183

the cost of producing each commodity. Rows (reading horizontally) show what happens to output.[1] The total for any commodity's column (e.g. column D, row J) equals the total for the same commodity's row (e.g. row D, column H), since the column shows the inputs into the total production, and the row shows the disposal of the same production. Column J sums the 'intermediate' demands (as shown in columns A to F) which is the term used for that part of a commodity's output which gets used up in making other commodities. The rest of its output is the 'final' demand, which enters into investment, Government use, services[2] and foreign trade. The sum of columns K through R constitutes final demand.[3] This, when added to intermediate demands in column J, gives the total output in column H. Column H is therefore the pivot of the table; to the left of H we add (vertically) to find out how much is available; to the right of H we add (horizontally, subtracting imports) to find out how the available amount is used.

The reader should note that the sum of the final demands (row J, columns K through R) is equal to the sum of value added (row H, columns A through F), and that these figures are merely an elaboration of those which appeared in Table XIII.

A similar elaboration yields all the figures required for projecting final demand in Year 10, except the figures for foreign trade. Table XIII gives us columns K through N, assuming more or less the same proportionate breakdowns in Year 10 as in Year 0, but making allowance for expected changes. Table XIV gives us column P, adjusted to bring its total to 631. This preliminary work is shown in Table XVI.

Alternative Procedures

We can now proceed along one of two paths. As can be seen in Table XIII, the foreign balance equals domestic final demand (right side) minus value added (left side). We know the domestic final demand for each commodity; if we project the foreign trade balance we shall then also have final demand for each commodity. Intermediate demand is related to final demand by the structure

---

[1] Columns and rows have been lettered instead of numbered because we shall use these letters as substitutes for names in the algebra which follows.

[2] Commodities used up in supplying services appear here as part of final demand, since services are not included in rows A to J.

[3] Column Q (Imports) is not added but subtracted.

of production represented in the matrix; once we have final demand, we can deduce intermediate demand, and therefore arrive at the total output of each commodity. This is one path: start with foreign trade, and end up with total output.

The alternative path is to start with the total output of each commodity, and end with its foreign trade. This involves much

TABLE XVI. *Domestic Final Demand, Year 10*

	K Fixed Inv.	L Stocks	M Government	N Services	P Consumption
A	—	4	7	—	268
B	—	2	10	—	146
C	—	2	4	36	—
D	—	2	6	8	43
E	12	2	5	15	102
F	71	2	6	26	72
G	163	—	—	—	—
	246	14	38	85	631

less algebra than the alternative, since intermediate demand follows automatically from output; write down the output of any commodity in row J, and one can at once fill in the vertical column standing above it, by applying its input coefficients. Hence, given total output we deduce intermediate demand, and subtracting this and domestic final demand will give the net export (or import) of the commodity.

As between starting with output, or starting with foreign trade, which path should we follow? This depends on whether it is easier to produce or to export. If it is easy to export, and we project a large export for any particular commodity, we will come out with a large output. The output may be impracticably large; in that case we would have done better to start by projecting output, knowing that we would have no difficulty in accepting the resulting export figure. In general, an industrial country can fairly easily increase the output of any of its industrial exports; the problem is to find buyers overseas. So an industrial country projects its foreign trade, and uses the input-output matrix to see what this involves for production. An agricultural country is in the reverse position; there are world commodity exchanges for most of its exports, and since its exports are only a fraction of world trade, it can usually sell all it can produce. Its problem is to raise production; getting an increase in agricultural output is the hardest problem in economic development. So an agricultural country normally proceeds by projecting outputs, and seeing what this involves in foreign trade. (There are exceptions; for example, India is the largest exporter of tea, and would have some difficulty in selling much more at favourable prices.)

We shall proceed along both paths. First we shall project foreign trade, arriving at a set of outputs which will prove to be unsatisfactory. Then we shall project outputs, and arrive at foreign trade.

Projecting Foreign Trade

All projections are guesswork. Guesses about foreign trade are even more prone to error than other guesses, because they require knowledge of what is happening in distant countries. Guessing cannot be avoided, since decisions for the future have to be made; but the planner has to recognize that he is working with an exceptionally wide margin of error.

Exports of a commodity are projected by studying trends in world demand and supply, projecting domestic demand and supply, and taking into account any specially relevant policies. It is easy, but fatal, to forget to predict the growth of domestic demand, which will reduce the surplus available for export unless output expands.

Imports are more difficult to predict than exports. The trend is misleading, since there is not a constant relationship between demand and imports. Development will increase the domestic supplies of some commodities more than others; import substitution will occur; importation of raw materials will take the place of importation of some finished goods; acceleration of growth will increase the imports of machinery; and so on. The volume of imports also depends on the volume of foreign aid. Since foreign aid increased sharply during the 1950's, projections which assume some constant relationship between imports and income come out with fantastic levels of imports by 1970, which merely reflect the underlying assumption that foreign aid will *grow* at the same pace between 1960 and 1970 as it did between 1950 and 1960.

The only reasonably satisfactory way of projecting imports and exports is to do so within the framework of an input-output matrix, with a predetermined overall net foreign balance. The method is one of reiteration in two stages. In the first stage one writes down for each industry the preliminary estimate of its projected imports and exports. When summed, these must yield the predetermined net balance of trade (40 in this example); so adjustments must be made to reach this total. The second stage is to check trade against production. The total output will always come out right, for the structure of the equations is such that a net import of 40 must yield a total value added of 974 (Table XIII), but individual industries may vary within this total. A set of foreign trade figures which looks reasonable may turn out to be impossible because it implies a set of production figures which is not reasonable. Trials must therefore continue until both the individual trade figures and the individual outputs projected for Year 10 seem to be feasible.

First Trial

Let us assume that the Planning Agency starts by making the following projections for foreign trade in Year 10:
- (i) the import of imported foodcrops will increase by 50 per cent; the export will increase by 10 per cent;
- (ii) imports of livestock products will be eliminated;
- (iii) imports (e.g. fuel) and exports (e.g. oil seeds) of raw materials will both double;
- (iv) exports of local manufactures can be increased to 20;
- (v) the increase in imports of 'other' manufactures will be held down to 40 per cent.

The fourth of these assumptions does not survive scrutiny. The Agency's industrial experts point out that though local manufactures are the easiest to produce they are also the hardest to export. They are based on heavy raw materials like clays and sands, which most countries have, and can exploit for themselves under the protection of high transportation costs. This assumption is therefore dropped, and the first projection of final demand in Year 10 appears as in Table XVII. Here the industries are represented by the letters of their rows.

The problem is to determine how much of each commodity is used up in the course of production; adding these intermediate uses to the final demands in column S of Table XVII will give the total output of each commodity. The solution can be derived from the relationships implicit in the input-output table. In

Table XV the figures in any commodity column can be expressed as percentages of the total output of that commodity, which appears at the foot of the column (row J). When this is done, an equation can be written for each row, based on the fact that the

TABLE XVII. *Tentative Final Demand, Year 10*

	K Fixed Inv.	L Stocks	M Govern- ment	N Ser- vices	P Con- sumption	Q Imports	R Exports	S Total
A	—	4	7	—	268	30	168	417
B	—	2	10	—	146	—	—	158
C	—	2	4	36	—	40	62	64
D	—	2	6	8	43	—	—	59
E	12	2	5	15	102	84	10	62
F	71	2	6	26	72	136	10	51
G	163	—	—	—	—	—	—	163
	246	14	38	85	631	290	250	974

output of each commodity must equal intermediate use plus final demand. Writing capital letters for the output of each commodity, and small letters for final demand, we get the set of equations in Table XVIII.

TABLE XVIII. *Input-Output Equations*

$$A = .04A + .40B \qquad\qquad + .173D \qquad\qquad\qquad\qquad\qquad + a$$
$$B = \qquad\qquad\qquad\qquad\qquad\qquad\qquad\qquad\qquad\qquad\qquad\qquad + b$$
$$C = .04A + .05B + .10C + .04D + .20E + .44F + .033G + c$$
$$D = .04A \qquad\qquad\qquad\qquad\qquad\qquad\qquad\qquad + .15G + d$$
$$E = \qquad\qquad\qquad\qquad\qquad\qquad\qquad\qquad\qquad\qquad\qquad\qquad + e$$
$$F = .03A + .05B + .082C + .08D + .073E \qquad\qquad + .10G + f$$
$$G = \qquad\qquad\qquad\qquad + .04D \qquad\qquad + .06F \qquad\qquad\qquad + g$$

This set of simultaneous equations is easily solved by substituting for a, . . . , g the figures of final demand which appear in column S of Table XVII. However, since it may become necessary to undertake several trials, with different final demand figures, it is better to solve the set of equations once and for all in terms of a, . . . , g so that different sets of final demand values can be tried with minimum labour. This process, known as 'inversion of the matrix', gives the results in Table XIX.

The first trial is made by the substitution for a, . . . , g in Table XIX of the final demands in column S of Table XVII. This gives the required output of each commodity; which is further translated into value added by applying the ratio of row H to row J in Table XVI. The result is shown in Table XX.

TABLE XIX. *Solution of the Input-Output Equations*

$$A = 1.049a + .420b \qquad\quad + .183d \qquad\qquad + .002f + .028g$$
$$B = \qquad\quad 1.000b$$
$$C = .069a + .111b + 1.158c + .104d + .269e + .516f + .105g$$
$$D = .043a + .018b + .001c + 1.014d + .001e + .010f + .153g$$
$$E = \qquad\qquad\qquad\qquad\qquad 1.000e$$
$$F = .041a + .074b + .096c + .100d + .096e + 1.049f + .123g$$
$$G = .004a + .005b + .006c + .047d + .006e + .063f + 1.014g$$

This proposal has to be rejected. First, it calls for an impossibly large increase in agricultural output. The original projection of output, in Table VII, bearing in mind the slow response of small farmers to technological change, postulated that agriculture could not grow faster than 3 per cent per annum, and put its value added

TABLE XX. *Tentative Output, Year 10*

		Output	Value Added
A.	Foodcrops	519	441
B.	Livestock	158	79
C.	Raw Materials	187	153
D.	Local Manufactures	106	71
E.	Processed Manufactures	62	45
F.	Other Manufactures	120	60
G.	Construction	175	125
		1,327	974

in Year 10 at 620. The corresponding figure in Table XX is the sum of A, B and C, which comes to 673. The capacity to export has been overestimated. It is not possible for agriculture to produce enough to meet domestic demands, plus a 10 per cent increase in food exports and a doubling of raw material exports. The exercise must be repeated, with lower export assumptions in Table XVII.

A second reason for rejecting this solution emerges when the outputs of manufactures are compared with outputs in Year 0 (Table XV). The output of processed manufactures is to rise from 55 to 62 and the output of 'other' manufactures from 50 to

120. This, the industrial experts advise, does not make sense. It is easy to expand the output of processed manufactures, which are industries based on light imported materials, and difficult to expand the output of 'other', which includes heavy industry. But this solution calls for a negligible increase in the former and more than a doubling of the latter. The next trial must therefore be based on much smaller imports of processed manufactures.

The student reader should go through another trial for himself, reducing the exports of agricultural products and the imports of processed manufactures in Table XV, and using the inverse matrix in Table XIX.

Second Trial

We shall now proceed along the alternative path. Since it is difficult to produce and easy to export, we shall assume the output of each commodity, and derive foreign trade by difference. For this we first construct a table which expresses the inputs into the production of each commodity as a percentage of its value added. This is done by expressing the figures in each column of Table XV as a percentage of row H. We use row H rather than row J because the master output projections by which we must abide (Agriculture=620, Industry=354) are given in terms of value added, and cannot be translated into ex-service prices until after the operation is completed. The matrix for this operation is given in Table XXI, which should be read vertically.

TABLE XXI. *Input Coefficients, Year 10*

	A	B	C	D	E	F	G
A	.047	.800	—	.260	—	—	—
B	—	—	—	—	—	—	—
C	.047	.100	.122	.060	.275	.800	.046
D	.047	—	—	—	—	—	.215
E	—	—	—	—	—	—	—
F	.070	.100	.100	.120	.100	—	.138
G	—	—	—	.060	—	.120	—
Value Added	1.000	1.000	1.000	1.000	1.000	1.000	1.000

Scrutiny of this matrix will reveal that its ratios do not correspond in every case to the ratios implicit in Table XV. We have increased the ratio of F entering into A, because more fertilizer will be used in agriculture ten years hence, and have reduced the ratio of C entering into F, because 'other' manufacture is expected to economize its use of raw materials. One does not have to use for Year 10 the same ratios as for Year 0; indeed the ratios are bound to change. Any changes which are foreseen should be made in Tables XVIII and XXI before calculating what the intermediate requirements of Year 10 will be.

Using Table XXI makes the calculation of intermediate requirements very simple. One can write any feasible set of value added's in row H, subject to making $A+B+C=620$ and $D+E+F+G=354$. Multiplying by the coefficients in Table XXI then gives the matrix for Year 10. It is not necessary to solve any equations.

Projections must be made in the light of the resources and potentials of the country, which vary from case to case. Nevertheless international comparisons are suggestive. Professor Hollis B. Chenery has compared the industrial structures of fifty-one countries at different levels of income, and has calculated regression equations which give the 'normal' size of each manufacturing industry, when allowance is made for both size of population and national income per head.[1] The same calculations show 'normal' growth elasticities, in relation to the growth of *per capita* income. No country is 'normal', but consultation of such figures may suggest possibilities that might otherwise be overlooked.

Conclusion

After trial calculations, we come up with the projections in Table XXII, which appear reasonable, in the sense that both the individual output figures and the individual export figures are deemed to be capable of attainment. The result is rather odd, in that exports increase by only 6 per cent over ten years. This is feasible temporarily while import substitution and foreign aid increase sharply, but ultimately output and foreign trade must grow at roughly equal rates. In the next Plan either the growth rate of agriculture must rise to 4 per cent per annum (the minimum for balanced growth) or else exports of manufactures must start to grow rapidly.

At this point the macroeconomic work, the work on individual projects and the work on economic policy come together. The macroeconomic work ensures consistency, but it does not ensure

[1] 'Patterns of Industrial Growth', *American Economic Review*, September 1960.

TABLE XXII. *Input-Output, Year 10*

'Ex-Service' Prices

	A *Food*	B *Livestock*	C *Raw Mat.*	D *Local Man.*	E *Processed*	F *Other Man.*	G *Construction*	H *TOTAL*	J *Intermediate*	K *Fixed Inv.*	L *Stocks*	M *Government*	N *Services*	P *Consumption*	Q *Imports*	R *Exports*
A. Foodcrops	19	64	—	20	—	—	—	485	103	—	4	7	—	268	30	133 R
B. Livestock	—	—	—	—	—	—	—	160	—	—	2	10	—	146	—	2 R
C. Raw Materials	19	8	17	5	29	40	6	171	124	—	2	4	36	—	40 R	45
D. Local Manufactures	19	8	—	—	—	—	26	113	45	—	2	6	8	43	—	—
E. Processed	—	—	14	9	11	—	—	145	—	12	2	5	15	102	3	9 R
F. Other Manufactures	28	8	—	—	—	—	17	96	87	71	2	6	26	72	178 R	12 R
G. Construction	—	—	—	4	—	6	—	173	10	163	—	—	—	—	—	10
H. Value Added	400	80	140	75	105	50	124									
J. Total	485	160	171	113	145	96	173		246	246	14	38	85	631	251	211

that the individual targets are themselves attainable. The macro-economic framework adds a dimension to individual project assessments; for only within the input-output matrix can one assess fully all the factors which determine the demand for an industry's product: specifically (i) the intermediate demands from other industries, (ii) the whole set of domestic final demands coming from investors, the Government and the consumer, which depend on macroeconomic decisions, and (iii) what the industry's foreign trade must be, if the overall trading requirements of the economy are to be met. If there must be targets, only the input-output framework can ensure their mutual consistency.

However, consistency is not all. Each project has to be assessed in terms of benefits and costs, and must be 'reasonable', in the sense that it represents an economic use of scarce resources. The attainment of industry targets depends on general economic policies; for example, there is no point in predicting substantial increases in agricultural output unless the Government is committed to adequate policies of land reform, irrigation, and so on.

When the work on projects is sufficiently advanced, its results and the results of the input-output analysis are matched. Adjustments have then to be made on each side. Some projects will be upgraded (or downgraded) because the input-output matrix shows a greater (or smaller) need for their output than the project specialists had estimated. On the other hand, the input-output matrix will have to be changed because some of its projections cannot survive the results of detailed project analysis. Thus the final matrix is based on projects and policies which have survived detailed assessment.

The policies are crucial, since the projected levels of output will require Government measures to stimulate the economy in general, and lagging industries in particular. Detailed study of these measures is essential, with realistic estimates of their cost, and potential effectiveness. In the last analysis the Plan is not the target figures, but the measures which are to be taken to reach desired goals.

Summary

1. An input-output matrix is the best framework in which to project output targets for individual industries, since it ensures

that projected demands, production, imports and exports be mutually consistent.

2. Given domestic demand, one may first project output and then deduce foreign trade, or first project foreign trade and then deduce output. It is more appropriate for industrial exporters to start with foreign trade, and for agricultural exporters to start with output.

3. Since development alters the structure of production, foreign trade should not be projected by applying to aggregate output some past propensity to import. Each industry's trade should be projected separately, within the input-output framework.

4. The potential cost and benefit of each project should be assessed in detail. The final input-output matrix should be based on the results of assessing each project separately.

5. Attainment of projected outputs depends on economic policy. The measures required for success should receive detailed study, and be indicated in the Plan, with their estimated cost.

6. LINEAR PROGRAMMING

We have now reached the stage of having a target output, import and export for each industry. Our targets are consistent, and seem to be reasonable. However, it would be possible to produce many other combinations which are both consistent and apparently reasonable. What the planner needs is the best of all possible combinations, in the light of current knowledge and expectations. Can this best be found? In theory it can be, though in practice our techniques are still rudimentary.

The best solution would be that which maximized net output at some constant set of prices. The appropriate prices are foreign trade prices. The final demand for each commodity is given; therefore the only question is whether to produce it at home, or to import it. The resources used for producing it could produce something else for export; if the income this would earn could in foreign markets buy more of the desired commodity than could be made at home with the same resources, domestic output should be cut and imports increased. If we know the quantity of resources required to make a unit of each commodity, the prices which exports would fetch, and the prices at which imports could be bought, we can calculate the most profitable output of each industry whose product can be imported or exported.

The mathematical technique for making these calculations is known as 'programming', whether 'linear' or 'non-linear' depending on the nature of the problem. Programming is a technique with many uses. For example, in development planning it can be used to choose between different techniques for making the same commodity; this is indeed the purpose for which it is most often used. Our example, in which it is to be used for choosing between home production and foreign trade is somewhat esoteric.

The choice between linear and non-linear programming depends on the problem. If cost per unit and price per unit do not vary with the size of output, the problem is linear, and is easily solved. But if cost or price changes as output changes, the problem is non-linear, and is more difficult. It is difficult, first, because it is not easy to find by established means the non-linear equations which express exactly how prices and costs vary with output; and secondly, because, even if one had the equations, they would be difficult to solve unless they were unrealistically simple. Mathematicians have given us easy methods for solving linear programmes, but are still trying to find easy ways to solve non-linear programmes. Though there has been some progress, we are in practice usually confined to the use of linear programming.

Now this is a great handicap, since our problems are definitely not linear. Whether the prices ruling in foreign trade will change with the volume of purchases or sales will depend on the country's size; a small country may be able to treat all foreign trade prices as given. However, even in a small country the quantity of resources per unit of output will depend upon the scale of production. Hence to use only linear programming to determine the allocation of resources would give the wrong answer.

We can escape this difficulty by programming not the use of all the country's resources, but only the use of the last 1 per cent or so. One thus assumes that an increase or reduction in the output of any commodity by 1 per cent will not affect its foreign trade price or its domestic cost. The prices and costs used for the calculations will not be average costs or prices, but the marginal costs and prices expected when the level of output of the final year has been attained. Having thus by programming found which are the more profitable commodities, one can increase what was proposed for them, and reduce the others, relying once more on knowledge of output and market conditions.

In what follows we shall proceed as if marginal costs and average costs are the same, since to introduce a new set of figures at this stage might only confuse the reader. We shall therefore be pretending that in this economy everything can be produced at constant cost. The result will be meaningful only if it can also be assumed that the prices at which this economy buys or sells in foreign markets are not affected by the amount of its trade. Because these are not realistic assumptions linear programming is not particularly helpful in allocating resources when making a Development Plan. The subject is included in this chapter merely in order to help the reader to see how programming might be used if we had better tools.

Technical Prelude

Something must be said about the way the figures are manipulated to get from Table XXII to the matrix in Table XXVI. This will interest only the student who already knows the elements of linear programming, and wishes to be sure that he can do this exercise for himself; other readers should skip this prelude. Experts in programming should skip the whole section.

For linear programming we deal not only with values of output, as we did in the input-output analysis, but also with quantities. Hence the first step is to reduce Table XXII from values to quantities. This is done by dividing the value of each commodity by its price, with the result shown in Table XXIII. (These are the same implicit ex-service prices which we have been using since Table XV. Hereinafter they are called 'Domestic Prices', to distinguish them from the foreign trade prices which we shall be introducing in a moment.)

TABLE XXIII. *Proposed Outputs*

Commodity	Value	Ex-Service Price per Unit	Quantity
A	485	48.5	10
B	160	160.0	1
C	171	24.43	7
D	113	45.2	2.5
E	145	29.0	5
F	96	48.0	2
G	173	55.8	3.1

Next we deal with the intermediate inputs, shown in columns and rows A through G in Table XXII. Dividing each row horizontally by its appropriate price turns values into quantities. Then dividing each column vertically by the appropriate quantity of the commodity (taken from the final column of Table XXIII) yields the input per unit of each commodity. These intermediate inputs appear in the first seven rows of the matrix in Table XXVI, on the left of the equal sign.

Next row H, Value Added, in Table XXII, must now be broken down into the primary inputs (factors of production), here assumed to be Land, Water, Stone, Unskilled Labour, Skilled Labour and Capital. The number of factors of production depends on the time horizon. In the short period labour and capital are highly specialized, so one has to work with a great many different kinds of labour and capital. But over ten years the amounts of new labour and new capital are very large, and these can be allocated to many different purposes before becoming specialized, so at the margin the number of primary units is small. At this stage capital is not the amount invested, but the annual capital cost of the required capital, using the standard formula given on page 56. The unit of capital is the amount which can be hired for one unit of the national currency. Water could be treated either as a basic factor or as an intermediate product. In the short run the amount of water is limited by reservoir capacity; in the long run more reservoirs can be built. Since we are supposed to be operating at the margin, water is treated here as a fixed factor. Stone would be an intermediate commodity; the term is used here as shorthand for metalliferous earths, which are a basic natural resource.

If an input-output matrix exists (as is assumed throughout this exercise) it will give the breakdown of Row H, Value Added. This is assumed to be as in Table XXIV on the next page.

We shall assume that the price of each factor of production is unity; thus the figures for value and for quantity are the same. To find quantities of input per unit of output, divide each column of Table XXIV by the appropriate quantity of output (last column of Table XXIII). This gives the figures which appear in the last six rows of the matrix in Table XXVI, with the total quantities of each factor on the right of the equal sign. Each of these six rows says on the left hand side how much of each factor one unit of each commodity requires; and imposes on the right hand side the constraint that total factor use must not exceed the amount available.

The object of the programme is to maximize the value which this set of factors can yield. Value is not the same as output, since part of output is used up in the course of production. The value to be

TABLE XXIV. *Primary Inputs, Totals*

	A	B	C	D	E	F	G	Total
Land	110	14	28	5	5	2	6.2	170.2
Water	10	4	7	2.5	5	4	3.1	35.6
Stone	10	2	14	5	5	2	12.4	50.4
Unskilled	230	44	63	27.5	30	14	58.9	467.4
Skilled	20	10	14	10	20	10	18.6	102.6
Capital	20	6	140	25	40	18	24.8	147.8
Row H	400	80	140	75	105	50	124.0	974.0

maximized is therefore Final Demand. This is given in columns K through R of Table XXII, except that the figures in that Table will have to be adjusted downwards because Final Demand there exceeds what is yielded by domestic production, since there is an import surplus of 40. We shall come to this adjustment in a moment.

In the matrix in Table XXVI the symbols A, ..., G are used to indicate output, while the symbols a, ..., g indicate the Final Demand for each commodity. The difference is used up in intermediate production. The first seven equations express this difference. Outputs have a plus sign; inputs a minus sign. Output is 1.0 if a commodity does not use up any of itself in production; if it does use up some of itself, this is subtracted.

It will be observed that instead of symbols d and g we have figures. This is because D and G are not traded in significant quantities. Value is to be maximized at foreign trade prices, on the assumption that it makes no difference to the country whether Final Demand is met from home output or from imports. We are assuming that G, construction, can be neither imported nor exported; and that though D, Local Manufactures, does enter into foreign trade, in practice heavy transport costs keep imports to zero and exports to a small, already known, amount. Hence Final Demands d and g are not unknowns. They are found by adding Row D, columns K through R of Table XXII, which, when divided by a price of 45.2 yields 1.504 units; and by adding the same columns in Row G, which, divided by a price of 55.8, yields 2.921 units. The other Final Demands are the five unknowns, which are shown also in the maximand at foreign trade prices.

The relevant foreign trade prices are not those of today, but those of the future, not the whole future, but such part of the future as is relevant to decisions which must be made during the period of the Plan. These prices are just guesses, but most decisions about the future have to be based on guesses. Fortunately, we need not guess absolute prices, but only changes in the ratio of different prices to each other.

Potential exports are priced at export prices; potential imports at import prices. In this exercise it is assumed that A, Food Crops and E, Processed Manufactures, are potential exports, and that they will fetch the domestic price when exported. Livestock, Raw Materials and Other Manufactures are potential imports, and are priced at import prices. Since our domestic prices are on an ex-service basis, our trade prices must also be on the same basis. Otherwise, if services enter into the commodities in different proportions, the differences in foreign trade prices will reflect differences in service inputs which are not included in our matrix. The foreign trade prices used in these calculations are shown below, for comparison with the domestic prices:

	A	B	C	E	F
Foreign	48.5	145	22	29	40
Domestic	48.5	160	24.43	29	48

The foreign trade prices appear in the maximand in Table XXVI.

When we have found a solution to this programme—the maximum value of Final Demand which this set of factors of production can yield—we shall have to compare it with the actual value of Final Demand which was planned in Table XXII. The final bit of preliminary work is to prepare this planned Final Demand for this comparison.

Two changes must be made. First, the Final Demands in Table XXII are in domestic prices; they must be revalued in foreign prices, since the programmed result will also be in foreign prices. Secondly, Final Demand in Table XXII exceeds domestic production by the amount of the import surplus; this excess must be eliminated by reducing each item of Domestic Use. This reduction could be based on many different assumptions, each yielding different results. Since the amount involved is small, the adjustment can be made simply by reducing each item proportionately. (In practice there would be disproportionate reductions, shared also by d and g.) These operations are performed in Table XXV. The first two columns show Final Demand at domestic prices; the next two show Final Demand at the foreign trade prices used in the maximand. The last two columns show the result of reducing each item of Domestic Use proportionately. Adding the figures in these two columns together gives the 'Planned Final Demand' which will be compared with the results yielded by linear programming.

TABLE XXV. *Adjusted Final Demand*

	Domestic Prices		Foreign Prices		Adjusted	
	Domestic Use	Net Exports	Domestic Use	Net Exports	Domestic Use	Net Exports
a	279	103	279.0	103.0	270.9	111.1
b	158	2	143.2	1.8	139.0	6.0
c	42	5	37.8	4.5	36.7	5.6
e	136	9	136.0	9.0	132.0	13.0
f	177	−168	147.5	−140.0	143.2	−135.7
	792	−49	743.5	−21.7	721.8	0

We now have all the data required for programming. The total quantity of each factor of production is known. What it takes to make each commodity, both by way of primary factors of production, and by way of intermediate use of other commodities, is known. The value of each commodity is also known. Now we have to find the maximum value which can be produced in this situation. This value is formally termed Final Demand, but the use of the word Demand should not mislead the reader. What we shall really get is net output (gross output of each commodity minus intermediate use), since Final Demand includes net exports.

The formal mathematical statement of the problem is given in Table XXVI.

This model cannot give a realistic solution, because of its non-negativity constraints

$$a \geq 0, \ldots, f \geq 0$$

These state that Final Demand cannot be negative. Now Final

TABLE XXVI. *Programming Model, Stage I*

Maximize $Z = 48.5a + 145.0b + 22.0c + 29.0e + 40.0f$

Subject to:

	A	B	C	D	E	F	G	
(1)	+ 0.961	− 1.320	..	− 0.165	..	..	..	$= a$
(2)	..	+ 1.000	..	..	..	..	..	$= b$
(3)	− 0.078	− 0.327	+ 0.901	− 0.082	− 0.237	− 0.819	− 0.079	$= c$
(4)	− 0.042	..	..	+ 1.000	..	..	− 0.186	≤ 1.504
(5)	..	..	..	..	+ 1.000	..	..	$= e$
(6)	− 0.058	− .167	− 0.042	− 0.075	− 0.046	− 0.054	− 0.114	$= f$
(7)	..	..	..	+ 0.029	..	− 0.054	+ 1.000	$= 2.921$
(8)	11.0	+ 14.0	+ 4.0	+ 2.0	+ 1.0	+ 1.0	+ 2.0	≤ 170.200
(9)	1.0	+ 4.0	+ 1.0	+ 1.0	+ 1.0	+ 2.0	+ 1.0	≤ 35.6
(10)	1.0	+ 2.0	+ 2.0	+ 2.0	+ 1.0	+ 1.0	+ 4.0	≤ 50.4
(11)	23.0	+ 44.0	+ 9.0	+ 11.0	+ 6.0	+ 7.0	+ 19.0	≤ 467.4
(12)	2.0	+ 10.0	+ 2.0	+ 4.0	+ 4.0	+ 5.0	+ 6.0	≤ 102.6
(13)	2.0	+ 6.0	+ 2.0	+ 10.0	+ 8.0	+ 9.0	+ 8.0	≤ 147.8

$a \geq 0,\ b \geq 0,\ c \geq 0,\ e \geq 0,\ f \geq 0$

Demand equals Domestic Use plus Net Exports. If Final Demand cannot be negative, imports cannot exceed Domestic Use; therefore intermediate uses cannot be supplied by importing. Such a solution cannot be accepted when programming for an underdeveloped country, for in practice there will be many commodities (e.g. crude steel) imported mainly for intermediate uses.

We get out of this difficulty by changing the non-negativity constraints to

$$A \geq 0, \ldots, G \geq 0$$

indicating that it is now Output which cannot be negative. The variables a, . . . , f are now redundant. We get rid of them by substituting in the objective function, using the definitions given in equations (1), (2), (3), (5) and (6). This produces the new objective function which appears in Table XXVII.

Now we are in a different kind of trouble. So long as we had an equation for each commodity, with Final Demand non-negative, the solution would have to yield some Output for every commodity which has intermediate uses. With these equations gone, the number of constraints shrinks drastically. Linear programming cannot yield outputs for more commodities than there are constraints. In this example there are seven commodities and eight constraints, but this is only because we are working with so few commodities. In realistic exercises, the number of commodities will greatly exceed the number of factors of production, if one is working with as long a horizon as ten years. The solution will then indicate that the economy should produce only an unrealistically small number of commodities.

This difficulty arises because we are applying linear programming to a situation which is definitely not linear. If costs were constant and prices infinitely elastic it would indeed pay an economy to specialize in very few commodities. One cannot hope to get the right answer if one uses inappropriate models.

One way round this difficulty is to apply additional artificial constraints. Assume that the planned output for each commodity is not far out from what it should be, and therefore do not let the programmed output vary from the planned by more than say 5 per cent either way. Putting a limit to the expansion of the more profitable commodities reduces the number whose output can fall to zero. This method can be used to produce sharp distinctions by reiteration at different levels; by imposing limits of say 10 per

TABLE XXVII. *Programming Model, Stage II*
Maximize $Z = 42.57 A + 67.11 B + 18.14 C - 12.81 D + 21.95 E + 21.98 F - 6.30 G$
Subject to:

	A	B	C	D	E	F	G	
(1)	− 0.042	..	..	+ 1.000	..	..	− 0.186	= 1.504
(2)	..	..	..	− 0.029	..	− .054	+ 1.000	= 2.921
(3)	11.0	+14.0	+4.0	+ 2.0	+1.0	+1.0	+ 2.0	≤170.200
(4)	1.0	+ 4.0	+1.0	+ 1.0	+1.0	+1.0	+ 1.0	≤ 35.6
(5)	1.0	+ 2.0	+2.0	+ 2.0	+1.0	+1.0	+ 4.0	≤ 50.4
(6)	23.0	+44.0	+9.0	+11.0	+6.0	+7.0	+19.0	≤467.4
(7)	2.0	+10.0	+2.0	+ 4.0	+4.0	+5.0	+ 6.0	≤102.6
(8)	2.0	6.0	+2.0	+10.0	+8.0	+9.0	+ 8.0	≤147.8

$A \geq 0, \ldots, G \geq 0$

cent, then 5 per cent, then 3 per cent and then 1 per cent, one can arrive at a rough order of priority for the commodities. This is only a subterfuge; a somewhat doubtful method of evading the fact that our model does not fit the situation we are analysing.

First Trial

We are now ready to proceed. The problem to be solved is given in Table XXVI in its revised form. Final Demand is to be maximised subject to eight constraints. The first two indicate that final demands d and g are already known. The other six indicate the maximum availabilities of the six factors of production.

The solution[1] of this problem is given in Table XXVIII. Programmed Final Demand comes to 732.0 whereas Planned Final Demand (Table XXVI) came only to 721.8.

TABLE XXVIII. *Programmed Final Demand I*

	Programmed FD	Adjusted Dom. Use	Programmed Net Export	Plan Net Export
a	360.4	257.9	102.5	111.1
b	169.9	146.0	23.9	6.0
c	66.3	38.8	27.5	5.6
e	212.2	125.7	86.5	13.0
f	−76.8	163.6	−240.4	−135.7
	732.0	732.0	0	0

Table XXVIII also translates the results into a programme for foreign trade. Final Demand equals Domestic Use (Table XXV) plus net exports. Domestic Use is first adjusted upwards to equal Final Demand in total. Net exports then follow by subtraction.

This, at first sight, is a most impressive result. The Agency does not need to guess what the outputs and foreign trade should be; given assumptions about prices and costs, it can calculate what

[1] As stated in the Preface, one of the objectives in the writing of this chapter has been to present the material in such a way that the average person likely to read it may check the estimates for himself. This cannot be achieved in this section on linear programming. To do all these calculations on a desk calculator would take too much time, and would almost certainly result in many arithmetical errors. This calculation was done on the Princeton electronic computer; I am grateful to my colleague Mr E. S. Pearsall, who programmed it for me, and to Mr John Hill, who programmed an earlier version. The work made use of computer facilities supported in part by National Science Foundation Grant NSF-GP 579.

outputs will maximize the national income, given available re-sources. The assumptions are heroic, but it is striking to find a tool which forces them to yield an answer.

Second Trial

Let us look more closely at the answer. What programming tells us is that given the resources which could produce the planned output, it would be better to produce the programmed output. But are the resources given?

Take unskilled labour. The sixth constraint in Table XXVII states that the amount of unskilled labour should not exceed 467.4 units. This constraint is needed if full employment is expected by Year 10, but in an over-populated country, with open or disguised unemployment, this constraint is not necessary. Similarly the third constraint limits the use of land to 170.2 units. This constraint is not required in sparsely populated countries. Even in over-populated countries more land can be brought into cultivation by reclamation, terracing and irrigation, in which case, instead of a land constraint one should simply add the cost of preparing the land to the cost of the commodities which it will produce. It is not necessary to introduce all the factors of produc-tion into the equations.

If unskilled labour is assumed to be abundant, we eliminate the sixth constraint in Table XXVII and solve again. The result is shown in the third column of Table XXIX. Then we replace the unskilled labour constraint and assume that land instead is abundant, removing the third constraint. The result is shown in the fourth column.

TABLE XXIX. *Programmed Final Demand II*

	Original Plan	First Trial	Without Labour	Without Land
a	382.0	360.4	372.4	536.6
b	145.0	169.9	291.2	..
c	42.3	66.3	−85.2	66.7
e	145.0	212.2	232.4	219.4
f	7.5	−76.8	−75.4	−74.7
	721.8	732.0	735.4	748.0

The choice of constraints obviously makes a great difference to the answer; in this example not so much difference to the total, but an enormous difference to the allocation among different commodities.

Third Trial

In the second trial we assumed that one or other of the factors was abundant. Now some other factors are not abundant, but can be made available at a price. The supply of skilled labour can be increased by training—which takes a long time—or by importation from abroad. The supply of capital can also be increased by importation from abroad. If more of a factor can be obtained at a price, we should not proceed as if its quantity were fixed. The correct procedure is to subtract the cost of the factor from the prices of the commodities into which it enters, and maximize the surplus.

We can tell whether to import more or less of any importable factor by comparing its price with its marginal product. When a linear programme is solved it yields two sets of solutions. One set, which we have been using, is the best combination of outputs. The other set, known as the 'dual', is the prices of the factors of production, *i.e.* the marginal productivity, corresponding to that combination of outputs. If the dual price of an importable factor exceeds the cost of importing it, the national income can be increased by importing more of it. We have been assuming that the price of each factor is unity. Table XXX shows the dual prices derived from the second trial when the unskilled labour constraint was removed.

TABLE XXX. *Dual Factor Prices*

Land	3.2
Water	0
Stone	0
Skilled	1.2
Capital	1.7

We cannot import more land, and the cost of importing skilled labour is likely to exceed the domestic price by more than 20 per cent, so we can ignore these two. But if capital can be hired for 1.0 when it yields 1.7, this constraint should disappear.

This is achieved by subtracting the element of capital cost in each commodity from the price of the commodity. One must subtract not only the direct capital input, but also the capital in the intermediate inputs. To get at the total capital input, one has to solve the input equations yielded by each column of Table XXVI, the typical equation being

$$0.961A - 0.078C - 0.042D - 0.058F = 2$$

the figure on the right side being the number of units of capital. Solving these seven equations yields the following capital inputs, intermediate plus primary.

A	3.6	E	9.2
B	13.6	F	11.9
C	2.8	G	11.8
D	12.1		

The price of capital being unity, we subtract these figures from the prices to get a new objective function, comparable with that of Stage I, Table XXVI.

Maximize $S = 44.9a + 131.4b + 19.2c + 19.8e + 28.1f$

This transforms in Stage II, Table XXVII, into

Maximize $S = 40.0A + 61.2B + 16.1C - 11.1D + 14.0E + 12.4F - 4.7G$

The solution is given in Table XXXI, except that, for the sake of comparability with the earlier solutions, the commodities are valued at prices which include the cost of capital. Both columns assume that unskilled labour is abundant. In the first column no additional capital is imported; in the second column unlimited capital is available at a price of 1.0 per unit.

TABLE XXXI. *Programmed Final Demand III*

	Limited Capital	Capital Priced
a	372.4	602.4
b	291.2	..
c	−85.2	−94.6
e	232.4	343.5
f	−75.4	−74.4
	735.4	776.9

What are we now maximizing? We are treating capitalists as if they were outside the economic system, and maximizing the surplus after they have been paid. This is obviously sensible if the capitalists are mainly foreigners—though the price at which they should be evaluated in the programme is their income after payment of taxes.

This treatment need not be confined to capitalists. The classical economists, *e.g.* Ricardo, Malthus and Mill, used to define the national income as the surplus left after deducting labourers' incomes. In some circumstances even this makes sense. In some countries the bulk of the people live in the countryside on a subsistence basis. Economic development is taking place in a relatively limited sector, which draws in from the subsistence economy such unskilled labour as it needs. The government of such a country may conceive of its problem as being to maximize the surplus available in the commercialized sector, after paying such labour as is required such wage as is necessary to bring it in; focusing attention on the surplus, because this is the major source of savings and taxes.

We have met these problems before, in Chapter II. We saw there that the quantity which has to be maximized is not necessarily current output. For example, in discussing techniques, we noted that the resident population might earn higher incomes with domestic-financed techniques than from more advanced techniques which use fewer domestic resources and pay more to foreign capitalists. At another point we noted that a smaller current income can be associated with a larger future income, if it distributes more to persons with a high propensity to save and invest. In calculating the cost of using the unemployed we had a choice of different formulas, depending on one's point of view. The quantity which is to be maximized is not a unique concept. It derives from political judgments. Linear programming is a tool which will maximize whatever it is set to maximize. Hence before using it one must decide what one's objective is.

Conclusion

We observed at the outset that while linear programming is a useful tool for solving many allocation problems, it is not particularly helpful for deciding what to import and export. This problem is not linear. Some of the prices remain unchanged as output changes, but others do not. Most of the costs change with output. A linear solution may show that it could be profitable to export more of a certain agricultural commodity, but the cost of getting the farmers to produce more of it cannot be put into a linear framework. Some Planning Agencies do these exercises, but the results are always misleading, unless handled with care, remembering espe-

TABLE XXXII. Revised Input-Output, Year 10

'Ex-Service' Prices

	A Food	B Livestock	C Raw Mat.	D Local Man.	E Processed	F Other Man.	G Construction	H TOTAL	J Intermediate	K Fixed Inv.	L Stocks	M Government	N Services	P Consumption	Q Imports	R Exports
A. Foodcrops	20	60	—	20	—	—	—	501	100	—	4	7	—	268	30	152
B. Livestock	—	—	—	—	—	—	—	148	—	—	2	10	—	146	12	2
C. Raw Materials	19	7	16	5	31	36	6	161	120	—	2	4	36	—	46	45
D. Local Manufactures	19	—	—	—	—	—	26	113	45	—	2	6	8	43	—	9
E. Processed	—	—	—	—	—	—	—	153	—	12	2	5	15	102	3	20
F. Other Manufactures	29	7	13	9	11	—	17	86	86	71	2	6	26	72	187	10
G. Construction	—	—	—	4	—	5	—	172	9	163	—	—	—	—	—	—
H. Value Added	414	74	132	75	111	45	123									
J. Total	501	148	161	113	153	86	172			246	14	38	85	631	278	238

cially that demand and supply elasticities are not infinite, as the linear model presupposes.

Handling what we have done with care suggests (Table XXIX) that if Land is a constraint we should plan to produce less of A, Foodcrops, and more of B, Livestock products; while if it is not, we should do the reverse. Assuming that we are planning for an African economy, with ample land, we therefore increase the output of A beyond the original intention. All solutions have recommended a greater output of E, Processed Manufactures, at the expense of F, Other Manufactures. These suggestions have to be considered in the light of what is known from other sources about markets and producers' intentions. There is no point in making a Plan to produce more of a commodity if there is no means of inducing people to produce more of it.

Let us assume that after taking everything into account the Planning Agency settles for the revised version of the Input-Output matrix for Year 10 given in Table XXXII. This becomes the basis of subsequent macroeconomic work.

Summary
1. Given production functions, foreign trade prices, and knowledge of available resources, it is possible to calculate how much of each commodity to produce at home; how much to export or import then follows by subtracting domestic demand.

2. The basic data are unreliable, being essentially guesses about future relationships.

3. The appropriate technique is non-linear programming, but the data are seldom suitable for this technique. Linear programming involves assumptions which add to the unreliability of the results.

4. The calculations yield different results according to whether what is to be maximized is current output, or the difference between current output and payments to some of the factors of production (e.g. to capital or to unskilled labour). These are political decisions.

7. THE CAPITAL BUDGET

The next step is to make a tentative capital budget, to test whether the capital expected to be available will be adequate for the postulated increase in income; and also to make tentative allocations to the different sectors.

Resources

For this part of the exercise estimates for terminal years will not suffice. It is necessary to estimate the total sum available over the whole ten-year period. Therefore it is necessary to begin by projecting GDP and savings in each year. This is done in Table XXXIII.

Rough assumptions will suffice for this purpose. GDP had been assumed to grow at an average rate of 4.2 per cent p.a. over the ten years, starting at 3.0 and ending at 4.5. It is now assumed further that successive annual rates are as follows: 3.0, 3.5, 4.0, 4.5, 4.5, 4.5, 4.5, 4.5, 4.5, 4.5. It will be observed that the maximum rate is already attained in the fourth year. The capital

TABLE XXXIII. *Capital Required and Available*

Year	GDP	Capital Required	Domestic Savings	Foreign Gap
1	1,030	155	146	9 R
2	1,066	176	154	22 R
3	1,109	200	162	38 R
4	1,158	226	171	55 R
5	1,210	236	182	54 R
6	1,265	247	193	54 R
7	1,322	258	204	54 R
8	1,381	269	215	54 R
9	1,443	281	228	53 R
10	1,510	294	243	51
	12,494	2,342	1,898	444 R

required rises from 14.3 per cent of GDP in Year 0 to 19.5 per cent in Year 10. Like the maximum rate of growth of GDP, the maximum capital requirement must be reached in the fourth year; assume some such regular growth as 15.0, 16.5, 18.0, 19.5 . . . 19.5. Domestic saving, on the other hand, grows steadily from 14.0 per cent in Year 0 to 16.1 per cent in Year 10; say, its

[1] Economists have produced a huge mathematical literature on optimal growth paths. Since development planners are not able to control the growth rate of an open agricultural economy from one year to the next, this literature is not yet ready for practical application. For references see Hahn, F. H., and Matthews, R. C. O., 'The Theory of Economic Growth: A Survey', *Economic Journal*, December 1964.

progression is 14.2, 14.4, 14.6, 14.8, 15.0, 15.2, 15.4, 15.6, 15.8, 16.1. The percentage dependence on foreign aid therefore reaches its maximum in Year 4. The absolute dependence begins to decline before the end of the ten-year period, and if the savings ratio continues to grow adequately, the economy should be nearly self-sustaining in terms of its capital requirements by the end of a further period of ten years.

Requirements

To estimate the sectoral requirements for capital we begin with commodities. Table XV shows the outputs in Year 0, and Table XXXII the outputs which have been tentatively set for Year 10. The requirement consists of two parts; that which is required for the increase in outputs, and that which is required to replace capital in use in Year 0 which falls ready to be replaced during the ten-year period.

The calculation is shown in Table XXXIV. Industries have been regrouped. The grouping used in Table XV was based on the convenience of distinguishing between net exports, net imports, and industries which do not participate significantly in foreign trade. Now we need a grouping which classifies industries more or less according to the amount of capital required per unit of output. (Output here means 'value added'; we could work

TABLE XXXIV. *Capital Required for Commodities*

	Output Year 0	Year 10	In- crease	Re- place	Total	ICOR	Capital Re- quired
Agriculture, large scale	90	140	50	54	104	2.0	208
Agriculture, small scale	380	480	100	114	214	0.5	107
Industry, light	70	146	76	42	118	1.6	189
Industry, heavy	40	70	30	24	54	4.0	216
Power	5	15	10	3	13	6.0	78
Construction	65	123	58	39	97	1.0	97
	650	974	324	276	600		895

equally well with factory or retail values, but the coefficients would then be correspondingly smaller.)

The first two columns of Table XXIV show the outputs expected in Years 0 and 10. The third column is the difference between those two. To arrive at the next column it is assumed that 60 per cent of the capital existing in Year 0 will fall due for replacement during the ten years; column 1 is therefore multiplied by 0.6. This assumption is not applied to small-scale agriculture; here it is assumed rather that producers of 30 per cent of the output of Year 0 will adopt new capitalistic techniques, so the multiplier in this row is 0.3. The column headed 'Total' combines the increase in output with the amount of output whose capital must be replaced. This in turn is multiplied by its appropriate 'incremental capital-output ratio', to give the total capital requirement in the final column. These ratios are tentative; the actual amount of capital required will not be known until the individual projects are approved.

Equally tentative allocations are now made to the service sectors. An average rate of investment in transport and communications is about 3 per cent of GDP. Housing is flexible, but with growing populations and rapid urbanization, less than 3 per cent of GDP is bound to be inadequate. The public service takes about 3 per cent of GDP; this applies only to the requirements for administration (including roads, schools and health). The Government also spends on housing and transport, and contributes to capital formation in agriculture and industry through the agricultural credit system and the industrial development agencies, but these contributions are already included in the respective sectors. Finally other services, including commerce, usually absorb about 10 per cent of gross capital formation. Using these ratios we get the capital budget shown in Table XXXV.

It should be noted that the budget is not confined to projects which will be started and finished within the ten-year period. In practice one would begin the budget by listing unfinished projects, and end it with a carry-over into the next period of projects started but not yet finished. Our first approximation to a budget in Table XXXV assumes that these two carry-overs cancel out in money values.

The result is encouraging. The sum required by sectors (2,378) is only slightly larger than the sum thought likely to be available

(2,342), so we shall adopt it as the sum available. At the same time, the tightness of fit serves as a reminder, especially to those making plans for expenditure in the public sector, that restraint is needed to keep plans within availabilities.

TABLE XXXV. *Ten-Year Capital Budget*

Agriculture	315
Industry	405
Power	78
Construction	97
Transport and Communications	375
Housing	375
Public Services	375
Other Services	238
Stocks	120
	2,378

Table XXXV should not be misread as indicating in any fashion that 3 : 1 is the 'normal' ICOR. In earlier discussion we have seen reasons why this ratio may vary widely, ranging between 2 and 6 to 1. A ratio of 3 : 1 is on the low side. It is reached in this example by making various favourable assumptions: especially, that agricultural output can be increased without heavy investment in irrigation, land reclamation or machinery; that there is still room for considerable expansion of import-substituting light industries, so that emphasis can be placed here instead of on more capital-intensive industries; that the population of towns is not exploding, so that housing can be kept down to 3 per cent of GDP; and that restraint will be shown in public service expenditures. If all these assumptions were reversed, the ratio would more probably be between 4 and 5 to 1.

The table is tentative; intended only for testing whether the ratio assumed at the start of these calculations still seems feasible at this stage. The final budget will incorporate the actual projects, at the costs reached by detailed analysis. Should this turn out to be much larger in total than is shown here, the whole exercise would have to be done again, starting from Table VII, with a lower rate of growth of GDP, or smaller expansion of public services, or a larger foreign deficit (higher taxation would not be feasible).

Flow of Funds

The next step is to prepare a table matching the various sources of funds with the various agents of investment. The sources are divided into savings, depreciation and foreign aid (including grants, loans and direct investment); the investing agents are here divided into Farmers, Business, Households and the Government, with Financial institutions (banks, savings banks, insurance companies, agricultural credit societies, etc.) serving as intermediaries. The result is shown in Table XXXVI. The sectors in which investment takes place have been reduced to five, by grouping 'Industry', 'Construction' and 'Other Services' into one; and by allocating 'Stocks' to the sectors to which they belong.

Table XXXVI is read like an input-output matrix. Read columns 1 to 5 vertically to find whence each agent derives its funds and read rows 1 to 5 horizontally to see how it uses them. Rows 6 to 8 are based on Table IX, put on to an annual basis and summed over ten years; 'Private Saving' in Table IX included the savings of unincorporated businesses, which are here divided between 'Farmers' and 'Business'; and 'Corporate Savings' included the savings of Government enterprises (in power, transport, housing, etc.) which are here added to other Government surpluses. Part of the postulated increase in saving was due to assuming that some investment could be financed by creating money, since all classes of the community would increase their holdings of money (currency and bank deposits) as real national income increased. This monetary saving is included in the table in the sums lent to the Government and to financial institutions.

Table XXXVI shows how big a financial burden falls on the Government when one assumes a high rate of capital formation in an economy with a low rate of private saving. In this example 7 per cent of gross domestic product passes through the Government's capital account (878). It gets 60 per cent of this from its own savings (including profits and depreciation), 26 per cent from foreign grants and loans, and the remaining 14 per cent from saving banks, treasury bills and domestic sales of Government bonds. It spends 44 per cent on the public services (narrowly defined), and 45 per cent on public enterprises and utilities, and lends the remaining 11 per cent to the private sector. Farmers impose the biggest financial burden, since they save and borrow abroad (320) less than they invest in farms and houses (390); on

TABLE XXXVI. Flow of Funds

	Farmers 1	Business 2	Households 3	Government 4	Financial 5	Agriculture 6	Industry 7	Power 8	Transport 9	Housing 10	Public Services 11	Total 12
1. Farmers	—	—	—	—	30	340	—	—	—	50	—	420
2. Business	—	—	—	80	30	—	740	—	195	55	—	1,100
3. Households	—	20	—	10	50	—	—	—	—	220	—	300
4. Government	—	—	—	—	100	—	70	83	190	50	385	878
5. Financial	100	50	40	40	—	—	—	—	—	—	—	230
6. Foreign	20	180	—	224	20							444
7. Depreciation	100	350	60	90	—							600
8. Savings	200	500	200	434	—							1,334
9. Total	420	1,100	300	878	230	340	810	83	385	375	385	2,378

the other hand they pay a large part of the taxes which contribute to Government savings. In this example the business community saves and borrows abroad more than it invests in its own enterprises (1,030 : 990); but there are great differences between businesses in this respect; some have to raise funds from households, and others borrow from financial institutions (including the Government's development corporations).

Table XXXVI is required for any Development Plan, even if the Plan is confined strictly to the public sector. A Plan does not have to undertake a comprehensive projection for the private sector in order to be good, but it cannot escape having to estimate how much money the Government will have to channel into the private sector through financial intermediaries. The information does not always appear in this systematic form, but somewhere the Plan must state how much finance the Government is going to need, how it expects to raise it, and how it expects to spend it.

Table XXXVI does not show repayment of Government debt, since this was not included in the 'real' capital requirements of Tables IX and XXXV. The Government is presumed in this example to have a separate sinking fund account into which it makes annual payments; provision for these payments has been made not in its capital account, but in the recurrent account in Table VIII, where they are among the 'Transfers', which include 'Debt Charges'. It would have been equally legitimate to include the repayment part of Debt Charges in 'Savings' in Table VIII, but in that case we would have had to take it out again before transferring Government savings to Table IX.

Regional Balance

The Plan must show the geographical locations of projects. The distribution of expenditure between regions is controversial, and must be shown in appropriate tables.

This work begins by setting out the current distribution of income and population between the regions, as is done in Table XXXVII. (For simplicity, we use only four regions.) A good Census will give the occupational distribution by regions; national income has probably not been calculated by regions, but the statisticians will benefit from having the exercise forced upon them, since it will improve their statistics.

TABLE XXXVII. *Regional Distribution, Year 0*

Region:	A V.A.	A Pop.	B V.A.	B Pop.	C V.A.	C Pop.	D V.A.	D Pop.	Total V.A.	Total Pop.
Agriculture	84	94	150	211	110	157	126	209	470	671
Industry	61	44	31	23	9	9	9	10	110	86
Power	2	1	2	1	1	1	—	—	5	3
Construction	36	20	15	10	7	5	7	5	65	40
Transport	28	16	18	11	8	7	6	6	60	40
Government	36	18	12	6	6	3	6	3	60	30
Services	98	57	61	38	22	18	19	17	200	130
Rent	14		11		3		2		30	
V.A. Pop.	359	250	300	300	166	200	175	250	1,000	1,000
Per cap.	1.44		1.00		0.84		0.70		1.00	

V.A.=Value Added. Pop.=Occupied Population.

Table XXXVII brings out the enormous disparity which exists among the regions. Output per head is twice as high in Region A as in Region D; indeed this region is almost untouched by such development as has already occurred: 84 per cent of its population is in agriculture. Similar tables for earlier years show that the disparity is increasing steadily.

From the political standpoint, this is one of the most difficult aspects of development planning. No Asian or African country is homogeneous; each has peoples of many languages, religions, or tribes, who distrust each other; and the fact that these differences tend to be associated with wide economic differences aggravates political hostility. Hence, if only for political reasons, most Governments are anxious to reduce regional economic disparities. The economic arguments (as we saw in Chapter II) run both ways. Some disparities are accidental, and can be corrected by creating new opportunities, especially by expenditure on roads, education and other infrastructure. On the other hand, when resources are so limited, there is a case for concentrating development in the areas which have the greatest immediate potential, and leaving attempts to level up incomes to a later stage, when resources are more ample.

Let us assume that, as a compromise, the Agency is instructed to plan on the following basis:

(i) The gap in output between the two richer regions should be reduced, by diverting rather more industrial and other investment to B. This will be achieved by a policy of subsidies, licensing, and improvement of B's infrastructure.

(ii) No attempt will be made at this stage to divert more industrial or agricultural investment to the two poorer regions C and D. However, in preparation for the next Plan, they will now receive a disproportionate investment in infrastructure.

The results of these decisions appear in Table XXXVIII, which shows the expected distribution of output and population in Year 10. Region B is expected to have the biggest proportionate increase in population, and in *per capita* output. (The table does not show what will happen to income, since that depends on changes in relative prices: e.g. if the prices of industrial products are falling, farmers can have higher real incomes even if their real output is constant.) *Per capita* output increases by 19 per cent in Region A, by 23 per cent in B, 17 per cent in C and 16 per cent in D. Thus the two poorer regions are still lagging behind in output. But their infrastructure is catching up. Expenditure on transport, Government services and power (taken together) increases by 126 per cent in these two regions, whereas the increase in A and B together is only 64 per cent.

Table XXXIX gives the regional distribution of the capital budget; this is linked to Table XXXV.

The *per capita* discrepancy in capital expenditure is even greater than that in annual output, because the most capital-intensive

DEVELOPMENT PLANNING

TABLE XXXVIII. *Regional Distribution, Year 10*

Region:	A V.A.	A Pop.	B V.A.	B Pop.	C V.A.	C Pop.	D V.A.	D Pop.	Total V.A.	Total Pop.
Agriculture	112	108	212	252	137	182	159	248	620	790
Industry	114	57	69	37	17	11	16	11	216	116
Power	5	2	5	2	3	2	2	1	15	7
Construction	59	28	42	23	11	7	11	7	123	65
Transport	39	20	30	17	14	9	11	7	94	53
Government	54	27	28	14	16	8	15	8	113	57
Services	138	74	91	55	31	21	27	18	287	168
Rent	19		16		4		3		42	
V.A. / Pop.	540	316	493	400	233	240	244	300	1,510	1,256
V.A. per cap.	1.71		1.23		0.97		0.81		1.20	

TABLE XXXIX. *Capital Budget, by Regions*

Region:	A	B	C	D	Total
Agriculture	88	134	58	35	315
Industry	226	145	18	16	405
Power	25	25	16	12	78
Construction	42	39	8	8	97
Transport	135	120	70	50	375
Housing	150	150	38	37	375
Public Services	160	110	55	50	375
Other Services	120	80	20	18	238
Stocks	50	45	15	10	120
	996	848	298	236	2,378

enterprises are concentrated in Regions A and B. In order to minimize adverse political criticism, the Government asks for a table showing sources of saving by region. This is still more difficult to devise, but is attempted in Table XL, which is linked to Table XXXVI. Government saving is distributed by estimating how much the Government gets in taxes, etc., from each region, and spends on current account for the benefit of each region. Foreign aid is distributed according to the region in which it will be spent.

TABLE XL. *Sources of Savings, by Regions*

Region:	A	B	C	D	Total
Depreciation	280	200	70	50	600
Savings by					
Farmers	40	65	45	50	200
Business	245	160	50	45	500
Households	95	60	25	20	200
Government	200	214	10	10	434
Foreign Aid	180	184	50	30	444
Total	1,040	883	250	205	2,378
Investment	996	848	298	236	2,378
Surplus	44	35	−48	−31	

This gives quite a different picture. The two poorest regions are now seen to be receiving funds, presumably mainly because the Government is spending disproportionately heavily there on current account. Residents of Region B are contributing to this, and may protest. However, the margin of error in such figures is so large that they are not an adequate basis for argument.

Summary

1. The capital budget must be based on detailed costing of projects. The total projected expenditure should not exceed the total finance expected to be available.

2. The capital-output ratio can vary between wide limits. Since at least half of investment is not for commodities but for services, there is no fixed relationship between the growth of commodity output and the ratio of investment to income.

3. It is useful to have a table matching savers and investors, by showing the channels through which finance will flow.

4. The Plan must show the location of each project; tables summarizing the regional distribution of expenditures will also be required.

8. THE MANPOWER BUDGET

Next the manpower aspects of the Plan must be examined, especially its dependence on various classes of skills.

Unskilled Labour

Let us begin with the labour supply as a whole. This Plan has postulated that GDP will increase by 51 per cent over ten years, while the labour force increases by 25.6 per cent. This involves an average increase of productivity per man of 1.9 per cent per annum.

Whether an average increase of 1.9 per cent is possible depends mainly on the agricultural sector. If we assume that productivity will increase in industry by 3 per cent per annum, and in services by 1.0 per cent per annum, we can deduce, as in Table XLI, the required increase in agricultural productivity.

TABLE XLI. *Output, Productivity and Population*

| | Year 0 | | | Year 10 | | |
	Output	Prod.	Pop.	Output	Prod.	Pop.
Agriculture	470	0.70	671	620	0.79	790 R
Industry	180	1.40	129	354	1.88	188
Services	350	1.75	200	536	1.93	278
	1,000		1,000	1,510		1,256

Outputs in Years 0 and 10 are derived from Table VI. Productivity and Population in Year 0 are assumed to be given in the statistical year book.[1] In Year 10 productivity has increased in Industry by 34.3 per cent, and in Services by 10.5 per cent; hence the labour force needed in these two sectors is derived by division. It follows that the labour available for Agriculture in Year 10 will be 790, and that productivity must be 0.785, having increased by 1.15 per cent per annum.

Agricultural productivity can rise by 1.15 per cent per annum

---

[1] The labour force here does not correspond to the number of units of labour in Table XXIV, since for the linear programming a unit of labour was defined as the amount of labour purchasable for one unit of currency.

quite easily if agriculture is overpopulated or mechanizing rapidly, so that output can be maintained or increased despite an outflow of labour. Most economies have some degree of underutilization of labour in one sector or another, such that when rapid industrialization begins, labour pours out of agriculture, or domestic service, or casual jobs, or petty retail trading, without a large adverse effect on output in the sectors which it abandons. Alternatively, married women pour out of the household into paid employment, thus increasing the proportion of the labour force at work. It is clearly necessary to check whether the supply of labour is going to be adequate for the Plan, but in the great majority of cases this is not likely to be a problem.

In the very early stages of development, before men have learnt to work for wages, persuading labour to leave the farms to seek work in factories or mines or plantations may well prove very difficult. However, most countries have long passed through this stage. In most of the poorer countries today the problem is rather that people are streaming off the land into towns faster than jobs can be created for them. There is therefore no difficulty in finding labour for manufacturing or for service industries.

The real problem is whether agriculture can achieve the required increase in total output while at the same time losing labour relatively to other sectors. If agriculture has in any case surplus labour, loss of labour will not affect output. But if agriculture has no labour surplus, attaining the required output may call for considerable mechanization and technological change. The scope for such changes is so wide in underdeveloped countries that a shortage of unskilled labour is not likely to be an obstacle to fulfilment of the Plan.

Unemployment

It is usually more important to ask the opposite question: does the Plan provide enough extra jobs to cope with existing unemployment and the expected increase in population?

The answer must depend partly on the labour situation in agriculture. If there is plenty of cultivable land, as in parts of Africa, an increase in population is met by bringing more land into cultivation: agriculture absorbs the increase. At the other extreme, if nearly all the cultivable land is already in use, and crowded with cultivators, as in parts of Asia, it would be desirable to be able to provide jobs outside agriculture for the whole of the increase in population. This cannot be done. For if 60 per cent of the labour force is in agriculture, and population increases by $2\frac{1}{2}$ per cent, to absorb all the increase outside agriculture would require non-agricultural employment to increase by 6.25 per cent per annum; which in turn means that non-agricultural output must increase by between 8 and 9 per cent. Since more than half of non-agricultural output is in services, such a rate of growth is not feasible. Any Plan for an already overcrowded country must show labour continuing to pile up in the countryside until a fairly late stage of development, when the ratio of agricultural employment has already fallen sharply.

More modest targets would be a 6 per cent rate of growth for non-agricultural output, and a 4 per cent rate of growth for non-agricultural manpower, which gives a 2 per cent increase in non-agricultural productivity. A country with surplus population or heavy unemployment should try to keep non-agricultural productivity *down* to this level. If analysis of the Plan shows that non-agricultural productivity is expected to increase by more than 2 per cent per annum, this is not an occasion for pride; on the contrary, it indicates that the programme should be re-examined most carefully to see whether a reduction in capital-intensity would not increase output as well as employment; since a smaller increase in productivity, employing more people, might give a larger national income. (In Table XLI non-agricultural productivity grows by 1.7 per cent per annum; the higher overall average is due to transfers from low productivity agriculture.)

Calculating the number of jobs required to cope with unemployment and population growth is no help in planning, since one cannot create more jobs than there are resources to support. Output is maximized by maximizing the product of the scarce resources, so the planning problem, where labour is abundant, is to make the best use of land and capital. However, the best way of using capital in these circumstances is to choose labour-intensive rather than capital-intensive techniques. For many reasons, listed in the preceding chapter, the capital-intensity of development programmes is usually excessive. When analysis shows that the Plan will provide relatively few jobs, the right reaction is not to blow up the rate of growth of output beyond what is feasible, but to look again more carefully at the capital-intensity of the projects.

THE MANPOWER BUDGET

Skilled Manpower

Analysis of the demand for skilled manpower can start by concentrating on three broad categories: graduates of institutions of higher education (hereinafter called university graduates), graduates of secondary schools, and skilled labour (defined as persons whose occupations require primary education followed by at least one year of special training or apprenticeship, whether on-the-job, or in institutions). At a later stage these three categories must be subdivided further into as many skills as require specialized training. It is not necessary to bother at this stage about semi-skilled workers, such as textile spinners, who acquire their skills on the job in the course of three to six months' training, since multiplying the number of such persons, as required, presents no special problem.

The starting point is an inventory of the number of such persons now existing in each industry. This material can be derived from a good Census of Population, if such a Census has been taken recently. The information one seeks may not have been published, but may be available on the Census cards, and if so can easily be run off on a machine. What is required is a cross-classification of industry and educational attainment; failing this, a cross-classification of industry and occupation, which most Censuses can provide, will do well enough, since the educational requirements for each occupation are not difficult to discover.

The next step is to express the figures in terms of ratios for each industry. Thus, instead of saying that the sugar industry employs 15,781 persons of whom 63 are university graduates, 324 are secondary graduates, 728 skilled, and 14,666 unskilled, we write that 0.4 per cent are university graduates, 2.1 per cent secondary, 4.6 per cent skilled, and 92.9 per cent unskilled.

Current Expectations

Now in order to calculate need, one has to use not existing ratios, which have been determined by past availabilities, and past opinions as to qualifications required, but rather the ratios which are currently used in recruiting. For example, in many West African countries graduates of primary schools have in the past been recruited for secretarial duties, because of the shortage of secondary school graduates; but today only graduates of secondary schools are taken for such jobs. Thus in calculating how many

225

secondary school graduates are needed to replace existing secretaries as the present incumbents die, retire, or leave their jobs for marriage or other reasons, one must regard all secretarial jobs as jobs requiring a secondary education. Thus one passes from a set of ratios showing how many people have secondary education to a new set of ratios showing how many jobs now require a secondary education, whether the present incumbents have secondary education or not, and these figures are all larger.

A table purporting to show how many jobs require secondary education is obviously subjective; not every employer demands the same qualifications; also what one demands is partly a function of what is available. Nevertheless, after surveying the market and consulting employers, it is possible to construct a table of expectations current in a particular place at a particular time. Table XLII has been constructed for Jamaica[1] in 1963. The ratios for secondary education are substantially higher than for most African countries (perhaps on the average twice as high) but substantially lower than for Western Europe (on the average only about one-third of the European ratios).

TABLE XLII. *Educational Requirements, by Industry*   Per Cent

	University	Secondary	Skilled	Other	Total
Agriculture, large scale	0.4	2.0	3.5	94.1	100.0
Agriculture, small scale	—	0.6	0.1	99.3	100.0
Mining	4.0	10.0	25.0	61.0	100.0
Manufacture, complex	4.0	10.0	25.0	61.0	100.0
Manufacture, simple	2.0	5.0	15.0	78.0	100.0
Manufacture, workshop	0.1	1.0	12.0	86.9	100.0
Construction	0.2	1.7	50.0	48.1	100.0
Communications	1.5	6.0	10.0	82.5	100.0
Commerce	1.5	11.0	1.0	86.5	100.0
Domestic Service	—	—	—	100.0	100.0
Other Services	4.5	35.0	2.0	58.5	100.0

One can see at once from Table XLII why Construction so easily becomes the bottleneck in development, for in this industry half the labour force consists of skilled workers, whose numbers take time to multiply. Another fact which stands out is the high proportion of secondary graduates required in services (especially teachers, nurses, technical assistants and secretaries).

[1] See my article 'Secondary Education and Economic Structure', *Social and Economic Studies*, June 1964.

Plans to expand the public services are easily held up for lack of trained persons in these categories.

Before we can proceed to make a manpower budget, we need a third set of ratios. We know (1) what proportion of people in each industry have (say) a secondary education. We also know (2) what proportion of jobs in each industry are now considered in Year 0 to require a secondary education. We now need to know (3) what proportion the jobs which now require a secondary education will bear to total jobs in each industry in Year 10. The difference between (2) and (3) does not lie in qualifications; required qualifications are assumed unchanged between Year 0 and Year 10. The difference lies in the relative quantitative importance of the jobs. For example, in the Services industry we may know that (say) 1 per cent are school teachers with a secondary education; that say 3 per cent are school teachers with or without secondary education; and thirdly that it is planned that the number of school teachers expand to become 5 per cent of the number of persons in services. The second ratio is required for calculating replacement demand; and the third ratio for calculating expansion of numbers.

Projecting Demand

We now assume that the Planning Agency calculates these three sets of ratios preparatory to making a manpower budget. To illustrate the technique we confine ourselves to calculating how many persons must graduate through secondary school to meet the requirements of the Plan. This covers the first two categories in Table XLII, because university graduates have to be included in the number who must pass through secondary school. Table XLIII sets out in the first column the percentage in each industry who now have secondary education; in the second column the percentage of jobs for which secondary education is now in Year 0 the required qualification; and in the third column what the percentage of jobs requiring secondary education will have become in Year 10, as a result of the expansion of secondary jobs relatively to others.

The number of secondary graduates (including university graduates) required by the Plan is calculated in Table XLIV. Column 1 shows the distribution of the working population in Year 0, and Column 2 its distribution in Year 10. These figures have to be

TABLE XLIII. *Percentage of Secondary and Higher Graduates*

	Actual Year 0	Jobs Year 0	Jobs Year 10
Agriculture, large scale	2.0	2.4	2.4
Agriculture, small scale	0.1	0.6	0.6
Manufacture, complex	12.0	14.0	14.0
Manufacture, simple	5.0	7.0	7.0
Manufacture, workshop	0.8	1.1	1.1
Construction	0.8	1.5	1.9
Communications	3.0	6.0	7.5
Commerce	5.0	10.0	12.5
Domestic Service	—	—	—
Other Services	12.0	24.0	30.0

consistent with the manpower, output and productivity projections already undertaken in Table XLI; this should present no new difficulty, since the basic data are the same.

Column 3 shows the actual number of secondary graduates in Year 0. These figures come from the Census. They can also be derived by multiplying the populations in column 1 of this table by the ratios in the first column of Table XLIII.

Column 4 shows the number of jobs in Year 0 for which a secondary education is now the required qualification. This is found by multiplying the populations in column 1 of this table by the ratios in the second column of Table XLIII.

Column 5 shows the number of jobs in Year 10 for which a secondary education is now the required qualification. This is found by multiplying the populations in column 2 of this table by the ratios in the third column of Table XLIII.

Column 6 is the difference between columns 5 and 4. It gives the increase in the number of jobs requiring secondary education.

Column 7 makes special allowance for countries (mainly in Africa) where a large proportion of the secondary educated are currently expatriates, who may be expected to return home within the next ten years. The figures are reached by assessing what proportion of the persons in column 3 fall into this category.

Column 8 calculates the number required to replace persons who will retire from the labour force during the next ten years, other than expatriates. Only retirement from the labour force counts, since moving from one industry to another does not

TABLE XLIV. *Secondary and Higher Graduates Required*

| | Occupied Population | | Graduates | | | Recruitment | | | |
	Year 0	Year 10	Actual Year 0	Jobs Year 0	Jobs Year 10	New	Replacement Expatriate	Replacement Normal	Total
	1	2	3	4	5	6	7	8	9
Agriculture									
large scale	7,100	9,100	142	170	218	48	90	16	154
small scale	60,000	69,900	60	360	419	59	—	72	131
Manufacturing									
complex	400	700	48	56	98	42	30	5	77
simplex	1,500	3,000	75	105	210	105	40	13	158
workshop	7,000	8,600	56	77	95	18	20	11	49
Construction	4,000	6,500	32	60	124	64	10	10	84
Communications	4,000	5,300	120	240	398	158	70	34	262
Commerce	6,000	8,300	300	600	1,038	438	120	192	750
Domestic Service	3,000	3,800	—	—	—	—	—	—	—
Other Services	7,000	10,400	840	1,680	3,120	1,440	400	512	2,352
Total	100,000	125,600	1,673	3,348	5,720	2,372	780	865	4,017

229

diminish the total number of graduates. The retirement rate among men is small; smaller than the death rate of the adult population, because the increase in the ratio of the educated results in the average age of the educated becoming lower than that of the adult population as a whole. The retirement rate of women is much higher; their working lives are much shorter because so many retire from the labour force soon after marriage. In this table it is assumed that the retirement rate over ten years will be 20 per cent, except in Commerce and Other Services where, because of the preponderance of women, it is assumed to be 40 per cent. These percentages are applied not to the number of educated persons in Year 0 (column 3), but to the number of jobs requiring education in Year 0 (column 4), minus the number of expatriates retiring (column 7).

The total number of new graduates required during the ten years is the sum of columns 6, 7 and 8, which is given in column 9. On the assumptions made, the Plan calls for 4,017 persons to graduate from secondary schools during the next ten years. This figure must itself be increased a little to allow for its own retirement rate. Thus total recruitment can be set in round numbers at 4,500 (the wastage rate of women is high). This recruitment can be translated into an age group percentage. A working population of 100,000 is associated with a total population of about 280,000. The number of persons aged eighteen in such a population is about 5,600, rising in ten years to about 7,000. To graduate 450 a year means that about 7 per cent of the age group must graduate from secondary schools, or, allowing for wastage, that about 12 per cent of the age group must enter secondary schools in each year. At the low level of productivity assumed for this economy, even in Year 10, the labour force requires only 4.5 per cent to have gone through secondary schools; but, because of the low starting point, and the high replacement ratios, the enrolment ratio is more than twice as high.

Similar calculations can be made for each category of skill—university graduates, building craftsmen, and so on. Where the category is small, and highly specialized, one can also, and perhaps better, use the alternative method of questioning prospective employers. The telephone company can estimate how many linesmen it will be employing in Year 10, the Ministry of Agriculture how many agricultural agents; the Ministry of Education how many elementary school teachers and so on. The questionnaire method has to be used for specialized categories, but breaks down when applied to wider groups. There is no point in asking business men how many secretaries they will employ in Year 10, or how many university graduates. Such wide categories have to be estimated by taking the Plan as a whole, estimating by means of what is known about ratios, and then checking this estimate by aggregating as many separate groups as can be deduced directly from the Plan.

Meeting Shortages

The resulting estimates of required skills must then be compared with estimated outputs. If the demand exceeds the supply, the Plan cannot be carried out with the existing supply. This may mean that parts of the Plan must be cut back; construction cannot exceed the supply of skilled workers; there is no point in building hospitals for which there are no nurses; and so on. But this can only at most be a short-term setback. The main point of a manpower budget is not to cut the Plan to the size of available skills, but rather to determine the resources to be allocated to the training of the skills required by the Plan. Training takes time, so the first year or two of the Plan must be tailored to available skills; but if training is given adequate priority, one should be able to assume that in the later years of the Plan skill will have ceased to be a bottleneck.

Even the early years of the Plan can be relieved by one of two expedients. Skills in short supply can be imported. One cannot make up a big deficiency of secondary graduates by importation; the numbers involved in elementary school teaching, nursing or secretarial work are too large, and the cost of imported secondary graduates is too high, for any big gap in these numbers to be met by importation. On the other hand, the number of university graduates required is small, so a shortage at this level need not hold up development.

The other expedient is to lower the qualifications demanded. If we need 4,500 graduates of secondary schools, and the schools will produce only 3,000, then one can continue to use graduates of primary schools for some of the jobs (nursing, teaching, typing) which one had intended to upgrade to secondary school status. Educational requirements are fairly flexible.

Conclusion

Economic development is not the purpose of education, so educational policy cannot be determined merely by assessing what skills are required to implement the Plan. Africa is still short of basic education, but in other continents the number of students seeking and receiving secondary and higher education in several countries already exceeds the levels which economic development alone would justify. Their manpower budgets need not therefore deal with general education, but can concentrate on specialized skills in short supply.

General education policy has already been considered in Chapter II. In the narrow field of the relationship between education and productivity, the essentials can be summed up in two propositions:

(1) The secondary school has priority over the primary school and the university.

(2) There cannot be too many technicians, engineers, or scientists.

The products of secondary schools are the officers and non-commissioned officers of an economic and social system. Secondary schools supply the persons who, with one or two more years of training (in institutions or on the job), become technologists, secretaries, nurses, school teachers, book-keepers, clerks, civil servants, agricultural assistants and supervisory workers of various kinds. The middle and upper ranks of business consist almost entirely of secondary school products, and these products are also the backbone of public administration. A country can manage with very few university graduates, because its better secondary school graduates can perform adequately most of the administrative tasks which university graduates otherwise do; and the few remaining gaps can be filled by imports. But one cannot meet the need for secondary school graduates by importing them: the numbers are too great, and the cost too high. If secondary school graduates are in short supply many desirable developments will be held up, and the cost of any scheme which relies on their skills will be excessive.

An adequate output from the secondary schools is also a necessary foundation for institutions which give specialized training (farm schools for agricultural assistants, teacher training colleges, nurses' training schools, and so on). If the secondary facilities are inadequate, the specialized facilities are misused. Young people then train as teachers or as agricultural assistants not because they wish to work in these capacities, but because this is a substitute for secondary education. Teacher training, especially, then becomes an avenue to higher-paid occupations, and the turnover is excessive. The soundest educational policy is to have an adequate output from the secondary schools; given this, shortages of more specialized skills will not last long.

Technicians are here defined as persons who, after receiving a basic education to age fifteen or sixteen, have received the equivalent of two years of full-time technical training—whether in a full-time institution, or whether over some longer period in some combination of on-the-job training and part-time study.

Most attempts to increase productivity involve either machinery or the application of scientific knowledge; they therefore involve technicians. At the present time the shortage of technicians is world-wide, but is most acute in underdeveloped countries. One reason is a high turnover; good technicians get scholarships to go on to university; or else they study for university degrees in evening classes. Hence a talented man tends to use the technician's training merely as a substitute for secondary education, on his way to higher achievements.

It is impossible to have a surplus of technicians. As more appear on the market, employers upgrade the qualifications of persons whom they hire for technical jobs, so all that happens is that trained technicians displace untrained ones, and in the process raise the level of productivity. Besides, even if there were more technicians than technical jobs, the surplus technicians could compete in non-technical areas with other graduates of secondary education, and would perform equally well in such jobs. Hence a Development Plan should give priority to multiplying the number of technicians as the surest way of raising productivity.

Some countries have difficulty in recruiting youngsters for technical training, in competition with the attractions of university courses. High school students prefer to go on to an institution which will give them a Bachelor's degree, especially if a Bachelor's degree will earn a higher salary than a technician's Diploma. Faculties of Law, Arts and Social Science are therefore flooded, while the technical colleges have empty places. The remedies are inherent in the problem: upgrade the pay of technicians, restrict entry into Faculties of Law, Arts and Social Science, and offer more generous scholarships and bursaries to students in technical colleges than to students in overcrowded Faculties. It is easy to have a surplus of Arts graduates, but impossible to have a surplus of technicians.

It is equally impossible to have too many engineers and scientists. Many countries have a surplus of university graduates in the humanities, law and commerce, but no country in the world has a surplus of engineers. Most of the jobs which graduates in the humanities fill—in administration, commerce or teaching— could be done equally well by engineers or scientists; but what engineers and scientists do cannot be done equally well by humanities graduates. Hence, in framing higher education policies there is no point in counting how many engineers or scientists the economy needs, with a view to keeping their numbers down; financial stringency may force strict control over the numbers admitted into faculties of humanities, law or commerce; but maximum encouragement should be given to students who desire to enter faculties of science, engineering, agriculture or medicine.

Summary
1. A shortage of unskilled labour is improbable; if it exists the remedy is to adopt measures to step up the output of agriculture while reducing its labour force.

2. In countries which suffer from pressure of population in the countryside, the annual increase in the productivity of sectors other than agriculture should be kept, in the interest of employment, *down* to the level which would maximize total output.

3. Requirements for skilled manpower of various categories should be projected several years ahead, and measures adopted to ensure adequate supplies.

4. Secondary education has priority over primary and university education.

5. From the economic point of view, it is impossible to train too many technicians, engineers or scientists.

9. THE GOVERNMENT BUDGET

Finally, we come to the Government budget (including central, provincial and local authorities). Capital expenditures are already accounted for in Table XXXVI. Here we deal with recurrent income and expenditure.

Planners began by planning capital expenditure only, or capital plus some recurrent items assumed to have special development significance, but this was soon seen to be insufficient. Most capital expenditures have recurrent counterparts; if hospitals are built, nurses and doctors must be found; if schools are built teachers must be found, and so on. The recurrent expenditure is often very large in relation to the capital expenditure; over five years the recurrent expenditure of a school may come to twice the capital expenditure. Neglect of the recurrent aspect therefore asks for financial trouble. Also, even without new capital expenditure, recurrent expenditure required merely to meet existing commitments tends to grow rapidly, and no assessment of available finances is possible without making allowance for the normal growth of recurrent expenditure. Discussion of foreign aid has tended to focus attention on the importance of capital; but in the public sector, the limitation tends to be recurrent expenditure rather than capital.

Existing Commitments

The planning exercise should begin by projecting what will happen to expenditures before taking into account new commitments to be made in the Development Plan. Even if one assumes that no new expenditures are undertaken, that there is no increase in staff, and that the general price level is constant, the cost of Government expenditure will rise. One reason for this is that productivity increases faster in the rest of the economy than in the Government sector. Since salaries in the Government sector must keep in line with salaries in other sectors, the 'price level' of Government services rises faster than the average price level. The difference may not be large; the price level of Government services certainly rises much faster than that of manufacturing industry, but productivity rises slowly in all sectors except manufacturing, so whether the rate of growth in the Government sector differs significantly from that of the economy as a whole, depends largely on whether the Government is mechanizing its office work, and allowing its 'organization and methods' men to streamline ancient procedures. Another reason why the price level of Government services may rise is the ageing of the staff. Civil servants work on scales which give them an increment every year. If nobody joined or left, the budget would increase each year by the sum of the annual increments. Given a normal age distribution, if people leave at the top of their scales only (through death or retirement) and are replaced by recruiting equal numbers at the bottom of the scale only, the average age and the total expenditure should be about constant. In developing countries the size of the staff has been increasing for some time, so the age distribution is not normal; the ratio of young to old is abnormally high, and the average age would continue to increase even if all vacancies were filled by recruitment at the bottom. Making a Plan in constant prices assumes that all prices will move in the same proportion. One can therefore ignore expected or possible changes in the general price level, but a divergence between the general price level and the price level of Government service has to be taken into account when assessing how much money is likely to be available. The upward creep of the budget for these reasons is quite significant. If population were constant, and the number and productivity of Government employees constant, and the cost of living constant, the money cost of the budget would increase by the same amount as *per capita* productivity in the system as a whole, if one were to keep civil servants' incomes in line with other persons', and by an extra half of 1 per cent per annum because of the rise in the average age of civil servants.

Then account must be taken of past schemes whose recurrent costs now enter the budget for the first time, or increase. Capital structures just being completed—roads, schools, hospitals, etc.— will bring recurrent costs. Promises already made—an increase in the number of scholarships, increased contributions to international organizations, commitments to meet a fixed proportion of the expenditure of other institutions, etc.—will have to be honoured. Loans borrowed with a moratorium on interest or sinking fund payments will now start to increase the public debt charges. Next, one must add recurrent commitments which do not involve capital expenditure. For example, the relentless increase of population will add to the size of the general administration—more policemen, more magistrates, more clerks, etc. This part of the exercise is easily overlooked. Commitments (old or new) which involve capital expenditure are included in the capital budget, so it is easy to check whether their recurrent counterparts are contained in the projection of recurrent expenditure; recurrent increases which have no capital counterpart are more easily forgotten.

Development Expenditure

The next stage is to link the public sector with what is projected for the private sector. This involves two different types of consideration. On the one side, public services are linked to output, as intermediate goods, or as part of the framework which stimulates growth. On the other side, public services are linked to personal income and consumption. In the first category comes the supply of water to factories; in the second category comes the supply of water to the villages. Different considerations arise when planning for these two different needs.

Linking the public service with projected output raises no special problems. The managers of the public utilities—electricity, gas, water, railways, harbours, telephones—will have been on the appropriate committees, and will have discussed with entrepreneurs both how much they plan to use, and where they plan to locate. Indeed, since the period between the decision to build and the date when the first output is obtained may easily be four years or more, they usually have to look beyond the next five-year Plan. Decisions on the location of capacity, or on the types of equipment to use, in some cases depend not on current demand but on the pattern of demand expected fifteen or twenty years ahead, so public utilities require long-term master plans (kept as flexible as possible) of which the current Development Plan is merely a segment. The same remark applies to roads.

Another group of agencies linked directly to the private sector is composed of the Government's financial corporations. The private sector now looks to the Government to an increasing extent for long-term finance for factories, agriculture and housing; and there are also numerous cases of partnership between private and public capital in starting new enterprises. Several factors drive the Government into financing private enterprise, irrespective of its ideology; the fact that it is potentially the largest source of saving in the economy, mobilizing through taxation resources which would either be consumed or sent abroad; the fact that it can raise money abroad (whether loans or gifts) more easily than its citizens; the fact that it is willing to take more risk than private lenders (though, by guaranteeing loans, it can avoid putting up much money of its own); and the fact that it may wish to participate in exploiting what may turn out to be very profitable opportunities (though here a suitable system of royalties and taxes is again a substitute for investment). If, in addition to the financing of the public utilities, and channeling finance to private activities through financial corporations, the Government wishes also to set up its own operating agricultural, industrial or housing corporations, it may easily happen that half the net investment in the economy is financed by the Government, even though the number of people directly employed by the Government may still be relatively small.

Other economic services may not be tied so closely to the private sector's projections, but are part of the general framework. Geological and other surveys are frequently undermanned. The agricultural services—research, training and extension—have a major burden to bear—since they play a major role in getting the increase in agricultural output on which the projections are based. Community Development is to help increase capital formation at low cost; and the Ministry of Labour is to ensure an incomes policy which does not result in continually mounting unemployment; the needs of these departments should have high priority.

The social services also have their link with output. The settling of new lands may require public health measures. The manpower survey yields some minimum targets for education. The need for welfare services is a by-product of the expansion of the modern sector. Unemployment relief not merely improves the social atmosphere (and therefore the willingness to invest) but, if it takes the form of employment on useful works, may contribute significantly to agricultural potential.

Most Government departments recognize the need to coordinate their services with the private sector. Surprisingly, coordination with one another is less frequent. It is not unusual to find that the water authorities have chosen villages A to G for development, the electricity authorities villages H to L, the medical authorities villages M to R, and so on. In discussing regional balance we saw that it was desirable to choose a limited number of locations to which new industries would be attracted, and that these should be equipped with the complete range of public services. The settlement of new agricultural lands also requires integrated planning of roads, water supplies, schools and so on. Apart from these special areas, co-ordination is not always necessary, or the best tactic; when it is not possible to give everything to every village, it may be politically wise to distribute what is available fairly widely. However, whatever the correct policy may be, it is not likely to be reached haphazardly; those who plan the location of services should exchange and discuss their plans.

The link on the side of output is relatively easy, but it does not go far in determining how much to invest in the various services. For over and above what is produced as intermediate goods, is what is produced for the consumer. The real problem with water or electricity or telephones is not how much industry wants, but how many villages to add to the system, when all want to be included and the money suffices only to finance a few. Similarly the problem in education may not be how many people to train to fill the jobs which development is expected to create, but how fast to continue expanding the system when there is already serious unemployment among school leavers. We considered these problems in Chapter II, and saw that there is no economic reason why the public should not have as much of these services as it is prepared to pay for. Thus the rate at which it is feasible to increase taxation is the only economic limit to the rate at which the social services should be expanded.

Fiscal Proposals
The budget projected for Year 10 is shown in Table XLV, which is an elaboration of Table VIII.

TABLE XLV. *Consolidated Budgets*

Expenditure	Year 0	Year 10	Revenue	Year 0	Year 10
Administrative	25	40	Import Duties	35	61 R
Economic	25	42	Excise	11	23
Education	17	38	Govt. Profits	−1	5
Health	10	23	Corporate Tax	20	39
Welfare	8	18	Personal I.T.	12	30
Defence	3	8	Social Ins.	3	9
Debt Charges	2	13	Local Taxes	15	30
Savings	25	45	Misc. Fees	20	30
	115	227		115	227

On the expenditure side, notable features are the more than doubling of Education, Health and Welfare (to 3.5, 1.5 and 1.2 per cent of GDP respectively), and the even larger increases in Defence and Debt Charges. It is very hard in these days to keep the recurrent budget under control, since the public's demand for social services is unlimited.

On the revenue side, the Government plans to turn the loss on state-owned enterprises into a profit; this may be a pious hope. Import duties are shown as a residual, because they are the most flexible item. However, this rate of increase will not be easy to achieve, especially as import substitution will be restraining the imports of consumer goods. As we have already noted, the Government is straining the economy by seeking simultaneously a large increase in investment and a large increase in public services. In absolute terms this is a modest budget, taking only 15 per cent of GDP; it is the rate of expansion that causes concern. Whether the tax revenue can be doubled (at constant prices) over ten years will depend as much on the quality of political leadership as on anything else.

Development Plans do not always publish a detailed forecast of future revenue, and whether they should do so is open to argument. A Government does not announce tax changes several months in advance, since this permits evasive action. But there is no harm in showing what tax changes will become necessary over the next ten years. On the contrary, this has some political advantage. There is the negative advantage that it is hard for the Opposition to make political capital out of a calculation showing that increases in Government expenditure will require increases in taxes over the years. And there is also the positive advantage of giving the public time to accustom itself to the inevitable.

Summary

1. The Plan must include a forecast of Government revenue and expenditure on current account.

2. The cost of existing commitments will increase even if no new policies are adopted; forecasting should begin with the cost of these commitments.

3. Many parts of the Plan have implications for public expenditure; these interrelationships should be worked out.

4. There is public pressure to expand the social services beyond

levels justifiable by their contribution to raising productivity. These are valid claims; the only economic limit to meeting them is the feasibility of raising the necessary taxes.

5. It is very difficult to keep recurrent expenditure under control, but the attempt should be made, since the financing of the Plan predicates a certain level of Government saving.

6. Detailed tax proposals need not be published, but the Government should have detailed ideas as to how it will find the necessary money.

IO. RETROSPECT

We have come a long way. As a result we now have a comprehensive framework, in which the tables interlock, and all the figures are consistent with one another. No Development Plan has ever been made with such a high degree of consistency, if only because no underdeveloped country has all the statistics which this kind of framework would require.

The reader who is unfamiliar with these techniques should not allow himself to be carried away by the arithmetic. In effect, we have made a Plan out of thin air. In practice, it is not possible to make a good Plan without having detailed knowledge of the country which is being planned. Innumerable decisions have to be made at every point; how much can be raised in taxes; whether the farmers are likely to increase their productivity; what new natural resources or technological opportunities await exploitation; what can be exported and what cannot; how urgent the housing situation is; whether current employment is more important than future income; and so on. Such decisions require not only intimate knowledge, but also political authority. What we have made here is not in any sense a 'model Plan', since the decisions we made as we went along were appropriate only to the circumstances which we assumed to exist in this particular place.

Moreover, as we have often reiterated, ultimately what matters are the individual projects chosen, and the economic policies adopted. One can make a good Plan without a macroeconomic framework, if the projects are well chosen and the policy measures well designed. Equally a Plan may be very bad, even though it meets all the tests of consistency.

Looking back on this mass of tables one may well ask how

DEVELOPMENT PLANNING

much of this would really be worth doing, if the statistics could be produced. Actually, the only controversial part is the fixing of targets for individual industries. Nobody disputes that planning adds order to Government expenditure, that Government programmes should be based on a careful projection of financial resources, or that manpower requirements should be examined. It is the attempt to forecast or control production in the private sector that raises dispute.

We have already discussed this subject in Chapter I. However, now that we have seen what forecasting involves, a further judgment can be added. The core of the argument is the usefulness or otherwise of the input-output matrix. This matrix enables the statisticians to bring together all the influences on the demand for a commodity, including the intermediate demands. How useful this is depends on where the engine of growth is located in the particular economy. If the economy is propelled by the rate of expansion of domestic demand, the input-output matrix is most helpful to investment planners. But if the engine of growth is located in import-substitution, the matrix, though relevant, is not necessary; and if it is located in the expansion of exports, the matrix is irrelevant.

If a country is still in the export-driven stage, the planners must concentrate on finding new natural resources, and on exploiting new techniques. If it is in the import-substitution stage, the basic data are the trade returns and consultants' reports on the feasibility and cost of manufacturing various commodities at home. The situation is different in an economy driven mainly by an expanding home market, in which intermediate demand plays also an increasing role; here the input-output matrix is a powerful tool. Expansion of domestic demand is the engine of growth in a few large underdeveloped economies, most notably India; but in general, comprehensive planning is more important to advanced economies than it is to underdeveloped economies.

FOR FURTHER READING: CHAPTER III

Barna, T. (Editor). *Structural Interdependence and Economic Development*. New York, 1963.
Chenery, H. B., and Clark, P. G., *Inter-Industry Economics*. New York, 1960.
Chenery, H. B., and Kretschmer, K. S., 'Resources Allocation for Economic Development', *Econometrica*, October 1956.

RETROSPECT

Haq, Mahbul ul. *The Strategy of Economic Planning: A Case Study of Pakistan.* London, 1963.

Hickman, B. G. (Editor). *Quantitative Planning of Economic Policy.* Washington, D.C., 1965.

Johansen, L. *A Multi-Sectoral Study of Economic Growth.* Amsterdam, 1964.

Prest, A. R. *The Investigation of National Income in British Tropical Dependencies.* London, 1957.

Reddaway, W. B. *The Development of the Indian Economy.* London, 1962.

Rosenstein-Rodan, Paul (Editor), *Capital Formation and Economic Development.* London, 1964.

Tinbergen, J., and Bos, H. C. *Mathematical Models of Economic Growth.* New York, 1962.

CHAPTER IV

The Planning Process

Planning involves every department of the Government. Normally a special Planning Agency is created, with the formal responsibility for making the Development Plan, and greater or less responsibility for seeing that it is carried out. However the work of assessing hundreds of projects, for which individual departments are in the first instance responsible cannot all be done by a Planning Agency. Where to draw the line between the functions of the Agency and the functions of other departments is an administrative problem which every country solves differently.

I. THE PLANNING AGENCY

The Planning Agency is a separate organization, with its own offices and staff. Ministerial responsibility for the Agency varies from country to country. Frequently the Agency works under the Ministry of Finance. This is not the best solution, because the outlooks of finance officials and of planning officials are dissimilar. A good Finance officer is interested mainly in keeping expenditure down, by ensuring that given objectives are secured at minimum cost; he is not a policy maker; policies come to him from other Ministries through the Cabinet. A Planning official should be equally concerned to minimize cost, but he is concerned more with making policies and establishing new objectives. His outlook is expansionary, while that of the Finance official is restrictive. So while the Planning Agency must collaborate closely with the Ministry of Finance, it should be independent of that Ministry.

The worst solution is to appoint a Minister of Development, and attach the Agency to him. Making a Plan involves the imposition of a centrally determined pattern upon all the Ministries, in the course of which each is forced to abandon or postpone several of its favourite projects. To get away with this, the Minister of Development must be superior to other Ministers. If he is just one among many, he is not likely to have the necessary authority. Occasionally a powerful man in the party is appointed to be Minister of Development, but this results in the presence of three super-Ministers in the Cabinet, and the jealousies to which human nature is prone detract from the efficiency of this solution.

By elimination we reach the common practice, which is to make the Planning Agency responsible to the Prime Minister, who may or may not appoint an under-Minister in his office to look after this function. As the Prime Minister usually has many other things on his mind, the success of this solution depends on having an executive head of the Planning Agency in whom the Prime Minister has confidence, so that he will intervene only on crucial issues, and will in general throw his weight behind the Agency's proposals even when he has not had time to study them in detail. Unless the Prime Minister backs the Planning Agency, achievement of its goals is impossible; the restraints imposed by scarcity, economic priority, inter-dependence and the need for consistency are likely to be ignored and sacrificed to the pet proposals of the more aggressive Ministers. So if the Prime Minister will not interest himself in planning, it is probably best to put the Agency under the Minister of Finance, as the strongest man available.

The size of the Agency's staff, and the qualifications of its employees, depend on how much of the planning the Agency must do itself. The staff must be competent to do the macro-economic work, but this by itself does not amount to much. It becomes formidable if the Department of Statistics is weak, for then the Agency finds itself drawn into the collection and analysis of statistical data needed to construct its macroeconomic framework, or to elucidate production trends in various sectors of the economy. At the other end of the scale, the formulation of individual projects is not normally the work of the Planning Agency. Planning begins by calling on each Ministry, provincial or local authority to submit detailed projects for consideration, and a similar call goes to organizations in the private sector. How much technical staff the Agency needs for individual project analysis depends on how well staffed these Ministries and organizations are. The Agency must have some technical staff of its own to help in project evaluation, especially at the stage when the number of projects is being cut to fit the available resources; some architects, civil engineers, agricultural scientists, and industrial experts are indispensable. How many will depend on whether Ministries are themselves so weak technically that the Agency has to lend a hand in drawing up the original project proposals. It must also be remembered that the Agency has not only to draw up the Plan but also to supervise its implementation. In particular it has every year to produce the segment of the Plan for the next fiscal year, and for this job it needs, mainly, financial officers of the kind one finds in the Ministry of Finance.

Generalization is impossible. A team of three (economist, agriculturist, civil engineer) could make a Development Plan for Barbados (population 250,000). In France the Planning Agency had in 1963 a professional staff of about thirty-five; in India, one of about 180.

Summary

A special agency of the Government should be created to prepare and implement a Development Plan. It should be responsible directly to the Prime Minister or head of Government.

2. PLANNING COMMITTEES

The Planning Agency acts in co-operation with other people, mainly through committees. This is not only or primarily because it cannot know everything. Obviously the Agency cannot hope to be more expert than everybody outside the Agency on every aspect of the economy; but even if it were, co-operation would still be essential. The principal reason is that a Plan is put into effect not by the Agency but by Ministries, provincial Governments, private entrepreneurs and other members of the general public. Even the most expert Plan will fail if it is not acceptable. The best way to ensure acceptance is to bring into the formulation of the Plan representatives of those who have to carry it out.

Governments are not always willing to share the planning process. Putting the matter at its lowest level, occasionally the Cabinet keeps plan-making to itself for no better reason than that each Minister has his own pet scheme (a road for his constituency, or an industrial plant for his cousin) which he does not want to see submitted to objective tests. This is particularly likely in new states where the politicians, the civil servants, and the general public are still unsure of the respective roles of each, and politicians are making, arbitrarily, decisions which more mature societies try to insulate against political considerations. But even where nothing 'fishy' is involved, a new Government may have fixed ideas of what it wants to do, and may determine to proceed without giving the sort of people who sit on representative committees a formal opportunity to criticize its plans. The Government may also fear regional disputes. The making of a Development Plan appears as an opportunity for the central Government to impose its programme upon the country as a whole, thus strengthening its position at the expense of provincial and local Governments, and if this is a touchy issue, as it is in many new states, the central Government is tempted to keep plan-making a private dialogue between itself and the Planning Agency. A Plan made in this way is not likely to succeed. Even if it is a good Plan, it is not likely to win the co-operation of the many people without whom it cannot be carried out.

Committees are needed at three levels; at the level of the design of individual projects; at the level at which the number of projects is matched to available resources; and at the Cabinet level.

Technical Committees
Individual projects are best considered at the start by technical committees, including civil servants and members of the general public who are involved. Committees can be established on different bases: on an industry basis (for electricity, textiles, livestock); on a public service basis (roads, ports, education, health, surveys); on a resource basis (manpower, savings, foreign exchange); on an institutional basis (company, law, banking law, co-operatives, registration of titles to land); or on a regional basis. The number of committees and sub-committees must depend on the country and its problems. In France there were established for the Fourth Plan 27 committees, with 991 members; these in turn set up a number of Working Groups bringing in a further 2,147 members. Of these 3,138 persons, only 781 were civil servants; the rest were members of the public providing voluntary service. The alleged success of French planning is usually attributed mainly to the fact that it is done so co-operatively. Those

who participate feel committed, and the knowledge that so many are committed increases the safety of investments which will pay off only if everybody else is doing his share of investing at the same time.

Such committees do not reduce the work of the Planning Agency; they increase it. No committee functions satisfactorily unless it is well serviced. The Planning Agency must prepare documentation, guide discussion, and keep the business moving. It must also judge which committees are fruitful and which are not, and decide what to do with those which are sterile—whether to abolish, subdivide, reconstitute, or put into cold storage. Some of the committees, especially those dealing with public services, can be chaired by Ministers, and serviced by their departments, but even these have to be watched.

The number of projects which get started in the Ministries or private organizations, and come for consideration before the committees, will exceed the number which can be incorporated into the final Plan. Committees therefore begin by asking for some indication as to how much is available for what comes within their terms of reference. It is seldom possible to have even an approximate answer ready before the committees start work. Planning is a long affair; it takes two to three years to make a Development Plan properly. Work has to start at both ends (the project end and the macroeconomic end) simultaneously. Besides, even if one has a general idea of the total resources available, allocation among the various sectors is not feasible without knowledge of the details of these sectors. One may tentatively allocate twice as much to Sector A as to Sector B, only to find, when the committees have done their work, that all the really profitable projects are in B and none in A. Moreover, it is important to resist the notion that time spent on studying projects which do not ultimately get into the Plan is time wasted. One cannot know the potentialities of an economy without a thorough search. Also, some opportunities which one would neglect if one concentrated only on what one thought were the highest priorities, turn out on detailed examination to be better than some of the projects with more superficial glamour. Finally, planning is a continuous process; even when designing the current Five Year Plan it is desirable to have some idea of what will enter the next Five Year Plan. Committees should therefore be encouraged to do a comprehensive job, and should not be subjected to restrictive quotas until a fairly advanced stage of the operation.

Cabinet Committee

While the committees work on individual projects, private and public, the Planning Agency should work at the macroeconomic end, determining what resources are available, and the broad sectoral distribution of the Plan. These matters involve Cabinet decisions. The size of the Plan depends partly on levels of taxation and current expenditure, and partly on arrangements for foreign aid. The distribution of resources also involves some high level decisions: whether to use some resources for relieving unemployment through public works, or to concentrate rather on commodity-producing investments; whether to import machinery or give priority to building up the engineering industries; whether to effect changes in the structure of agriculture; and so on.

The Planning Agency therefore needs a special committee of the Cabinet which will interest itself in major planning strategy, and issue directives. To this committee it will take schemes showing possible alternatives with their repercussions, and from this committee it should receive basic instructions as to the general shape of the Plan.

The next stage is to bring together the results of these two sets of labours: the individual proposals of the committees, and the macroeconomic framework emerging from the Cabinet. This the Planning Agency does by reducing the number of proposals to fit available resources and strategy. Thereby it produces the first draft of the Plan. It will have to go back to the committees, for each committee to comment on the details of what has been accepted or rejected in its sector, but first the draft must be considered from the viewpoint of the balance among sectors. That is the task of a second level committee.

National Planning Council

This second-level committee links the work of the technical project committees at one end, and of the Cabinet committee at the other. It is therefore best composed of representatives of both: say the Ministers on the Cabinet committee plus chairmen of some of the technical project committees. The mixture of Ministers and independent members is important, for if the Plan is to succeed, it must have both Government and public support. This committee is the crucial planning body, and is usually given a grand name, such as 'National Planning Council.' We have reached it last, because we have followed the sequence of work step by step. But often the planning process begins by establishing the National Planning Council, which then appoints subordinate committees and staff.

The Planning Agency modifies its first draft in the light of discussions in the Planning Council, and then goes back to the committees for comments on the individual projects chosen, in comparison with those excluded. From this point on the Plan goes back and forth among the Agency, the committees, the National Planning Council and the Cabinet committee, until it is finally ready for Cabinet approval, publication, and submission to Parliament.

All this takes time. Two to three years is not too long a period for the preparation of a Development Plan. Some Governments expect a Plan to be ready in six months. They come into power, denounce the existing Plan, and demand a new one. Planning does not fit well into the timetable of political manoeuvring. Every Government has some ideas that it wants incorporated into a Plan, but a Plan is made not for a Government but for a people, and most of the problems with which it deals are unaffected by changes in the Government. Such modifications as the Government wishes to make can usually be accomplished without demanding an entirely new Plan.

The proposition that a Plan is made for a people rather than for a Government also explains the committee structure described in this section, which requires the public to participate in all stages of the Plan's construction. As already indicated, the utility of this procedure does not depend specifically on a commitment to democratic processes, though it would also follow from such a prediliction; it follows rather from the desire to make a Plan which stands a good chance of implementation. Implementation does not rest only on the Government; the Plan pre-supposes that the public will undertake a host of activities which development requires. So the Plan is more likely to succeed if those who are to carry it out have a hand in drafting it, than if it is made in ignorance or defiance of the public's wishes or intentions.

Because the design of a Plan is a co-operative undertaking,

involving the public, the Government and planning specialists, the final product does not bear a personal stamp. The Planning Agency is engaged in diplomatic negotiation, rather than in decision-making. Its integrity is involved; it is the guardian of the Plan's rationality: its internal consistency, its efficiency, and its relevance. It has to fight for these standards while at the same time conceding that other aspects—its size, direction, regional balance, etc.—require political decisions beyond its competence. The talents of the head of the Planning Agency must include not only expertise in planning techniques, and ability to administer a complicated process, but also the capacity to get along with a lot of very different kinds of people.

The machinery described in this chapter pre-supposes that it is intended to make a comprehensive Plan, including both the private and public sectors. How elaborate an organization one needs depends on how comprehensive the Plan which is undertaken. If a Plan consists only of a list of proposed public expenditures, the number of committees can be minimal. The Agency then deals directly with the Ministries. Even with such a limited Plan, however, the public should be brought into consultation, and a system of committees to consider each of the public services is as good a way as any of achieving this.

Summary
1. If the Plan is to be accepted when published, all important decision-makers, public and private, who will have a hand in implementing it must be represented in its preparation.

2. The Cabinet should appoint a special committee of its members to make major decisions on the objectives of the Plan, and on priorities.

3. The Planning Agency needs the assistance of technical committees to study individual projects as well as various other problems of resource utilization.

4. A National Planning Council is useful for considering the first draft of a Plan taken as a whole; it serves as a link between technical committees and the Cabinet committee.

3. FEDERAL PLANNING

In a federation responsibilities are shared between the centre and the states. A single Planning Agency for the centre and the states is therefore inappropriate.

The problem is fairly simple if the states are responsible both for administering and for financing a particular service; the difficulties arise where administration is shared between the centre and the states, or where the states administer, but part of the finance for the service comes from the centre.

The state must make its own plans for services which it administers and finances entirely. The centre may have interests in co-ordination; it may be seeking to persuade all the states to pursue a common policy; or it may have to co-ordinate a service maintained by the states (e.g. secondary education) with a service maintained by the centre (e.g. university education). But the centre is not likely to have much influence over services and policies for which it is not putting up any money. The effort of co-ordination is worth making, but excessive optimism would be out of place.

Co-ordination is often easier at the professional than at the political level, so is best done by bringing together officials of the state and central Planning Agencies, rather than by setting up Ministerial committees. Professionals have common standards and objectives, and speak a common language; hence they reach agreement more easily than politicians.

The centre cannot impose its will with regard to services which it does not finance, and need not try to do so. The serious problems arise where centre and states share responsibility for finance, since this requires agreement on common policy. The centre may be financially involved even if it does not contribute out of its own revenues, for the centre may be the only channel for funds from the outside world. If only the centre can borrow abroad, whether *de jure* or *de facto*, or if foreign Governments or foundations making grants insist on dealing only with the central Government, then the centre may become involved in the plans of the states because it has to decide on their relative priorities when seeking external aid.

Administration is as important as money. The centre may set aside money for a service, but if the states will not expand the service, whether because they do not like the centre's plans, or because they do not have the staff to carry them out, or even simply because they are apathetic, then the centre's plans come to nought.

If the state has to administer a service, it is better for the plans to be made by the Planning Agencies of the states than by the Planning Agency of the centre, since this is the first step to ensuring that the plan has local support, and therefore stands some chance of being carried out. The idea that each state should have a Planning Agency of its own may seem to invite excessive proliferation; but federations which have avoided such proliferation have notably failed to solve the problem of federal-state relations. The centre makes plans, and the states fail to carry them out. Actually, not much duplication is involved, since the state's Agency is concerned only with matters which enter into the state's budget, or call for policy decisions by the state. Whether there is a central Plan or not, every major spending unit, private or public, needs some machinery for looking ahead.

The centre cannot abdicate responsibility for functions which it shares with the states. Apart from the constitutional position, the centre has a moral responsibility because it tends to monopolize leadership. The best politicians tend to go to the central parliament, and the best officials tend to work in the central agencies. Hence the states need leadership from the centre in preparing plans, no less than in financing them. However, there is a fundamental difference between a Plan compiled by the central Agency in collaboration with the states' Planning Agencies, which commits the states to no more than the states are willing to perform, and a publication to which the states are not committed.

The centre and the states are jealous of one another, and seldom see eye to eye. This tension cannot be removed by mere formula. Setting up adequate machinery for consultation and participation in the planning process helps—especially machinery for co-operation between Planning officials. But co-operation is essentially an attitude of mind, which reflects itself in courteous and co-operative behaviour. The prime requisite for success is that the planners at the centre—official and political—respect those in the states, and genuinely seek a meeting of minds. The absence of this respect is usually the chief reason for the failure of good relations between the centre and the states.

DEVELOPMENT PLANNING

Summary

1. In a federal constitution each state or province should have its own planning machinery.

2. Projects for which the centre and the states share responsibility (either financial or administrative) must be planned cooperatively.

3. The centre will need to give a lead to the states in planning, but it is fruitless to publish a Plan allocating to the states projects which they are not prepared to undertake.

4. PREPARING PROJECTS

In an underdeveloped country the making of a Development Plan usually begins with the Cabinet requesting each Government department or Ministry to submit its proposals for the next planning period. Thus a mass of material reaches the Agency's office: how many schools the Ministry of Education would like to build, how much the geologists want to spend on air surveys, what industries the Industrial Development Corporation is planning to finance, and so on.

All these proposals must be studied in the Planning Agency, and the more important will also go to the Planning Committees. What does each proposal claim to achieve? Is it likely to achieve what it claims? Is the cost estimated properly (too low or excessively padded)? Would the achievement be worth the cost? It is always hard to get out of the Ministries the materials on which to base such judgments, when the first Development Plan is being prepared, because most of them do not have the necessary statistics or expertise. Planning improves from Plan to Plan because the Ministries become familiar with the process, and also because the Planning Agency begins regular evaluation of development expenditures and policies.

The policies are more important than the expenditures. The Planning Agency will find itself reviewing the whole range of public policy—in education, housing, health services, local government reform, import substitution, exchange control, corporation law, tax incentives, land tenure, land reform—all is grist to its mill.

This wide range determines the range of the Agency's staff. It will need not only economists, but also men with wide experience in other professions. How much work falls on the Agency will depend on the competence of the Ministries, and this varies. The better Ministries will produce proposals which need little vetting by the Agency. In dealing with poor Ministries, the Agency not only has to examine programmes in detail, and recast them, but may even find itself filling gaps by making new proposals of its own. Thus, in weak administrations a Planning Agency may acquire substantial power, if it is well staffed, because it becomes by default the powerhouse of development ideas. This is unhealthy. A good Planning Agency is essential, but so also are good Ministries. The Ministries should be stengthened to the point where each is capable of making good programmes for itself.

However good the Ministries may be, the Planning Agency cannot escape a co-ordinating function. The Plan must be mutually consistent. For example, if some new geographical region is to be developed, all the Ministries concerned must prepare to supply adequate services. Ministries are not good at getting together when preparing their programmes, and even if they were, changes are made after the proposals have been through the Agency and the Planning Committees, which require further co-ordination.

The bulk of the material coming from the Ministries will deal with the expansion of Government services. The amount of money sought will be too large, and much time will have to be spent on cutting out the less important, suggesting new schemes or improvements in those which have been submitted, and re-costing the acceptable proposals. This may take 80 per cent of the Planning Agency's time, though it is in fact the less important part of its work.

The rate of economic growth depends primarily on the rate of growth of commodity output, and only indirectly on the rate of expansion of Government services. This is not because commodities are more important than services, for they are equally important. It is because, whereas the output of services grows easily in response to the output of commodities, the latter does not necessarily grow in response to services. Hence the Planning Agency must pay a great deal of attention to proposals for expanding commodity output.

Every Planning Agency begins work on a new Plan by trying to discover the potential for developing new industries or expanding the output or productivity of existing industries. Intensive sessions with the soil scientists may reveal new cultivable areas ready to be opened up for settlement. Sessions with the agronomists assess the prospects of new crops, or ways of increasing the output of existing crops. Sessions with the geologists examine the prospects of new mines. Work on the trade returns leads to feasibility studies of import substitution. Work with the input-output matrix shows up expected increases in intermediate output; and so all along the line.

How much work of this kind the Agency must do for itself will depend on the quality of the economic Ministries and the Development Corporations, who are charged in the first instance with responsibility for this side of development. If they are well staffed, the Agency will simply rely on what they say. If they are weak, it must seek to strengthen them, and meanwhile will have to do some of their work.

However ably the Planning Agency may perform in sorting proposals for the expansion of Government services—for more schools, or roads, or prisons—it has not really made a *Development* Plan until it has pinpointed the industries on whose expansion it is relying to carry the economy forward.

Project Analysis

If private enterprise is active in promoting new economic activity, detailed analysis of new enterprises can be left to the private sector. Usually it is not possible to leave all such analysis to private enterprise, whether because private enterprise is seeking Government participation, or Government support; or because private enterprise is shy, and waits for Government agencies to prove the feasibility of projects; or because the enterprise is to be financed by the Government. Then the Planning Agency will find itself dealing with feasibility studies, made by itself or others, which seek to establish the costs and benefits of proposed enterprises.

Assessing the cost of a project is relatively easy, when compared with assessing its benefits. The exercise begins with the technologists preparing preliminary figures of costs. However there are different ways of producing output, and the choice between these ways is an economic problem. There may be a choice of locations, or a choice of techniques; estimates must be made for each choice within the feasible range. If factor prices reflect the true relative scarcity of factors of production, the technologist's estimates will show the true costs, and the cheapest mode of production is easily ascertained. If factor prices do not truly reflect social costs, 'accounting' or 'shadow' prices must be used instead; all this we have already discussed in Chapter II.

Assessing benefits is more difficult, first because of the greater element of uncertainty, and secondly because of the difficulty of assessing external economies.

Take first a commodity which is to be produced for sale at a normal profit, and which does not involve external economies. Here the problem is simply to estimate what the demand will be, in quantity and price. For quantity one uses the material at hand. The volume of imports is a good starting point, if the purpose is import-substitution. Figures may be available showing the trend of demand; these have to be corrected for expected changes in population, in taste, or in income per head. For new products a market survey may be required. Demand will depend on price, so some estimate of the elasticity of demand is needed. As for the price, the easiest case is that which permits the producer to fix a price which covers his cost, without fear of competition from close rivals. At the other extreme, the price is set by the market, *e.g.*, for exported commodities. Guessing what the price will be then involves speculating on the future of world demand and supply, and is obviously hazardous.

In theory, the analysis is completed by finding the most profitable price to charge and quantity to sell in each year; subtracting each year's cost; and finding the rate of discount which will equate future net yields with present outlay. In practice, all these figures are highly speculative. Nevertheless, such calculations have value. Governments of underdeveloped countries tend to make industrial investments hastily and optimistically, so many projects are started which could not pass any reasonably competent attempt to assess their viability.

To complicate the analysis, take next a commodity which will be sold below cost, as a matter of deliberate policy. Let us continue to assume that there are no external economies. The problem therefore reduces to assessing whether the benefit to the individual consumer will exceed the cost. If one also assumes that the consumer knows best how to spend his money, this is the same as asking whether he would be willing to pay the cost if this were charged, and how much he would then be willing to buy. Evidence from other countries at a similar level, where a price equal to cost is charged, may help. However, if the Government has reasons for wishing to sell below cost, its attachment to the project is likely to be too great to be shaken by cost-benefit analysis.

Assessing the external economies can be the most difficult part of measuring the benefit. As we saw in Chapter II, if there is no restriction on charging a price, and if there are also no economies of scale, then changes in rents do not count; if the consumer is not in these circumstances willing to pay a price which covers cost, the project should not be undertaken. If there are economies of scale, and the product is to be sold not at average cost but (as it should be) at marginal cost, a deficit will result. It may be possible to cover this deficit by some sort of supplementary levy on the consumer, varying not with his consumption, but with some other index of his capacity to pay (*e.g.*, a two-part tariff). Then the problem is to assess whether the supplementary charge will raise enough revenue to meet the deficit. Alternatively the deficit falls on the Government budget, and the assessment becomes more vague. In extreme cases, where the project is very large, and will greatly affect the level of output of a whole region (*e.g.*, irrigation, transportation) it becomes necessary virtually to project the increase in national income which will result from the project, and subtract all additional costs required to produce this increase (more capital, more labour, more public services and so on) to arrive at the net benefit attributable to the project.

It is important to avoid double counting; if one uses a low shadow wage in valuing labour, when calculating costs, one must not also, when calculating benefits, give extra credit to the project because it will relieve unemployment. Shadow pricing may be applied to costs or to benefits; the same item should not appear in both. Again, annual values and capital values should not be added together. Examples of what to avoid were given in our earlier discussion of interdependence of investments.

In project analysis what counts is not technique—the techniques are straightforward—but knowledge of the industry. It takes detailed knowledge to give confidence in assessing either costs or benefits. This work is for specialists. Planning Agencies

---

[1] For the details of project evaluation see Otto Eckstein, *Water Resource Development: The Economics of Project Evaluation*, 1958.

have to use consultants, and also get some members of their staffs to specialize on particular industries. Without such specialized knowledge, project analysis is bound to be wrong.

Summary

1. Every proposal must be assessed separately, to establish its feasibility, cost, benefit, and degree of priority. This is the time-consuming part of development planning.

2. The sharing of this work between the Ministries and the Planning Agency will depend on the relative competence of each.

3. Assessing the cost and benefits of new industrial enterprises is highly specialized work, which is best left to experienced consultants.

5. THE ANNUAL PLAN

Yearly Schedules

A Five or Ten Year Plan shows in the first instance the total sum to be spent on each project over the period. For effective work, however, these totals have to be broken down to show separately the amount to be spent in each year. These yearly schedules may or may not be published in the Plan, but they need to be communicated to the officials implementing the Plan. Preparation takes time. Blueprints must be drawn and redrawn, tenders advertised, the contract awarded, and the contractor installed on site; two years may elapse between the decision to go ahead with a project and the turning of the first sod. Some preparatory work is therefore always being done two or three years in advance of the year in which the project appears in the annual capital budget.

This advance work is facilitated by preparing as a companion to the Development Plan a document which shows details for each project in each year; when construction of each project is due to start and to end; and the timing of all the preliminary stages of each project, including dates for Parliamentary approval, tendering, and award of contract. The Development Plan is the 'master' document, but the working document for the planners is the one which gives this material year by year.

Capital expenditure does not fit neatly into budgets approved separately for each year. The exact amount that will be spent on any given project cannot be predicted. Hence it is normal to ask

DEVELOPMENT PLANNING

Parliament to approve in each year more than can be done in that year, retaining the latitude to advance some projects and to retard others. The point where capital budgeting most often tends to fall down is the transition from one Five Year Plan to another. Some of the projects to be executed in the first year of a new Plan need to have been decided two years earlier, and to have had two years of solid preparatory work. Even Parliamentary approval may have been necessary in the previous year. As likely as not, the Development Plan is not in final shape until the final month before the new period begins, so the first year's projects cannot wait for approval of the Development Plan. The Planning Agency begins work on a new Development Plan two or three years ahead of time. At a very early stage it must settle what will be done in the first two years of the new period, and get approval for preliminary work.

Control

The Development Plan does not authorize expenditure. It lists projects to which the Government intends to accord priority, but it does not authorize Ministers to spend on those projects. Ministers derive their authorization from the annual capital budget which is passed by Parliament along with the annual recurrent budget. The Development Plan provides a framework, but what really matters is the annual budget.

The crucial test of the effectiveness of the Development Plan, and of the influence of the Planning Agency, is the extent to which the Development Plan really controls the annual budget.

In its efforts to implement the Development Plan, the Agency may be defeated by other officials or by Ministers. It was noted earlier that all important decision-makers must participate in making the Development Plan if it is to be effective, since they may otherwise ignore it. This was the purpose of creating a network of committees where they could all have their say. How easy it is to ignore the published Plan will depend to some extent on the Prime Minister or President. The Plan may survive if he insists that it be followed, but if he is willing to let Ministers introduce new schemes into the Cabinet, without proper vetting by the planners, the Plan has little chance. To say this is only to say that a country is not ready for development planning until Government procedures have settled down in a way which ensures proper administrative control over finance. Alas, many underdeveloped countries are still not ready for serious development planning for this very reason. Plans are published for political propaganda purposes, without any real intention of adhering to what they say.

Planning and a disorderly Cabinet do not go together. Nowadays there is enough business to justify creating a special Cabinet sub-committee for economic affairs, meeting once or twice a month, and including the leading economic Ministers. The Cabinet should refuse to discuss any economic matter which has not first been through this sub-committee. And this sub-committee should refuse to make any recommendations without first receiving proper documentation from civil servants and technical advisers. This should not need saying; but in truth in many new states planning is rendered impossible by the Cabinet's habit of taking important decisions without prior investigation.

If the Plan is to be effective, it is usually necessary to allocate to the Planning Agency the responsibility for making the annual capital budget, since this prevents departments from slipping in schemes which have already been given low priority. If the Planning Agency prepares the Development Plan but has no control over the annual capital budget, the Plan will almost certainly be ineffective.

The Planning Agency has to collaborate closely with the Ministry of Finance in preparing the annual capital budget. They may easily run afoul of each other unless their responsibilities are clearly demarcated, and machinery for co-ordination kept working smoothly.

Thus the Budget Bureau of the Ministry of Finance prepares the budget for recurrent expenditure; the Planning Agency prepares the budget for capital expenditure. These two are linked; this year's capital expenditure (on schools or hospitals) involves next year's recurrent expenditure (on teachers or nurses). If the Development Plan has been prepared properly, it includes a forecast of recurrent expenditure which takes account of proposed capital expenditure, but things may not have turned out as expected. Again, the financing of capital expenditure, which the Agency controls, depends on the raising of sufficient taxes in the current budget, which the Ministry controls. Clearly these two must collaborate. At the official level the Planning Agency must be sure to have on its staff some people who are trained in budget work, who speak the language of the Ministry officials, and who are acceptable to them as equals. Officials making the current budget and officials making the capital budget should meet together regularly in committee, for the purpose of co-ordinating their work. Failures at the official level will have to be rectified at the Cabinet level.

Finance

Control of the public sector has two sides—control of expenditure and control of revenue. The Planning Agency is deeply involved in the first, but the second is outside its control. Yet, however ably expenditure may be controlled, the Plan will come to nothing if revenue is not also properly managed. The Plan is predicated on the availability of finance—including a budget surplus of a certain size, and a certain level of profits in public enterprises. If the, Minister of Finance does not raise enough in taxes, or the public enterprises do not charge adequately for their products, the resulting deficiency of resources will either produce inflation, or force the abandonment of some proposed expenditures, or both.

Development planning was started to bring order into proposals for public expenditure; control of public revenue is an unintended by-product. Planning Agencies have no direct responsibility for revenue: this aspect remains firmly with the Minister of Finance. However the Plan influences the situation by showing what the revenue should be; the appropriate size of the Government's budget is an important by-product of the macroeconomic arithmetic. In the absence of planning, governments tend to fix tax levels haphazardly from one year to the next, in the light of immediate budgetary needs. The existence of a Plan helps to force the Minister of Finance and the Cabinet to think of public revenue in a wider context.

Evaluation

Apart from preparing the capital budget, the Planning Agency has also to keep a check on its implementation. It requires from the Accountant-General's department of the Ministry of Finance up-to-date figures of capital expenditure. It must also be in touch with the Ministry of Works, and know the latest position on preparation of drawings, acceptance of tenders, work-in-progress, changes in expected cost, and so on. Such information is required even if only to know what figures to put into the next budget. But the Agency probably has also a supervisory function. The Government expects it to find out what is holding up the implementation of the Plan, and either itself to push matters on, or else to make recommendations for speeding up the work. The duties of the Planning Agency are not always made clear in this respect. Sometimes it has no responsibility, beyond making the Five Year Plan; even the annual capital budget is made not by the Planning Agency but by the Ministry of Finance. At the other extreme the Planning Agency finds the Government looking to it to see that the Plan keeps on schedule; it then has a general responsibility to prod, without necessarily having effective instruments for dealing with Ministries whose inefficiency is holding up the Plan.

One can take it for granted that the Plan will fall behind schedule unless the Planning Agency is responsible for reporting on its progress. Ministries may be good at spending money on current account; they are seldom good at spending capital funds, which require a long process of previous planning to which they are not accustomed. The Planning Agency must therefore have on its staff experienced 'progress chasers' (engineers are better at this than economists) who follow each project through from design to completion, and report when anything is falling behind schedule.

Reporting and evaluation should always be put on a regular and systematic basis, since this helps to ensure implementation. Reports should cover both progress in the private sector (how many new industrial plants, indices of industrial and agricultural output, how many houses built, and so on) and also the extent to which the public sector is on schedule (how many new schools, miles of road built, and so on), with special reports from time to time on how new policies are working out (Community Development, agricultural training, etc.). Governments are sometimes reluctant to publish such information, because it shows up their deficiencies; on the other hand, it is not easy for the Government to discipline its own Ministries: exposing the laggards and praising the good performers publicly helps the Government, as well as giving the public information which it needs. Whether such reports are published or not, the Planning Agency should have a separate division charged with evaluation of the progress of the Plan, and its reports should be studied seriously by the Cabinet's sub-committee on economic affairs.

Public reporting cannot be avoided if the Plan is made democratically, using private persons on a network of committees. By the third year of a Five Year Plan the committees will again be in session to work on the next Five Year Plan; they will not take the exercise seriously unless the Government is taking the existing Plan seriously, and reporting on its implementation.

Revision

Implementing a Plan is more difficult than making it. Making a Plan is an exercise of the imagination, while implementation is a struggle with reality. Before crossing the Atlantic, the pilot of an aircraft plots his course in relation to expected weather and winds. Once aloft, reality is found to differ from expectations; the plan must be modified continually to cope with changing facts.

The annual capital budget provides the opportunity to keep up to date with changing circumstances. To be bound by the figures in the Development Plan would lead to misallocation of resources. It would also destroy the authority of the Planning Agency. Decision-makers, private and public, would find the planners' documents increasingly irrelevant to immediate needs, and would either ignore them, or lobby against the Agency. A Plan without relevance soon ceases to carry authority.

The simplest procedure is for the Planning Agency to draft each year, for its own purposes, a capital budget for the current and two succeeding years. This solves two problems mentioned earlier—the need to do preparatory work two or three years ahead, and the need to prepare the carryover from one Plan to the next. It also provides a framework for continual revision.

As time passes and circumstances change, the annual capital budget will diverge increasingly from what is predicted in the published Development Plan. This can be handled in various ways. The Plan may be formally revised, and a new document issued; the publication of Evaluation Reports provides an unobtrusive opportunity for doing this. Or the Plan may simply be ignored, the annual budget taking its place completely. Or the Plan may be formally scrapped, and a new one issued before the old one was due to expire. A Plan has not necessarily failed because it has grown out of date. If useful when first issued, it would have failed only if it continued to govern policy after it had ceased to be relevant.

THE PRIVATE SECTOR

Summary

1. A Development Plan usually covers several years. Proposed expenditures should be broken down on an annual basis. Much time elapses between approval of a project and the start of building operations. The planning authorities must keep a time schedule with dates for the various stages through which each project must pass.

2. The Planning Agency must be given the responsibility for preparing the annual capital budget if the Development Plan is really to take effect. In this task the Agency must work closely with the officials in the Budget Bureau who prepare the annual recurrent budget.

3. The success of the Plan depends on the Minister of Finance taking steps to raise the necessary revenues. The macroeconomic arithmetic of the Plan exerts pressure in this direction, but responsibility lies with the Cabinet.

4. Progress of the Plan should be evaluated at regular intervals.

5. Proposals in the Plan should be revised continually as circumstances alter and new information becomes available. A three-year capital budget, revised each year, is a useful planning tool. Considerable divergence is to be expected between proposals in the published Plan and annual authorizations in the later years of the planning period.

6. THE PRIVATE SECTOR

Development Plans do not all contain targets for commodity output, but most of them are as much concerned with expanding commodity output as with expenditure on public services.

Production Targets

The seriousness with which the Government takes targets for commodity output will depend on whether the commodity is produced wholly by private enterprise or in establishments in which the Government participates financially. If the commodity is to be produced by a public enterprise, or by a public-private partnership, the targets tell officials what they are supposed to do (though authorization as distinct from advance notice will be communicated separately). Governments are also interested in the targets for some privately operated industries which they consider basic, whether because these industries supply intermediate goods and services to a wide range of other industries, or because they are a prime source of foreign exchange, or because their availability and cost matter significantly to the cost of living. Apart from such special cases, the Government is more interested in macroeconomic quantities than in the behaviour of individual industries—in the rate of growth of the economy as a whole, in overall financial resources (saving, foreign investment, foreign exchange and taxes), in employment, in the price level and in regional balance. Whether 5 per cent per annum growth is achieved by the projected doubling of the output of peanuts, or by the unexpected discovery of silver, is a matter of secondary importance.

Even those targets which are thought to be important must be subject to constant revision. As time passes, more or less than was predicted becomes appropriate; policy must adjust to this. To adhere to predictions is especially silly if this prevents possible new developments. The Plan may propose a factory for making bicycles; nobody can be found to set up a bicycle factory, but along comes a man who wishes to make radios, which were not in the Plan. In the absence of licensing there is no problem with the Government; he just goes ahead. In a nightmare state, he is unable to get a licence, because radios are not in the Plan. Licences should not be based on what is said in a Five Year or Ten Year Plan. The licensers need their own three or six or twelve months plans, kept up-to-date in view of current resources and opportunities.

Licensing

Licensing is one of the obstacles to development in the poorer countries. Since market prices give the wrong signals, one can make a perfect theoretical case for substituting licensing as a method of allocating resources. However, good licensing requires a good civil service, which understands the purpose of the system, is free from corruption, and is accustomed to prompt execution of business operations. Instead, in most poor countries licensing means inordinate delays, and inexplicable decisions. If licensing cannot be administered promptly and efficiently, the country is better off without it.

For a few years after the Second World War progressive thinkers acclaimed rationing and licensing as inevitable and desirable instruments of economic democracy; but this was only a passing phase. By the middle 1950 all the leading social demo-cratic parties in the world had come to realize that licensing is an inefficient and corrupt way of allocating resources, and had dropped it from their programmes. Today even in the USSR powerful and authoritative voices are urging greater reliance on the market, and less use of administrative direction. If licensing is inefficient and corrupt in advanced countries, with first class administrations, it is even more harmful in less developed countries.

After food rationing, the next most tiresome area of licensing is general exchange control, because it affects so many people directly, and therefore offers so much scope for delay, corruption and arbitrary decision. Some countries have had exchange control for so long that they have persuaded themselves that it is an inevitable accompaniment of economic development. This is not so; most countries have developed without exchange control; it is rather a sign of failure to allocate sufficient resources to main-tenance of the foreign balance, whether by paying more attention to exports, or by investing more in import substitution. Countries which make adequate plans for exportation and import substitution do not need exchange control (apart from restrictions on export-ing capital). Failure to keep export costs in line with world prices—whether through lack of an incomes policy, or through failure to balance the budget, or through maintenance of an incorrect foreign exchange rate—is both a symptom and a cause. Since it is difficult to keep an economy running smoothly any country is liable to have failures of this kind; but they should be recognized as failures calling for rectification; not promoted as a subject for pride and self-congratulation.

Some direct control of investment is inevitable—whether through the licensing of the importation of machinery or through the issue of building permits—because of the imperfections of the market. It may be necessary in some countries to prevent invest-ment in factories which will displace handicraft workers, without increasing the national output. More commonly—perhaps even universally—building permits are necessary to give effect to a zoning policy (to keep factories out of residential districts) or to a policy of regional balance (to prevent excessive concentration in one or two towns). It is possible in these policy areas to make regulations which are precise, and leave little room for personal assessment and interpretation. This minimizes the delay in issuing permits, as well as the opportunity for arbitrary and corrupt decisions.

One of the least attractive aspects of licensing is what it does to the small business men who, added together, make as great a contribution to development as the big men, or greater. Licensing always hurts the small men most. The big firm can keep specialists who become familiar with the regulations, and with the men who administer them, and who can therefore get the big firm's business through. The big firms also have more influence and—if bribery is involved—more money. Licenses are usually based on past performance; this helps the established firm, and prevents the small firm from growing. A licensing system is inevitably biassed against small business.

Such a bias is difficult to avoid even without licensing, especially if committees have participated in drawing up the Development Plan. The representatives of business on the committees will usually be from the larger firms. These are the men best known to civil servants and Ministers, so, even with the best will in the world, their problems naturally receive attention most easily. Every Development Corporation and every Ministry of Trade and Industry should have sections specially charged with the interests of small business.

Building permits apart, almost any other desired control of the economy can be achieved without licensing, either by taxing the activities one seeks to discourage (e.g. import duties, excise duties on luxury consumption) or by subsidizing those one seeks to encourage. Manipulation of prices through taxes and subsidies is the smoothest way to influence the allocation of resources in the private sector.

Most Government intervention in the private sector of a developing economy should be expansionist, rather than restrictive. The other important area for restrictive action, apart from building, is the control of those imports which are cheaper in money but more expensive in real terms. This can be done through exchange control or import licensing, but these are inferior forms of control since they require a separate administrative decision for each importation, and thus open the door to much delay and corruption. Undesired imports can be cut or excluded by the imposition of import duties of suitable magnitude. The most efficient way to protect import substituting industries is to establish an independent Tariffs Commission to hear cases and make recommendations, and to keep under review all industries which are receiving tariff protection, to ensure that protection is not a cloak for profiteering or inefficiency. Although each industry is studied separately, the Commission is guided by a general rule: the case for protection is based on the argument that factor prices are wrong; if one can establish by how much they are wrong, one can deduce how much protection is justified across the board. The Commission should thus establish what degree of protection it considers generally desirable irrespective of conditions in the individual industry, and should exceed this rate only in very special cases. Experience shows that the absolute independence and objectivity of a Tariffs Commission is vital if it is to hold public confidence. It may have to take some evidence in camera, but its reports should always be published.

The Planning Agency does not administer licensing, but may become involved. It is involved if (as happens in badly administered countries) the licensing authorities are refusing to release resources (e.g. foreign exchange to purchase raw materials) to enterprises built in accordance with the Plan. It is involved if major changes of policy are required, since it had a hand in devising the policies set out in the Plan. It is also involved with major investment projects, especially if there is a considerable deviation from what was originally projected. In practice, therefore, it is almost certain to find itself participating in some of the bigger administrative decisions, such as whether to give the licence for the steel mill to the German firm A, or the French firm B; or whether to accept the contractor's claim that Government delays raised the cost of the dam 40 per cent over the contract price, or take the issue to arbitration. An agency involved in so all-embracing a process as economic development, and known to have direct access to a powerful committee of the Cabinet, will find it hard to limit its activities within a narrow framework.

Promoting Enterprise

The fundamental task of development planning is to release the energies of the people so that they may do what needs doing to raise the rate of economic growth. The things to be done are productive decisions to be made by a very large proportion of the country's inhabitants. Industrialists are to build factories; farmers are to adopt new technologies; labour is to move to new jobs; research workers are to find new solutions; perhaps as much as 20 per cent of the population must change its ways somehow or other—learn, invest, accept new institutions—if the rate of growth is to move from 3 to 5 per cent. The planner's job is to find out what stands in the way of these productive decisions, and to introduce measures which make such decisions more likely.

Emphasis is placed upon the high proportion of the population involved. The Government cannot by itself, or through its officials, raise the rate of growth from 3 to 5 per cent. Such an exercise involves a wide section of the people. The Government can persuade, threaten or induce; but in the last analysis it is the people who achieve.

What stands in the way of more rapid growth is not the same in every country. Sometimes it is mainly lack of natural resources, or of knowledge of resources, or of knowledge of how best to exploit known resources; then one must look to science for remedies. Sometimes it is poor infrastructure—lack of roads, harbours, water supplies, electric power, or other basic services. Deficiencies of technical skiols and of basic education are universal. Sometimes the fault lies in institutions which hamper or discourage initiative: inadequate commercial laws, inadequate marketing or credit facilities, an inefficient bureaucracy, or a mass of restrictive licences. Or it may lie in price policies, especially the chronic tendency of some countries to price themselves out of the world market, by continually inflating domestic costs, while holding the foreign exchange rate at an unrealistic level.

If one were asked to pick a single factor as the most common cause of a low rate of economic growth it would have to be the absence of a vigorous agricultural policy. As we have seen before, agricultural stagnation is the main constraint on the rate of growth. It keeps down the living standards of the great majority of the people, and in restricting their purchasing power, restricts also the scope for industrialization. It is the prime cause of a low taxable capacity and a low rate of saving. It contributes to a shortage of foreign exchange, either by failure to earn more, or by failure to supply the growing urban demand for food and raw materials, which must then be imported. Except for countries which have rich mineral resources, no underdeveloped country can grow rapidly in which farm output is stagnating. Hence a vigorous agricultural policy must head the list of development measures. Given good institutional, price and agricultural policies, the chief difficulty which remains is the shortage of large scale entrepreneurship, especially for mining and manufacturing. There is no shortage of small scale enterprise, or of willingness to exploit opportunities. The will to do business and make money shows up in the hordes of traders; and in the rapidity with which small enterpreneurs take up small business opportunities as soon as the opportunities are opened up—motor transport, cinemas, building and contracting, small flour mills, printers, softdrinks—there is no shortage of small business types in underdeveloped countries. The shortage is of men who can build and run a large modern factory or mine or ship.

Development planning includes measures designed to increase the domestic supply of managerial talent. These attack the main causes of the shortage, viz. lack of opportunity, lack of technical training, and lack of money. To remedy lack of opportunity pressure is applied to foreign firms to employ more nationals in high positions, and give them better training. Sometimes foreign firms are not allowed to operate unless they take nationals as partners—though this measure is frequently little more than a racket. Sometimes, too, domestic entrepreneurs are sheltered from the competition of foreign rivals, by licensing the foreigner or keeping him out altogether—a policy which has point where the cliquishness of established foreigners is a factor preventing nationals from getting a foothold in a business, but which also has the danger of removing the competitive spur to improvement. Lack of technical training is met partly by placement in establishments in overseas countries; partly by offering classes in subjects relevant to business management (accountancy, personnel management, merchandizing, commercial law, etc.); and partly by providing some sort of consulting service to help small business men. Finally, lack of money is met by applying pressure to the commercial banks to lend more freely to nationals; and also by establishing development banks of various sorts, with private or public funds.

In time such measures, plus the currently high prestige of business management, will increase the supply of domestic managers for large scale enterprises to the point where there is no longer a crucial shortage. But the current domestic supply is not adequate to produce a 5 per cent rate of growth. If such a rate is to be attained, some importation of foreign management is inevitable, whether in the form of foreign enterprise or in the form of hired management.

Finding investors who are willing to start businesses, whether on their own, or (if foreigners) in partnership with domestic entrepreneurs, or in partnership with the Government is one of the chief aspects of Plan implementation. For this purpose it is usual to create one or more Development Corporations, to study new projects, find potential investors, and negotiate. Potential investors in new industries look to the Government for many kinds of assistance. Some Government agencies help in securing additional information (geological survey, industrial research, agricultural research). Some help in widening the market (protecting the home market, or negotiating to lower foreign tariffs). Some help in recruiting and training labour, or developing suitable industrial sites, or encouraging farmers to grow a raw material for processing. Others are expected to make loans (industrial bank, agricultural credit, mortgage finance). And the Ministry of Finance may be asked for subsidies (to meet the cost of running in factories, to encourage farmers to use fertilizers or conserve soil, and so on).

Every country has to decide for itself whether to encourage private enterprise, what framework to establish for private operations, and whether to discriminate between domestic and foreign enterprise. Some underdeveloped countries have decided to put the emphasis on public enterprise, and in those sectors where foreign management is essential, they either hire it for salaries and fees, or insist on partnership between private and public funds. The result depends largely on the amount of domestic administrative skill available for tapping. Given adequate resources of finance and skill, and a sound administrative framework, public enterprise can be as dynamic as private enterprise. However these conditions are not fulfilled in the majority of underdeveloped countries, and most of those which have decided to rely on public enterprise are plagued with waste, inefficiency and corruption. Whether the benefits outweigh the disadvantages each person must judge in the light of his own political philosophy.

Countries which have decided on a mixed economy must follow through the consequences in the private sector. The amount of private enterprise, and the amount of risk private entrepreneurs will take, depend partly on the extent of freedom from administrative control, and even more on the opportunities for making profits. In several of these countries official spokesmen appeal frequently for new private investment, and publish Plans predicated upon large amounts of private investment, but since at the same time they hedge private investment round with restrictions and licences, and take steps to keep private profit low, these appeals and Plans come to nothing.

It is no part of the purpose of this book to argue whether a 3 per cent rate of growth is better or worse than a 5 per cent rate of growth; our concern is not with ends, but with means. Given that the end is rapid growth, the main point to be stressed is that this end cannot be achieved without offering high incentives to individuals. Rapid growth involves decision-making not merely by politicians and civil servants, but also by a large proportion of the population. Exhortation and symbolic rewards help to put people in the right frame of mind, but only an infinitesimal proportion of any population will decide to incur costs and take risks without the possibility of substantial material reward. *The possibility of higher individual earnings is the fuel of economic growth*, whether in the form of profits, salaries, wages, higher farm incomes, or otherwise. Economic growth cannot be produced by legislation, administrative regulation, or exhortation, without the accompaniment of high material incentives. Hence the crucial test of the quality of development planning, in that part of the economy which is left to private initiative, is how effective are the incentives offered to the population to make decisions which will result in economic growth.

Summary

1. Most of the targets for commodity output are not to be taken seriously; what matters is the level of total investment and output, rather than the growth of individual industries.

2. Targets which matter should be revised continually, in the light of changing resources and other circumstances.

3. Licensing is an inferior instrument of planning, symptomatic of failure to use the price mechanism efficiently.

4. Some licensing is inevitable; publication of precise regulations and principles speeds administration, and reduces uncertainty and arbitrariness.

DEVELOPMENT PLANNING

5. The fundamental task of planning in the private sector is to remove the obstacles in the way of legitimate private initiative, by increasing the knowledge of resources and their potential utilization, and by improving infrastructure and the institutional framework of economic activity.

6. This requires to be supplemented by measures inducing a larger flow of entrepreneurship.

7. Economic growth depends on a large proportion of the country's inhabitants—farmers, wage earners, professionals, entrepreneurs—responding to opportunities for improving their economic conditions. Incentives are the key to economic growth.

FOR FURTHER READING: CHAPTER IV

Eckstein, Otto. *Water Resource Development: The Economics of Project Evaluation.* Cambridge, Mass., 1958.

Hanson, A. H. *Public Enterprise and Economic Development.* London, 1959.

Lewis, W. A. *The Principles of Economic Planning.* London, 1949.

Mason, E. S. *Economic Planning in Underdeveloped Areas: Government and Business.* New York, 1958.

Swerdlow, I. (Editor). *Development Administration: Concepts and Problems.* Syracuse, 1963.

Walinsky, L. J. *The Planning and Execution of Economic Development.* New York, 1963.

Waterston, A. *Planning in Pakistan.* Baltimore, 1963.

INDEX

DEVELOPMENT PLANNING

Singer, H. W., 71 *n.*
Social services, 95–6, 100–15, 168,
238. *See also* Welfare services
Standard of living, *see* Consumption
Subsidies, *see* Public finance
Swerdlow, I., 274

Tariffs Commission, 269
Taxation, *see* Public finance
Technology, 19, 22, 26–7, 35–6, 45–8,
56–8, 64–8, 99, 233, 242, 256.
See also Productivity, Research
Terms of trade, 39, 49–50, 51, 166
Tinbergen, J., 24, 243
Trade unions, 52, 78, 81, 84, 90, 91–2,
94, 162
Uganda, 122
Unemployment, 29–31, 40, 57–8,
63–4, 67, 72, 76–87, 131, 205–6,
223–4; disguised, 31, 76–7, 83,
223; seasonal, 84

USSR, Russia, 48, 125, 132, 159,
182
United Nations, 24, 50, 146. *See also*
Foreign aid
USA, 17, 57, 88, 104, 107, 108, 111,
118, 125, 142

Venezuela, 45

Wages, 28–30, 40, 57–8, 72, 76–81,
84, 90–6, 113, 120, 132, 134–5,
136, 161–2
Wald, H. P., 146
Walinsky, L. J., 274
Water supplies, 17, 27, 28, 32, 40, 68,
71, 73, 80, 84, 103, 159, 160, 238,
239
Waterston, A., 274
Welfare services, 32–3, 86, 114, 123,
162, 170, 172, 238, 239, 257–8
Witt, L. W., 145